"Engrossing and well researched . . .
Solid, fascinating, and multi-layered."
The Cleveland Plain Dealer

"Compelling, provocative, poignant . . .
Barker's courageous book should be read by anyone who seeks to understand the psyche of Indian America five centuries after Columbus.
Researched with a skilled reporter's meticulous
craft, written with eloquence, jammed with insight, it is a tremendous accomplishment."
The Arizona Republic

"A chilling and haunting exploration of red and
white relations in the contemporary West . . .
With a well-balanced cultural sensitivity, Barker
reveals the harsh details of daily life for Native
Americans and introduces us to the mystical
world of Navajo witchcraft."
St. Louis Post-Dispatch

"[Barker] tells the story with skill and sensitivity,
revealing the cultural and psychological truths
behind the sensational material."
Santa Fe New Mexican

"Effective . . . Anyone interested in Navajo ver-
sus Anglo justice and modern Navajo affairs is
strongly encouraged to go directly to their nearest bookstore and buy a copy of this book."
Navajo Times

Also by Rodney Barker:

THE HIROSHIMA MAIDENS

THE
BROKEN
CIRCLE

A True Story of Murder and Magic
in Indian Country

Rodney Barker

IVY BOOKS • NEW YORK

Ivy Books
Published by Ballantine Books
Copyright © 1992 by Rodney Barker

Library of Congress Catalog Card Number: 91-39402

ISBN 0-8041-1147-2

This edition published by arrangement with Simon & Schuster, Inc.

Manufactured in the United States of America

First Ballantine Books Edition: June 1993

For Star

CONTENTS

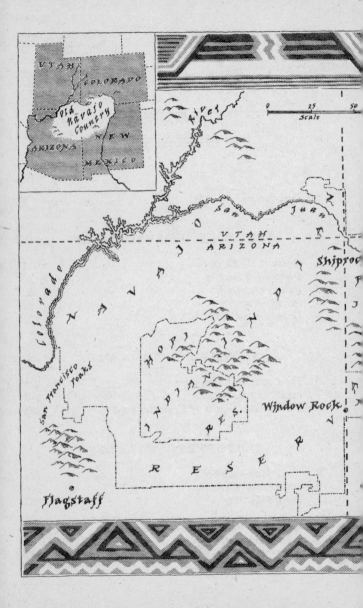

UTAH
COLORADO
Old
Navajo
Country
ARIZONA
NEW
MEXICO

River

0   25   50
Scale

San   Juan   R.

UTAH
ARIZONA

Shiprock

Colorado

N A V A J O

San Francisco Peaks

HOPI

INDIAN

RES.

Window Rock

R E S E R

Flagstaff

INTRODUCTION

You might call it a contemporary twist on the frontier tale of the white man who goes and lives among the Indians and through that experience becomes one: On a summer Saturday in 1974, an extraordinary series of events began that would teach me what it meant to be an Indian in the American West in the last quarter of the twentieth century.

I was not well acquainted with Farmington, New Mexico. Usually I would swoop through on my way to a day hike on the Navajo Reservation, several miles to the west, pausing only long enough to gas up. But on this occasion, as I approached the main part of town and found all traffic detoured and crowds packing the sidewalks, after asking a portly patrolman what was going on and being informed the Sheriff's Posse Parade was about to start, I decided to park my car and observe the festivities.

The first I was aware that something out of the ordinary was happening was when I realized that no sooner had the parade begun to roll down Main Street than it stopped. Then I heard jeers and catcalls and whooping imitations of Indian war cries. Threading my way through the throngs of people, I approached a scene so in keeping with my idea of a Western-style show-down, it could have been staged. Perhaps a half-dozen young Indians wearing cowboy hats and red headbands and enough militant touches to identify them as modern warriors were faced off against a six-man contingent of horsemen dressed in Old West cavalry uniforms. Only the aggressive movements of the mounted men, who seemed ready to spur their skittish horses forward, and the menace of the Indians, who wore sunglasses that wouldn't let you see their eyes, just your own bulging reflection, said this was not a scheduled performance.

As a Farmington policeman approached from the opposite side of the street, I too moved closer to the center of action. The Indians were ordered to get out of the street and let the parade proceed. They said not until the U.S. Cavalry unit left the parade. They were then told they were unlawfully interfering with a lawful assembly. They countered with a lecture on the brutal role of cavalry soldiers in Navajo history.

As several helmeted policemen armed with black batons rushed up, the officer issued an ultimatum: The Indians had until the count of five to clear the street.

Most of the people bunched around me were Indians who had massed in a general show of support, but now they began to retreat. The militants held their ground, however. So did I. Attribute it to a reckless faith that innocence would keep me out of harm's way, or the journalist's presumption of invulnerability—in all the excitement I missed the danger, and stood there taking everything in.

Afterward, the police would be quoted in the newspaper as saying they had warned that tear gas would be used if the Indians did not disperse. I don't remember hearing that. The first I knew the conflict had taken a violent turn was when I watched a grenade arch overhead. The next thing I knew I was tasting the sour tang of tear gas.

Just like that, a disturbance became a riot. People were screaming and stampeding wildly in all directions, shoving and knocking one another to the ground where they were trampled by others trying to escape the gas. The escalation made no sense to me, innocent bystanders were getting hurt, and giving it no more thought than that, I circled swiftly to the upwind side, made a short run at the hissing, smoking canister, and kicked it like a teed-up football.

Like an instant replay in slow motion I can still see that canister as it skitters across the pavement into the middle of the street toward the startled expressions of the Farmington policemen who had yet to don their gas masks, just before they are swallowed by fog.

I suppose I shouldn't have been surprised when two burly cops grabbed me roughly by the arms and ran me like bar bouncers to the corner, where they slapped my pockets for weapons, cuffed my hands behind me, and pitched me in the back of a paddy wagon. But surprise was the least of my reactions. This was one of the more extreme moments of my life. As the door slammed shut and I was left lying face-down with my arms wrenched behind me, I almost cried out in rage. Nothing can upset one's faith in the social order quite like being arrested and manacled for an act of conscience, as rash as it might be.

There was a grilled window between the cab and the back of the van through which the guards could inspect their prisoners, and crawling toward it on my knees, I looked out. The view, cropped to the size of a TV screen, was a replay from the evening news. Streets cloudy with tear gas. People staggering along sidewalks, coughing and wiping their eyes. A tough pack of policemen in riot gear fighting over the last scraps of a disturbance. I could have been watching a special report on civil unrest in Selma or Johannesburg.

Suddenly the back doors swung wide and two Indians with hair to their shoulders and hard but watery eyes were heaved in by four cops who hustled around to the front of the van, jumped in the cab, and we lurched forward. I braced myself as the driver careened around a corner in hot pursuit of several Indians sprinting down a side street. There was laughter and cursing from in front until the van slammed to a stop and the men leaped out. Through the window I watched a spectacle of police run amok. All four patrolmen charged through the area, rounding up an Indian each and holding him until a ranking officer appeared and pointed out who should be released and who tossed in the police van, without reference to their specific transgressions. One man had been standing in line at a hamburger stand when he was picked up.

As I watched it seemed to me the police were continuing to arrest randomly as a way of building up numbers in order to justify their overreaction at the parade. And with that realization came a sense of purpose about all this. I found myself concentrating on police improprieties, the use of excessive force, recording images and impressions as if I anticipated that someday a prosecutor would put me on the witness stand. A desire to see right done and wrong overcome went deep with me.

From the time I had been arrested to when we were finally driven up to the Farmington police station, perhaps a half-hour had passed. Twenty or thirty of us were crammed in a holding cell so tightly we could only stand. Looking around me, I couldn't help noticing I was the only white man on the wrong side of the bars; a fact that many of the Indians likewise noted, as did a roomful of sneering policemen.

After we were booked we were taken to a large cell I imagined to be the drunk tank because most of those already incarcerated were slumped in sodden states of inebriation. Passing a single stopped-up toilet, I went over to a sink to wash my face and discovered that water burns skin that has been gassed. For a moment I thought I had splashed acid on my face and that it was a joke perpetrated by the jailers.

Sitting on the floor, my back against the wall, I waited for what would come next and listened to the conversations of my cellmates. Some spoke in English, exchanging their arrest stories, but most conversed in Navajo. Since I couldn't understand what they were saying I listened to the pitch and tone of their voices and decided they were simply making small talk. It struck me then that while for me this was a major event, for many of them it was business as usual.

When I realized that this was where I would be spending the night I removed my shoes, shaped them into a pillow, curled up on the floor, and tried my best to crawl into a hole inside myself.

In the morning we were lined up and led into a cafeteria where we were served burnt oatmeal and boiled coffee, which I ate and drank with relish. Until this time I had been avoided by the other prisoners as if I were a poorly disguised informant planted among them, but now I found myself approached by two intense young Indians who plunked down across from me and point-blank asked who I was and what I was doing there.

One of them was almost comically rotund and so nearsighted the magnification of his thick glasses made his eyes fairly pop out of his broad, stolid face. He introduced himself as Wilbert Tsosie. The other was tall and heavyset and his wire-rimmed spectacles and fatigue jacket gave him the look of a sixties war protestor. His name was John Redhouse. I didn't recognize them from the confrontation the previous day but, as I soon found out, they were the leaders of the militant group that had stopped the parade.

For the rest of that morning we talked, and from them I learned that for several months Farmington had been in the throes of a civil-rights struggle. They talked about racism and discrimination in Farmington, and the tensions that had preceded the parade incident: In the late spring three Navajo men had been mutilated and murdered by three Farmington High School students. Just the day before a judge had ruled the youths would not be tried as adults for their crimes, and sentenced them to a couple of years in the state reformatory. For murdering three Indians the white boys had been given a legal spanking, was the way it was put to me. And the Indian community was damned angry because it was one more example of the way white man's justice shorted Indians.

All of this was told to me as a way of putting their actions at the parade in context. Every weekend for a month they had marched through downtown Farmington demanding justice, but a parade permit had been denied them this particular weekend. They interpreted the appearance of the Old West soldiers—dressed in the same uniforms worn by government troops when they had ruthlessly defeated the Navajo in the nineteenth-century Indian wars—as an analog to the tradition of calling in the cavalry when the Indians "acted up."

After hearing their side of the story I was not prepared to join the revolution, but I was convinced that these individuals believed in the morality of their cause and were committed to making lasting improvements for their people, no matter the personal sacrifices. And that induced a powerful sympathy.

Just about this time a guard came for Wilbert Tsosie and he left the cell. I continued to talk with Redhouse so I was present when Tsosie returned with news from the outside. He said he had just talked to his attorney, who had told him crowds had gathered and were maintaining a vigil; there were TV crews standing by and a report of the "riot" had been broadcast on national network news. The whole world was watching, he said.

That information sent spirits soaring. Everyone, myself included, suddenly saw himself as part of something important, of history in the making. . . .

Well, it was like that, and it wasn't. By the time I was released later that day (on $200 bail, charged with obstruction of an officer, trial set in two weeks) the cameras and crowds were gone. But I read all about the incident in the paper and caught the regional coverage on the six-o'clock news, and for several days afterward I was called and interviewed by members of the media.

But somehow that wasn't enough. After reflecting on the entire experience, and reading the newspaper reports, I felt that an essential point was being overlooked. In too many of the accounts the militants were labeled as street agitators, and I believed their radical actions could be justified in light of their pursuit of political empowerment.

I decided that I had been given this experience to make use of in some way. And taking that thought a step further, I decided that I had been selected to help shape its meaning.

I became an advocate for the Navajo. I penned a vitriolic op-ed piece in the local paper that purported to tell the "truth" of what had happened in Farmington. I contacted a radio talk-show host and went on the air to give voice to their grievances, as if hearing it from a white man would somehow make a difference. Knowing that one lesson of the civil-rights struggle was that a small group of activists has on occasion been able to achieve important goals and political objectives, I arranged for public meetings so people could see that the leaders of this movement were not irresponsible rabble-rousers. I went so far as to seek out the widow of one of the murdered Indians with the intention of writing something that would make her sorrow justly noticed.

Soon enough it became clear to me that the ethnic furies loosed that summer in Farmington were not going to reverse a century of oppression and injustice. And as the "movement" seemed to lose momentum, so my dedication to Indian issues waned. Fourteen years would pass during which I would move on and away, traveling many places but never back to Indian country, dusting off now and then my memories of the brief role I played in the Indian-rights fight like a war story become quaint over time.

In the spring of 1988, at, of all places, the Gene Autry Hotel in Palm Springs, California, I attended a Western art show and was moving from painting to painting when I was stopped by a portrait of Shiprock Peak. Jutting jaggedly out of desert sands west of Farmington, Shiprock is a volcanic plug that bears a startling resemblance to an old black ship under full sail, turned to stone, which is why it has been painted almost as many times as the Grand Canyon.

The artist, a lanky, affable fellow dressed like a ranch hand, moseyed over.

I nodded toward his painting and asked, "Are you from the Southwest?"

"Farmington, New Mexico," he answered, firing up a cigarette. "Ever heard of it?"

For a moment I just looked at him. "Yeah. I've heard of it," I replied. And then, because the patrons filing through were few in number, and he seemed interested in what I would say next, I told my Farmington Story.

When I was done, the artist chuckled richly. Not only that, he raised the ante with an unanticipated contribution: He said he'd gone to school with the three boys who had murdered the Navajo men.

"No kidding?" Then, almost rhetorically, I wondered aloud what had become of them.

"You haven't heard?" he asked.

Something in the way he said it put me on the alert. "No."

"A Navajo shaman put a curse on them and they're all dead."

I didn't know what to think. I am not one who believes only in what is scientifically explainable—I think the universe is infinite in its mysteries—but neither am I someone particularly partial to such notions.

"Come on. You don't believe in that stuff, do you?" I said to him.

His one-sided grin made it difficult to tell how honest he was being when he answered, "Let's say I keep an open mind about it."

I snorted. "That almost sounds like you do."

All kidding was put aside when he said, "What I know of Navajo witchcraft and how it works leads me to think if you mess with Indian spirits, you'd best beware."

As I say, I didn't know what to think; but the more I considered it the more my curiosity was piqued. Questions formed. What had been the outcome of all the dissent? Had the militants made a positive difference? I remembered one of the leaders telling me he wanted nothing less than to bring about a spiritual reawakening within the Navajo tribe that would lead to a restoration of some semblance of their ancestral greatness. Had that happened? And the juveniles who by all accounts had gotten away with murder: Who were they? What kinds of families did they come from? What had prompted them to commit such evil? Were they really dead and were their fates truly connected to Navajo witchcraft?

For fourteen years my interest in Indian affairs had lain emotionally dormant. The news that magic was part of the updated story, and the possibility that justice had finally been obtained through an Indian court of supernatural appeals, re-freshed that interest.

I was intrigued—enough to consider a return visit. Who knows what will come of it, I mused. Perhaps nothing. Then again, perhaps my role as a chronicler in this saga wasn't over yet.

1

THE CHOKECHERRY MASSACRE

1

DEATH IN
THE DESERT

The trip to Farmington, any way you go, crosses vast expanses of high desert grassland, shot with sagebrush and checkered with mesas that bore the eye like camouflage. Peering out through tinted windows, you can't help but admire the grit of the early pioneers who kept their horses' heads pointed down the trail to San Juan County to reap their share of the bounty they imagined the American West offered freely to those willing to make the trek. The number of automobiles pulled to the roadsides, hoods popped and radiators steaming as though they've stopped to catch their second wind, reminds you the journey is still an adventure in endurance.

These are peripheral areas to the northern Navajo frontier whose ownership is mixed among Navajo herders, Anglo ranchers, and the U.S. government, but Indians are the only people who actually live out here. All along the route you pass dirt roads that are little more than weed-choked wagon tracks striking off toward mud-and-cedar hogans just out of sight, or twenty miles away, there is no telling. Look closely and you are apt to see a Navajo shepherd trailing a flock of sheep that rolls like fleecy ground fog across slick rock and up a dry wash. Pause and you will hear the tinkling bells of marker sheep, the whip-whistle of the herder, the yap of a mongrel: musical notes of a pastoral symphony.

The views extend for a hundred miles out here—farther if you look north to where the mountains in Colorado are piled against the skyline as if New Mexico's canyons had been dug out and the dirt flung there. And there are no towns, unless you count those populated by prairie dogs. Just an occasional old-time trading post that stands its ground like it grew there, the ramshackle pens in back reminders of the annual sheep dips,

11

when Navajo sheepmen brought their flocks in to be immersed in vats of boiled lime and sulfur to prevent the spread of scabies. In the corner of your eye you can almost see them in their high-crowned hats pushing the bleating stock into solution-filled troughs with forked poles, while the women, in long skirts and necklaces, cook fry bread over an open campfire.

Driving toward a horizon that seems to maintain its distance, you feel the immense vastness of the ocean, of endless sky and pure space, so that when you finally do top a rise and see the "bright lights" of a town on the far side of what looks like open range forever, you know the feeling of sighting land after a long sea journey.

Farmington is still an hour away—in this country, "down the road apiece" can mean a day's drive—which leaves plenty of time to ponder the significance of its geographic isolation. How does the fact that this is the only major Anglo community for hundreds of miles shape the general mentality of its citizens? What is it like to live next door to the largest Indian tribe in the United States? A "foreign" nation with its own language, customs, and traditions? A defeated people whose tribal enmity toward the white man simmers just below the surface?

Farmington is a main-street town, running east to west, and is curiously flat—the tallest buildings stand two and three stories high; the commercial district grew in the direction of horizontal expansion rather than vertical thrust. The downtown blocks also lack a distinctive historic or cultural design style. Some of the store fronts are capped by territorial-style decorative brick-work, and many of the buildings were constructed out of adobe and sandstone blocks, but there is no Early Spanish and Old West ambience to Farmington, either of which would be traditional to the Southwest. What does show is the semi-modern glazed aspect of a town that once tried to make way for what was generally considered "progress," and in trying to serve a second master lost its regional character. Farmington has always reminded me of one of those landmark Victorian hotels whose lobby was once graced with marble wainscoting, sparkling chandeliers, and hand-carved oak fixtures, all of which has been removed and the lobby redecorated to cater to tourism and its developing trade.

It helps to know the history of this town.

The story is told that a Mormon pioneer traveling this way with two good wives in a covered wagon found himself surrounded by Indians on the warpath and decided, "We'll just have to stay here until we outnumber them." A more reliable version of the town's provenance has it that in the 1870s this area was a wintering spot favored by gold prospectors. They were followed by Mormon colonists, *gringo* ranchers who fattened their stock on the grama grass that carpeted the mesas, and pioneer farmers who put the river valleys under irrigation, and out of the commerce that ensued a farming town evolved that was appropriately named Farmington.

Over the next half-century, as farmers began to raise produce on a marketable scale, a substantial fruit industry flourished. Farmington advertised itself as "The Home of the Big Red Apple," but in spite of this prosperity it managed to retain a rural character, keeping its small-town ways. As late as 1949, if you had stopped an average citizen and asked him to peer into the future and describe what he saw, he would have seen cows and chickens in the backyard, his neighbor hauling wood and hay, and beyond that, more of the same. He would not have imagined big-city businessmen hurrying in and out of buildings with lease agreements in their briefcases, having to dodge automobiles to cross the street, a sky crowded with airplanes, his own chamber of commerce issuing brochures that promoted his hometown as "The Energy Capital of the West."

Within a few short years advanced technology and increased energy demands in the urban West changed the Farmington scene, bringing on an oil and natural-gas boom that multiplied a population of 3,000 persons tenfold, and turned a "cowtown" into a metropolis. Apple orchards were swallowed whole by housing developments. Dirt streets were paved; paved streets were widened. To attract as well as accommodate business, office buildings were built, along with supermarkets, shopping centers, and a country club with an eighteen-hole golf course. To serve the wings of commerce, the municipal airport was expanded to handle commuter flights from Denver, Salt Lake City, and Albuquerque and was dubbed "La Guardia of the Desert."

For almost ten years the town revved up for a 1950s vision of Tomorrowland that evaporated like a mirage when the boom peaked around 1960, and was followed by a slump that continued to sag until about 1970. In the depressed aftermath worried city officials tried to come up with a plan that would make them less vulnerable to fitful periods of growth and decline. And like many another Western town that abandoned its agricultural origins for the dream of becoming an energy empire, Farmington decided to cultivate a tourist-town identity. Advertising efforts by local boosters now focused on drawing vacationers to "The Gateway to Navajoland."

Drive through the main part of town and you see the Indian presence everywhere. Each block houses curio shops specializing in Indian arts and crafts. In addition to the usual tribal kitsch by way of Hong Kong—headdresses that look feathered with the down off Easter chicks—there are Navajo sandpaintings, baskets, pottery, and silver jewelry for sale, and rugs hang in the windows like the hides off New Mexico sunsets. The streets are filled with Navajo men dressed like cowboys driving pickup trucks, while Navajo women, as many in slacks and jeans as in traditional flowing skirts, stroll the sidewalks. You are even apt to spot an inebriated Indian stretched out on a park bench, sleeping away one wine hangover while dreaming of the next.

In spite of the fact that Indian resources and trade are essential to Farmington's economic livelihood—most of the oil and gas wells were located on Navajo land, and Navajos comprise an estimated one-third of the town's shoppers—Anglo attitudes toward Navajos have always been rooted in racial arrogance. Once the days passed when pioneer prerogatives gave white men lawless rights over native populations, Indians became a resource to be exploited. As far back as 1893, the *Junction City Times*, the town's newspaper, called it right when the editors wrote: "There can be no doubt that some strict course must be pursued in order to place the dominant White race in a position of safety and quietude, with respect to our dusky and uncertain neighbors. The tide of immigration will be stayed, the stream of settlers cease, men of enlightened ideas and ample means who must inevitably seek the lower San Juan for homes and prosperity, must be assured. Denizens of the cold and inclement east whose natural foresight shows them that right here in this country is the spot where fortune is to be made and ruddy health regained, will pause until shown that a stern line of demarcation exists between them and the Indian, and that over that line the Redskins shall not advance . . . and across which he himself should not be allowed to stray, except for the sole purpose of commerce, with an immediate return incumbent upon him."

Over the next eighty-odd years only the external appearances changed, as the prevailing attitude toward Indians continued to be dominated by nineteenth-century imperialistic views in which a strong profit motive was the primary rationale for good race relations. White merchants welcomed Navajo business, but not their presence. Navajos were denied full participation in the social, economic, and political affairs of the city, at the same time that their indigence, privations, and naïveté were taken advantage of. It was an attitude that tolerated casual discrimination, over time bred an atmosphere of hostile contempt, and in the end courted violence.

If a single incident can ever be cited as being representative of the racial attitude of a community, in Farmington it would probably be an event that took place in the late fifties. Several intoxicated Indians were walking past a fire station one evening, a couple of firemen were sitting outside, and they took a bucket of red paint and poured it over the Indians, covering them from head to toe. Because of the symbolism implied, they thought it quite a good joke. But when it was reported in the local press, an administrative proceeding followed and the result was a mild reprimand with the reminder, "These people are citizens too." Afterward, an informal poll of the community found that approximately 75 percent thought it was a humorous incident and punishment was not deserved, 15 percent were repulsed by the act and felt the firemen should have been terminated, and the remaining 10 percent had no opinion. According to an attorney close to the case at the time, who is still in practice today, this incident could be viewed as a radiograph of the heart of Farmington's attitude toward its Navajo neighbors.

There are many earnest people living in Farmington who will swear this is not a racist community, and that it would be libel against the town to call it one. But in 1974 it was put on trial for that very charge and, like it or not, Farmington is to the Indian-rights fight what Selma is to the black civil-rights movement. In this context, Farmington is remembered for its belligerent resistance to the recognition of justice and equality for all, and is held responsible for the personal tragedies that followed.

I returned to Farmington in the spring of 1988. My first stop was the local newspaper, the *Farmington Daily Times*, where I spent the better part of a day looking at microfilm. After locating and copying every article, editorial, and letter to the editor that pertained to my research, I made a list of each person mentioned by name. Then I checked into a cheap motel that let its guests make unlimited free local calls, opened the phone book, and started calling.

Although I still was not sure there was enough to write about in all this, I felt it was important to be able to justify my interest and, early on, I developed various rationales for why someone should bother to answer impertinent questions posed by a stranger. Depending on who I was talking to, I would use different appeals. When speaking with civic leaders, for instance, I might say, "When a community is bitterly fractured by controversial events the way Farmington was, there are always going to be questions and issues left unanswered and unresolved. Few communities have the luxury of an official historian who can provide a transcendent understanding of what happened."

With others I would customize my explanation to meet their specific concerns, but the phrasing followed similar lines. There is a distinction to be made between reflecting on the past and digging it up. A mix of misinformation, rumor, and gossip has distorted the healing process, preventing highly charged emotions from settling. It is time for someone to come in, talk to all parties, set the record straight, and put a proper ending to this tale.

Very quickly it became apparent to me that elaborate statements of purpose were unnecessary, and could even induce suspicion. To an extent that surprised me, I found people open and willing to share their thoughts and memories of that time. Indeed, virtually no one I spoke with was wanting for an opinion or lacking an anecdote. There were times when I felt as if I had come along just as a communal statute of limitations had run out and people suddenly felt free to speak their minds about an event that had been suppressed for years.

Another fact became obvious. As Indians will name a year for a memorable occasion and talk about it thereafter as the year such-and-such took place, so 1974 is remembered in Farmington. Many refer to it as "The Year of the Riot on Main Street," but ask around and you will hear personal variations that are poignantly expressive of the tension, anxiety, and fear that seized the residents of this community during that time. "The Year I Started Carrying a Gun." "The Year I Walked My Children to School." "The Year I Worried Every Time My Dog Brought a Strange Bone Home."

Before making too many inquiries, I wanted to determine what in fact had happened to the three youths charged with murdering the Navajo men. After all, the key to my interest in returning to Farmington had been the tantalizing tale of vengeance through witchcraft.

About the "boys," I heard all sorts of stories. One was killed in a freak car accident, I was told. Another was supposedly struck by lightning that bolted out of a blue sky, somewhere near El Paso. The third, I was informed, had been crushed to death by a trash compactor after passing out in a dumpster. From several sources I heard that a drug overdose somehow figured in. Then I heard one boy was still alive, but had sustained severe motor-nerve damage as a result of injuries received when he was working under a car and the jacks had mysteriously collapsed. "He limped into the hospital dragging one side, and that's the way he walks today."

Confirmation of the particulars would be forthcoming if I decided to pursue this story, I knew, but even at this point it was interesting to observe the way people in town reported on the fates of the youths. No one seemed to know for certain what had become of them, but most seemed willing to believe that some righteous force had caught up with them. Some called it Karma. Others quoted the passage in the Bible that says we reap what we sow. And more than a few mentioned the Indian curse. Each had his or her own interpretation for the strange workings of fate, but all had arrived at the same conclusion—"You can't tell me there's no justice in the world"—and the idea of a curse lived on in the lore of the town.

It was time to get in touch with Rena Benally. Back when I had first become involved in this story, it had struck me, after reading the scanty information about the victims in the paper, that a fuller presentation of who these individuals were would restore a vestige of dignity to their memory. Through my Navajo contacts I had met Rena Benally, the widow of one of the murdered Navajo men. Acculturated more than most Navajo women—she had spent much of her early life in the company of white missionaries—she was nonetheless a shy and inward-looking woman, full of hidden sentiments, and it took many conversations before she felt comfortable enough to cooperate with my desire to write an article about her husband and their life together. Neither one of us knew how much good it had done, but I believe it provided her with a sense of conclusion, and in the process we had become good friends.

Over ten years had passed since we had last spoken, but when I heard Rena's voice on the phone I knew the familiarity we had established then had created a bond unbroken by the passage of time. I did not tell her my reason for getting back in touch; I saved that for the lunch date we arranged to have at a Farmington restaurant.

Rena was in her late forties now and twenty additional pounds had rounded her figure in the intervening years, but her face had changed very little. She still had the natural almond-eyed raven-haired beauty that Anglo artists tend to romanticize in Indian-maiden paintings.

We played catch-up. I asked her about her life today. Then, after we had finished eating and were sipping coffee, I brought up The Curse.

"Rena. There is something I would like to ask you. Have you heard any witch-talk about those boys?"

I know it probably sounds a little hokey, put that way. But knowing little about the subject other than that it was linked to Navajo ritual and religion, I wanted to be respectful and convey an openness and ability to enter into the spirit of other people's beliefs. In no way did I want a hint of skepticism on my part to make her feel I already had formed an opinion on the matter.

When I asked, I had no idea what she would say next. I did know that an almost impenetrable wall of secrecy surrounds the subject of witchcraft, and that most Navajo, even acculturated Navajo, are reluctant to talk about it in any specific way, especially with non-Navajos.

She took a long time before answering. "At first, like everyone else, I wanted revenge too. . . ." Her voice trailed off.

I waited until I couldn't bear it any longer. "Does that mean there's something to this witching rumor?"

She hesitated, then said, "I've heard people say things."

She was obviously uncomfortable with the direction of our conversation, but I needed to know. "You've heard people say things like what?"

"That they were going to work on those boys, one at a time."

"Who was going to work on them?"

She wouldn't say.

"How does it work?"

She didn't know.

"Do you believe it worked?"

"I heard it did."

"From whom?"

She wouldn't say.

I sat there staring at her for a moment. Then, deciding not to push her any harder, I changed the subject.

Back at my motel that evening, I stood in the doorway to my room basking in the lavender afterglow of a desert sunset while waiting for the heat of the day to subside. The sunburnt air, like a tongue depressor, left me trying to lick the dry away. Overhead, a neon cowboy spinning a lariat flickered and snapped like a bug zapper. Recalling my conversation with Rena, I didn't think she was telling me all she knew, but that was okay. There had been enough mystery in her answers to make a compelling case for a deeper probe. And if my quest was to be successful, I sensed her cooperation would be pivotal.

Going north out of town, the road draws a straight line through middle-class subdivisions that have claimed the desert in the name of suburbia. For several miles the pavement is bordered by a rich variety of plant life. Just as cottonwoods and tamarisk trim the riverbanks in this country, grasses and flowers, watered by runoff, flourish along the roadsides.

At the entrance to what locals call Chokecherry Canyon the surface turns to packed dirt where gas companies have bladed a trail through sand and sage and scattered piñon trees. In all directions drip tanks, well heads, and pipelines loop out of the ground like busted guts. Where it crosses the dry washes, the road suddenly goes soft. Sand is worse than mud. Spin your tires twice and you'll walk out.

For years this desolate region has been a popular place for family outings. Parents bring their kids out on weekends and holidays to pick chokecherries, to picnic, and to hunt for potsherds and arrowheads. Some say the area is haunted by its native past. Whether you are superstitious or not, anyone who has spent much time out here will admit the land is strangely charged.

Standing in the loose fine dust of an arroyo, you will sometimes think you hear the trickling of water over rocks and feel a refreshing coolness wash over you.

Great crinkled rock formations that look like immense scaly

lizards basking in the sun seem peculiarly alive in another dimension, and appear to follow you wherever you go.

A coyote grinning at you from a ridge will disappear without a track, as though it ducked down an anthill.

The senses belie and magic abounds, as at the start of some mythological creation.

And everywhere, Indian artifacts lie buried in the earth— spear points, stone tools, carved fetishes. There is just no telling what secrets these windblown sands and sun-scorched hills might yield.

On a seasonable springtime Sunday in 1974, Jim and Carolyn Hastings, lifetime residents of Farmington, packed their Ford with kids and cooler and headed north to make good on their promise to someday take their three sons on an expedition to Chokecherry Canyon. While Jim drove, Carolyn read aloud from *Jonathan Livingston Seagull*, a book she was enjoying so much she wanted to share it with her family. There were only a few pages left by the time they arrived at Brown Springs, a place in the canyon where a spring bubbled up beneath a range of sandstone cliffs, and Carolyn thought the book was too good to put down so she continued to read to the very end. But the boys were too excited to listen any longer, and all three jumped out of the car, scrambling up a rocky shelf to begin their artifact hunt.

When she was finished, Carolyn stepped from the car and answered the "Hey, Mom!" call of one of her sons with a big wave.

"Is it the same as when you were here?" Jimmy, her oldest at thirteen, yelled down from the top of the eroded stone formation.

Glancing swiftly around at a sheer overhang of smooth rock streaked black with seep that seemed to cradle a solitude that was the natural way of the world, Carolyn sighed in remembrance. It had been years since her last visit and she thought very little was different. "The same," she sang back. But upon a closer survey of the surroundings she noted that in fact it *had* changed, becoming in the interval a teenage party area, its popularity documented by broken glass, crushed beer cans, and .22-caliber bullet hulls. The litter also included a pair of black workboots she suspected must have been left behind after a wild time the night before.

As they had driven up, Carolyn had been conscious of the way the scent of fresh-cut sage sweetened the air blowing in the car windows. She loved the smell of sage. As a young girl she would strip the branches clean with her hands, press the petals to her face, and breathe in deeply. At the time she had wondered about its source, and now, as she and her husband started to collect firewood, she found herself walking along the rim of a small dike that had been pushed up by a sheepherder to catch springwater, following a perfume trail as she looked for kindling.

Spotting what appeared to be a clump of sagebrush piled on a mound of rocks, she headed that way to see if there were any dry pieces. Her eyes roamed the area as she walked because the smell of sage was stronger here, so she was standing beside the brushpile before she looked down and saw that those were not rocks underneath.

She jumped back, letting out a horrified cry. "Jim!"

Her husband was standing about twenty-five feet away, down a sandy wash, and he started running toward her. So did her kids. They all thought she had been bitten by a rattlesnake.

She felt her husband's hands on her shoulders. "What's wrong, honey?"

Swallowing deeply to steady herself, she gestured toward the sagebrush. "There's a dead Indian over there."

He looked at her closely, and when nothing in her eyes backed off, without saying a word he turned and started walking slowly in the direction she pointed.

As she watched him go, what she had seen under the sagebrush began to take a clearer form in her mind, developing like a Polaroid print. Without checking vital signs she knew the man was dead. Anyone would have known that just by looking at the body. Because it was naked she had been able to see how it was mottled with bruises, and the bloody damage to the head looked like she imagined it would if that was where the man had been shot.

For an instant she sagged under a sadness. Her feelings for Indians ran deep. As a young girl she used to see three and sometimes four generations huddled together in a horse-drawn wagon, creaking along the roads leading to and from the reservation. Their ancestry, culture, and traditions had seemed to give them something to belong to, a close sense of kinship she had grown up wanting for her own family. Apart from the shock of stumbling upon a gruesome death, she felt a deep hurt that one of a people she so admired had come to such an awful end.

The sweet smell of sage brought her out of her reverie, reminding her that this was something that had probably happened very recently. As it also dawned on her that the person who had done it might still be around, she turned in a slow circle, sweeping the ridge of bare rock and desert brush with her eyes. Though she saw nothing out of the ordinary, there were many places a watcher could remain hidden, which lent an air of menace to the quiet. She was straining for a muffled cough, the sound of footfalls, the click as a firearm is cocked, when she heard her three boys clattering down the cliffside.

"Get back to the car," she shouted. "Now!" And as she hurried toward the Ford herself, she could hear her husband, who had seen all he needed to see, coming up fast behind her.

It had been a slow month for crime in San Juan County. Arson was suspected as the cause of a fire at the Herman Miller farm that destroyed 3,000 bales of hay. Deputies were investigating a report that a seventeen-year-old girl had run away from home. There was an attempted break-in at the Red Garter Cafe, and vandalism to a county-owned Caterpillar. But nothing out of the ordinary until the dispatcher at the Sheriff's Department received a frantic call from Carolyn Hastings.

Deputy Bruce Brimhall, who thought of himself as a farmer and this as moonlighting, responded, and because this was not your normal Sunday afternoon check-it-out, Undersheriff Doug Brown was also called. It took something sensational to bother the sheriff on a weekend, and the discovery of a dead Indian didn't qualify. Hardly a day went by that the sheriff's office wasn't called to pry one out of a car wreck, piece by piece, or scrape one off the highway where he'd wandered like game that didn't know better. Some wiseguy once cracked that the Highway Department ought to post caution signs warning motorists to watch out for Indians, never mind deer.

The undersheriff lived in Aztec, fifteen miles to the northeast, so by the time he pulled up at Brown Springs not only had the deputy taken a statement, the medical examiner was inspecting the corpse and the ambulance from the mortuary was backing up to the scene. Doug Brown, Jr., a crew-cut, square-jawed former sergeant with the Farmington Police Department whose angled features were given a boyish set by his heavy black-framed glasses, tipped his Western hat for maximum shade as he approached Deputy Brimhall, who stood sweating in the chocolate-brown uniform of the department.

"What do we have?"

The deputy gestured with his head to the far side of Brown Springs. "Another good Indian."

Set in permanent sunsquint, Brown's pale blue eyes took on the hard sheen of old pawn. "Show me."

When the deputy lifted the branches of drying sage, gingerly, as though they formed a blanket on a sleeping man he did not want to wake, the undersheriff grimaced and exhaled quickly, as if to rid himself of bad air, so strong was the odor of alcohol.

Taking a step back, he inspected the lifeless form lying face down in the dirt in front of him from a remove that allowed him to take in the entire body at a glance. It was an Indian all right, an obese, powerfully built man. The medical investigator would give him the precise cause of death, but Brown didn't need an official report to tell him the obvious: The man had been beaten, he'd been burned, and his head had been crushed with rocks. His brooding eyes settled on one grisly detail—the face was puffy and mashed at the same time, like a pumpkin carving after a freeze; then another—rocks, stained with blood and hair, were lined up along one side of the body as if someone had had it in mind to make a bonfire of the man—pausing long enough on each to allow the implications as well as the specifics to sink in. His guess was the victim had been dead less than twelve hours because he wasn't all that discolored yet, and the swelling was minimal.

It was a difficult crime scene to work. There was trash everywhere, and it was hard to separate what tracks had been left by kids out partying previously, what had been put down by the Hastings family, and which were pertinent to the crime. Combing the area for physical evidence, Brown was able to determine what had become of the man's clothing. The black workboots appeared to belong to the victim, and between them and his final resting place were several fire sites where, among the ashes, he found the burnt remains of a nylon shirt and blue jeans.

At a certain point, when he felt that searching further was not going to yield anything useful, the undersheriff tried to add up what he had. Standing on a jut of rimrock from which he could see great distances of windswept desert given a loose nap by the sparse vegetation, he lit a Winston and pressed himself to come up with some theory that would explain such a grotesque act of homicidal violence. Any time you found your

victim undressed you suspected you were faced with a sex
crime, and there was no doubt sexual overtones were present
here. As the body had been rolled onto a stretcher, Brown had
noticed that the man's groin had been gigged by a sharp in-
strument and the tip of his uncircumcised penis charred like a
candle wick. Trying to imagine what would have driven someone to such extreme brutalization of the private parts, he speculated that possibly the fellow had been caught fooling around
with the wrong man's wife, and this had been a way of evening
the score.

Grinding a hole in the sand with his boot heel, Brown buried
the Winston butt so it wouldn't be mistaken for evidence by
others who might rework the scene. There was nothing else he
felt he could do until the dead man had been identified. There
being no pockets to search for a wallet, he knew that knowledge wouldn't come until fingerprints were matched or a family member reported the victim missing.

The undersheriff glanced at his watch. It was almost five. If
he didn't hurry he'd be late for a family get-together at his
mother-in-law's. After instructing the deputy to take in the
evidence that had been gathered, he said he'd compile a written
report in the morning, and returned to his day off.

It was 6:20 and Brown had just sat down to eat when the
phone rang.

"For you, Doug," his mother-in-law called.

"Who is it?" Brown asked.

"The dispatcher."

"What is it this time," he growled as he took the phone.

"You're not going to believe this. . . ."

He listened to what she had to say, and she was right.

"I'm on my way," he said and hung up. But first he called
Lieutenant R. B. Miller, next in command under him. As
Brown would comment later, "When things double up, I want
hands."

To a sheriff's office that prided itself on Western informality—
some deputies suited up, some were known to go plainclothed,
depending on what they had clean to wear—Lieutenant R. B.
Miller brought an impeccable militaristic bearing. The "R"
stood for Rufus, but everyone called him Bob, and he was a
hefty six-footer, forty-four years of age, whose drawl identified
South Texas as his birthplace and whose jowls and dewlaps all
but fitted him in bib overalls. But you weren't going to find

straw in the pockets of his uniform. From the spitshine on his Western boots to his snappy cream-colored Stetson whose brim had been trimmed down to three inches ("Case a wind come up, it don't blow off as easy"), he embodied the average person's idea of Western Peace Officer.

A gentleman who owned a moral streak that referenced a decade of honorable service in the Marine Corps before he turned to law enforcement, Miller brought the same high standards to his police work. You want to be a good cop, rookies were told, watch the way Bob Miller does his job. When he walks away from a crime scene, every scrap of evidence has been collected, all vital information has been properly recorded, and precise measurements have been taken. Even a lawyer could reconstruct the scene from his diagrams.

Some said his obsession for thoroughness was also his downfall when the time came for promotions because it showed up his superiors. But come a showdown or a shoot-out, or whenever it was time to tighten things up at the Sheriff's Department, Lieutenant Miller was called to the rescue.

Miller arrived at the scene at 6:57 P.M. In a small black book he jotted quick notes on the physical surroundings. It was a remote area, two and a half miles north of the city, a small basin dotted with cedar and piñon trees and indented in a thirty-foot-high sandstone bluff like a bay in a rocky coastline. The location was approximately a mile and a half east of Brown Springs.

While the undersheriff briefed him on the details of the case he had investigated earlier in the day, Miller scanned the area, a grim expression remarking silently on the situation that had developed prior to his arrival. Apparently the report had been received by the dispatcher at the Farmington Police Department, and when she had broadcast a request for assistance on the police radio band, everyone with a badge and a gun—highway patrolmen, city police, off-duty deputies—had headed north, trailed by a volunteer force of private citizens who had nothing better to do with their Sundays than monitor the police frequencies on scanners, picking up on a fire or accident and racing out to the scene. And doing what came naturally to a car-driving crowd converging on a spectacle, they had driven as close to the scene as possible before parking and walking right up to the object of curiosity.

Someone in authority should have taken charge, cordoned the area off, initiated the appropriate steps to protect the integ-

rity of the crime scene. That was elementary. And that had not
been done. So it was with dismay that Miller observed at least
two dozen citizens swarming the area, paying no attention to
where they were walking, carelessly flipping cigarette butts,
possibly destroying evidence, certainly contaminating the
scene; and more uniformed officers milling about than there
was any need for.

Approaching the center of activity, Miller wondered who
was responsible for the fiasco. Then he saw his boss, Sheriff
Dan Sullivan, storming around, and it all made sense. Although the sheriff was blooded in law enforcement (his grandfather had served as sheriff when New Mexico was still a
territory), Miller had always thought of the man more as a
politician than a lawman. In his opinion, Sullivan's folksy
good-ol'-boy manner had won him four elections to high office, not his crime-solving abilities. It wouldn't have surprised
him to find the sheriff selling tickets.

"Bob." Sergeant Gill of the Farmington Police Department
greeted him with a friendly salute. Though he had been the first
officer to arrive on the scene, Gill knew the primary jurisdiction belonged to the county. Nodding toward two young men
in T-shirts and Levi's, he said, "Those there are the ones who
found him." Then he tossed his head in the direction of a group
of uniformed officers standing thirty feet away in a loose hud-
dle around a figure lying on the ground.

The undersheriff headed that way, while Miller strode over
to the two men. "I'd appreciate if you'd go over what happened today. From start to finish."

They said they had come up the canyon to go for a hike.
They had parked their car about a hundred yards west of here
and were walking along the top of the bluff when they saw the
body below. They left immediately, notified the police, and
drove back with an officer.

After he had taken it all down in his notebook, Miller asked,
"Did you see anyone else in the area while you were here?"

Both nodded. They remembered seeing a Ford pickup, a '72
or '73 model, white top and blue base. It stayed in their mind
because the driver had made several passes before stopping
near their car and looking it over. That made them suspicious,
but then he drove off and that was the last they saw of him.

"You get a look at him?"

"Too far away."

"Anything else?"

A shake of the head.

After thanking them, Miller strode over to where the officers stood watch over a light-framed male Indian stretched out full length with his head to the north, feet to the south, face-down in the dirt, emitting a strong alcohol stench. His top half was dressed in a white undershirt, a brown pullover, and a blue jacket, all partially burned, and he was naked from the waist down. There were three large rocks lying on the east side of his head, two river rocks and one sandstone type. Each was stained with blood and tufted with hair, identifying them as instruments that had probably been used to bludgeon the man to death. Adding a grotesque touch to an already ugly scene, a glob of melted plastic filled the crease in the man's buttocks, which were also splotched where the skin had been scorched by fire.

When he had finished inventorying the hard facts of the killing, Miller looked up and noted the way those standing around stared uneasily at the lewdly exposed corpse, as if they were embarrassed to be looking so intently at a naked man, found his condition repugnant, but were unable to take their eyes off him. He could tell that some were sickened, while others thought it was no big deal because the victim was an Indian. To him all victims were alike in that they were human.

"A carbon copy of the other," Undersheriff Brown submitted.

A fact that was apparently lost on someone, Miller reflected.

This line of thought gave way easily to a completely different one, as Miller realized by the slant of the shadows off the piñon trees that he had barely a half-hour of good light left.

When he asked several gawkers not to touch anything until he'd had a chance to look the area over, the undersheriff picked up on the cue and diplomatically attempted to assert some semblance of control over the crowd. "You, you, and you, get back down yonder," he barked to civilian and officer alike as he tried to get the idea across as reasonably as possible that he had a job to do and they were in the goddamn way.

While Brown played the part of traffic cop, cursing under his breath and shaking his head when he wasn't ordering people around, Lieutenant Miller went to work. He was familiar with the particular challenges presented by an outdoor crime scene. It was far more complex and fragile than an interior because there were more elements to consider, each of which could be impinged upon so easily—by rain or blowing winds, by the media or cops, whose curiosity was a crime scene's worst enemy. You had to get what you could while it was there, because the evidence wouldn't last long and once it was gone there was no getting it back.

His starting point was the site of the body, where the crime had ended, and he worked backward from there. Leading away from the body were two sets of footprints that Miller felt were involved in the crime. But it was hard to get a fix on their size and shape because the ground here was loose, leaving depressions, not impressions. Careful with the placement of each step he took, he followed a rough trail of marks back across a sandy flat, stopping every few feet to squat on his heels for a closer look.

He was good at this. Since he'd tracked small game as a boy, few details escaped his eyes when he was determined to read the record left by creatures passing across a landscape. He knew, for instance, that dating a track depended on the time of year. In this country in the spring, when temperatures dropped below freezing at night, thawing in the daytime, a track that looked fresh in the morning could be a month old. Likewise, in the summer when it was breezy, it didn't take long for a track to age or disappear. Even the way a track was put down could be telling. He'd caught a fellow once on a $20,000 vandalism case because the man had just started wearing Western boots, and instead of walking on the heel would shift his weight to the outside, leaving a print that was deeper on one side than the other.

Miller stood up. He took a step in the general direction he had been going and stopped. Just to one side of his own foot, at a spot where the caliche had formed a crust, he spotted an identifiable print. It was only a partial—the corner of a heel, a section of the sole—but it was enough for him to feel he was looking at the patterned design typically found on the bottom of a hiking boot.

A preternatural hush seemed to surround him during the next several minutes as the intensity of his inspection combined with the circumstances of this being a crime scene to create an intricate, under-glass stillness. It was almost as if, by asking all the elements to testify, every rock, bush, tree, and grain of sand was afraid to move for fear of being put in the witness box next. Even the evening breeze seemed to hold its breath.

He took several more steps and stopped again, staring down at a complete print whose distinct markings identified it as a boot that was described in the popular vernacular as a "waffle-stomper." On his hands and knees now, he studied the markings and was able to make out six distinct stars in the sole and one in the heel.

Miller looked up and around. The sheriff and an entourage of officers were off in another area entirely. It was the wrong place to look, and for once he was grateful for Sullivan's incompetence.

After framing the track with tree limbs so no one would accidentally trample it, the lieutenant moved on with his search. Several feet farther on he discovered a fresh depression in the ground of approximately the same dimensions as one of the large rocks by the body; around its edges, positioned in a way you would expect of someone who had retrieved the rock, were a series of prints that looked to have been made by a boot with a slick sole and a pointed toe. Looking back toward the body, Miller saw the likelihood that the soft prints he had previously found indistinguishable belonged to someone wearing cowboy boots.

So there were two of them, he was thinking when he heard his name urgently called by the undersheriff.

Approximately 200 feet from the body, Brown had discovered evidence of where the whole macabre business had probably started: A scooped-out place where someone had wallowed in the sand. A pair of light-brown sunglasses broken in half. One black leather low-quarter shoe. Two socks. More large rocks splashed red. And a puddle of blood in which the tread of a waffle-stomper was imprinted like a fossil in mud—a single four-pointed star in the heel, six of the same in the sole.

"Lieutenant. Over here."

Just west of where they were standing, at a place where cars could park but none had on this evening, another deputy had located a set of tire tracks as pronounced as skid marks. And beside them, drawn in the dust like a diagram for a dance step, more sets of waffle-stomper prints that Miller would recognize anywhere now.

Glancing at the fading light, Miller's long legs took him swiftly to his vehicle where he retrieved a pack of plastic evidence bags and his camera. He knew, moving this fast, that he had only picked up on the obvious and there were probably many things overlooked. But he also felt that what had been found was important and a record should be started immediately.

It was while walking back that he saw, to his consternation, a county judge lean over the body and withdraw the hardened plastic from between the dead man's buttocks. Miller was not about to walk over, take it from him, and stick it back; but he did feel that the body should not have been tampered with, and it distressed him no end to think that other relevant details had already been altered or lost.

He started at the tire tracks, first taking measurements of the distance between the tires, both width and length, from which he would be able to tell if he was looking for a mid-size or full-size vehicle. Next, after laying a wooden ruler across the track and his gold star beside it for identification purposes, he snapped several pictures using his Polaroid flash camera. He knew this information wasn't the lock-and-key type and wouldn't do him much good until he had an idea who the vehicle belonged to, but once he did have a suspect it could turn out to be an incriminating link to the crime scene. Any tire was going to have certain cuts and nicks that differentiated it from every other tire, sort of like fingerprints. A good photo of a tire print could be absolutely matched to an actual tire.

From different angles he then photographed the bloody bootprint, making sure the camera caught its distinctive markings, and once again using the wooden ruler to show its exact length and width. He came up with a bootprint that measured 3½ inches across at the heel, 4 inches across at the sole, and 12½ inches from heel to toe. Setting the camera aside, he collected blood and soil samples. If he ever did manage to find the boots that had left the print, he knew he would find trace elements of the same.

Knowing where the crime had begun, and having a body to inform him where it had ended, made it easier to track its course. From the pool of blood, twin grooves, suggestive of drag marks, extended for almost 100 feet, and where they stopped there were indications a struggle had taken place. Staring at a blood-soaked patch of sand and a black pile of ashes from a wood fire, Miller bent over and stirred the debris with a stick, turning up several small pieces of brown material charred at the edges. The texture suggested the material came from a pair of brown Levi-type pants. He sealed the sample in another plastic bag.

From the evidence available it was difficult to determine how the victim had gotten from the fire site to where his body was found. Miller felt he either was moving under his own power or was carried, as there were no drag marks present. There were signs he was down on the ground at least twice before reaching his final position, however. More blood. More charred material.

After photographing the first print he had found, the lieutenant moved to the body itself, taking three pictures of it as it was found and one after it was turned over on its back. He had gazed into the faces of more dead people than he cared to remember and usually had no problem with adults. It was when kids met their premature ends that he was capable of a strong rush of sentiment. The exception was a homicide where excessive brutality was involved. If a fellow wanted someone dead there were any number of quick and easy ways to get the job done. Here, it was apparent the killing time had been intentionally drawn out. As his imagination choreographed the crime out of the props that had been left behind, and one dead actor, he saw two mean men chasing a smaller third, pummeling him with rocks when he was down, torturing him with fire, and God only knew what else had gone on before plastic had been melted on the man's naked buttocks.

He went no further with this line of thought. He knew enough to know that this man had been made to suffer, and it had been a prolonged and terrible suffering before he had been allowed to die. And that changed the character of the crime for the lieutenant. No murder was excusable, but some evoked a special obligation on his part to see his work through to a conviction. With these cases he put the muscle of a full commitment into action no matter how many extra hours or how much legwork it took. Though it was of little comfort to the man at his feet, this became one of those cases for Lieutenant Miller.

It was while calculating the distances between the different significant points with a tape measure that Miller noticed two Farmington Police Department officers, following Sheriff Sullivan's orders, attempting to make a cast of the complete bootprint. Watching them slop plaster directly into the impression without preparing it properly first, and knowing the minute the moist mixture hit the sand it would change the shape of the print drastically, he was relieved that he had gotten to it first. He had a feeling that what they came up with would be worthless, and he would be right.

As the sun disappeared behind the Chuska Mountains, dusk settled into the basin like a cloud of purple dust. A certain coolness came with it. Strangers in this country might think it was going to rain, but locals knew it was a typical April night.

Sheriff Sullivan asked several of his deputies to lend a hand carrying the bloody rocks up to the trunk of his vehicle. And then, after everyone who had no business being there in the first place had gone home, a core group of officers congregated and tried to make sense of the mystery. Two men, both Indians, had apparently been murdered by the same person(s) on the same day. Who did it? Why?

Everyone seemed to agree that this was probably something Indians had done to their own. Violent death was no stranger to those raised on the reservation. Drunken brawls, knife fights, and general mayhem were a fact of Indian life. Although none of the officers had seen such sadistic cruelty before, it was well known that Navajos distrusted justice through the white man's courts, preferring to settle grievances in their own way, with their own means of enforcement. Now that there were two victims, Brown wasn't so sure about his triangle theory, which was replaced by the sheriff's suspicion the dead men might have been involved in a rape of some young girl. Although there were no active rape cases involving Indians currently under investigation, Sullivan speculated that the victim and her family might have preferred to keep the crime a secret rather than face publicity, exacting revenge in their own time and fashion.

Among the deputies present was an older man everyone called Shake. Of old New Mexican stock, he'd run a trading post on the reservation in his early years, knew the Navajo people and their ways, and spoke the language better than most of them. Just by looking at a Navajo he could tell you what clan he belonged to. As the theorizing went on, Miller sidled over to Shake and, dropping his voice to keep the conversation just between the two of them, asked, "Shake. You ever seen an Indian with a size twelve and a half foot?"

Shake didn't have to think about it. "Nope."

Miller nodded in the dark. "Me neither."

For most of those present, the evening ended when the plaster cast of the bootprint had hardened, and Sheriff Sullivan discontinued the investigation until the next morning. Lieutenant Miller was unable to let go just yet, however. He had not had a chance to check the victim's clothing for possible clues, and he knew better than to assume that anyone else had. So he proceeded to the Lee and Oviatt Mortuary, where both bodies had been taken.

The results were negative. What he did establish positively, after examining the victim who had just been brought in and the one found earlier in the day, was an identical pattern to the beatings and burnings, down to the scorched genitals.

Impatient to get started on the identification process, Miller called for a deputy, and when Bruce Brimhall showed up he instructed him to roll fingerprints tonight. While this was being done, Miller stepped outside for a cigarette and to think things over.

So far, other than a lot of tracks, none of which were going to lead them to a suspect, all they had to go on were the bodies. But there was an old saying, "When you're at a loss on a homicide investigation, go to the body," and he considered that. Both victims were probably Navajo. There were indications both had liquor in their systems. Because the reservation was dry, that meant the men most likely had been drinking at one of the bars in town at an earlier time. As anyone familiar with the situation in reservation bordertowns knew, Indians had their own favorite drinking establishments. So if you wanted to get a make on one of the habitués, that was where you went.

When he finished his cigarette, Miller went back inside.

"Done?" he asked the deputy.

"Just about."

"Good. Then let's go see if we can turn up someone who knows these men."

It was a tactic he had used before to accelerate the identification process when there was a highway accident involving Indians and no IDs could be found. Round up a bunch of the bedraggled bingers from Farmington's Indian bar scene and walk them by the victim. A strained procedure at best, it was often productive and sometimes served a dual purpose, turning up a name *and* issuing a warning about drinking and driving.

As with most reservation bordertowns, Farmington had its own skid row district that catered to a native clientele that on any given day or night appeared to be drinking its way to oblivion. Picking them up in twos and threes and escorting them to the mortuary, Miller and the deputy walked them into the room where the two bodies were stretched on tables, draped with a sheet. One at a time Miller pulled the coverings back far enough for them to get a good look at the face, no more.

Miller did not have a trace of superstition in his bones. In his mind, people were attached to earthbound agonies that ended at death's door. The idea of ghosts reaching out from the grave to haunt or hurt the living belonged to the realm of fantasy—and Navajo superstition. He knew that the dead were objects of horror for the Navajo, because they believed an evil spirit remained in a corpse. So the Navajo reaction to one had always struck him as half-comic. No matter their state of drunkenness, it shocked them sober. Their eyes would bulge as if they were seeing someone *returned* from the dead to claim them, and they couldn't get out of the room fast enough. But before he let them out they had to cooperate with the program.

On this night, on the third run-through, he got lucky. A bleary, blunt-faced Navajo man came fully awake before looking quickly away when Miller pulled the sheet down on the first individual who had been found.

"You recognize this man?" he asked.

The Navajo glanced again. He wasn't sure, which was understandable given the battered condition of the face.

"Any idea who he might be?"

The Navajo mumbled something that included the name "John Harvey."

"John Harvey? Is that what you said?"

The Indian nodded and Miller wrote it down.

"And this other?" He snapped the sheet down. "You know him?"

The Navajo was a man of fewer words than the lieutenant. He shook his head and left the room before Miller could offer him a ride back or to buy a round of drinks.

On the chance that the victim had been picked up for a prior offense, and with a name he could check the file and compare prints, Miller drove up to the Farmington Police Department, which sat on a bluff overlooking the city. The prints matched. The first victim was indeed a Navajo named John Harvey. He had a string of arrests, all alcohol related. His age was thirty-nine; his last known address was Fruitland, New Mexico, twelve miles to the west.

Now that he knew the identity of at least one of the victims, Miller was satisfied with the progress he had made in a few short hours, and scribbled "Pending further investigation" in his notebook. There was no guarantee the mystery of the other man's identity would be solved as easily. It was possible the men didn't know each other, hadn't been together the previous evening, and were randomly selected simply because they were available at the time the killers decided to go on a rampage. But he had a feeling that an ID on the second victim would not be long in coming. Certainly not as long as the answers to the questions, What is happening? And why?

By car it was less than a five-minute drive home for Miller, and as he navigated back streets made even darker by unlit houses, his thoughts turned to the town asleep around him, and the murderous air that would rise on the morrow. He had lived in Farmington for almost twenty years and always considered it a friendly community. He'd met his wife here, raised kids here, planned to retire here. It was home. But knowing there were cold-blooded killers at large made it seem like a dangerous place tonight.

And especially hazardous for Indians.

2

DISQUIETING
DETAILS

The silver threads of three rivers, fed by melting snows from Colorado's mountains, braid into a single strand at Farmington, where La Plata and the Animas rivers join the San Juan River. Cross the San Juan and you leave the ditched and irrigated lowlands made artificially suitable for farming by the pioneers and arrive at thirsty plains of bare rock and sand. The river mostly follows the modern northern boundary of the Navajo Reservation, a place as different in feeling from Farmington as it is in physical characteristics. To many non-natives, there is a rich and natural beauty to the landscape of the reservation, but to the author of an anonymous poem written at the turn of the century,

Beyond the San Juan River, are paths that lead to death
To the desert's scorching breezes, that feel like Satan's
    breath,
Beyond the white man's outposts, where the poisonous
    reptile waits
Are the Devil's own possessions, his original estates.

Beyond the San Juan River, are paths as yet unknown
With a tarantula 'neath each pebble, a centipede 'neath
    each stone,
Behind the dreaded cactus, beneath the noxious weeds
Are ever-present perils, of a million different breeds.

Beyond the San Juan River, 'tis said the story's told
Are paths that lead to mountains of purest virgin gold,
But 'tis our firm conviction, whatever else they tell
Beyond the San Juan River, all paths lead straight to hell.

36

To the Navajo this is holy ground. And if the scenery seems barren and inhospitable to "white eyes," to Navajos it is both heaven and home. This is their designated corner of the universe. According to their origin myth, here, between the four sacred peaks of Mount Taylor, Blanca Peak, Mount Hesperus, and the San Francisco Peaks, is the place of emergence, where the Holy People came up from the underworld to slay the monsters that roamed old Navajoland before they created the *Dineh*—The People—as the Navajo refer to themselves. It is the center of their ancient history, sacred beliefs, and curing ceremonies. All that takes place within its borders is strengthened and blessed, while everything that goes on without is dangerous and disruptive.

Anthropologists tell a different story, linking the Navajo to a nomadic tribe who migrated south from Canada around A.D. 1500, gathering plants and hunting game, before settling in scattered camps in the canyon country of the American Southwest, an area abandoned by the Anasazi centuries before for reasons that still remain a mystery. The Navajo way of life became specialized for survival, and their readiness to adapt the techniques of others would become a tribal trait. From the Pueblo tribes they learned small-scale farming methods. When the Spanish entered the region in the 1600s, bringing horses and sheep, the Navajo began raising stock for food and clothing, and this activity increased their mobility and efficiency as mounted marauders. Over the next 200 years they coexisted uneasily with their neighbors, alternately raiding or trading with other tribes in the region and warring over land and resources with Spanish and Mexican colonizers. When the Americans arrived in the nineteenth century and western lands were opened for settlement, continuing rounds of raiding and military retaliation prompted the U.S. government in 1863 to send in the famous Indian fighter Colonel Kit Carson to implement the national policy of destroying "pesky redskins."

Never well armed—their warriors carried more bows than guns—the Navajo were masterful guerrilla fighters who used the canyons, mountains, and desert as allies. But Carson's ruthless "scorched-earth" tactics defeated them in less than a year. He burned their crops, slaughtered their livestock, salted their fields, and starved the Navajo into submission.

Some 2,400 *Dineh* eventually surrendered and were herded on the hellish "Long Walk" 300 miles to Fort Sumner, a remote military outpost in eastern New Mexico. After several months the total number forced to relocate came to 8,000. The incarceration of the Navajo was to be an experiment in forced acculturation: There they would be domesticated into sedentary farmers. But it failed miserably. Neither punishment nor indoctrination nor hard work could convert them to a way of life not inherently their own. Beggared by deprivation and new diseases, the spirit of The People outlasted the patience of the white authorities, and in 1868 the U.S. government abandoned the experiment and agreed to a treaty that allowed the Navajo to return to a reduced portion of their majestic but desolate homelands. They were granted lands that were uninteresting to whites because there was not enough water to grow anything on them and no resources worth exploiting—lands that fit the formula for avoiding white-settler encroachment: Give Indians the badlands to share with the sagebrush and coyotes, lands that lay protected by their gods within the four cornering sacred mountains.

In that sense the Navajo are lucky. Unlike many other native tribes whose military defeat in the nineteenth century resulted in permanent banishment from their ancestral grounds, Navajos can enjoy ongoing cultural traditions in familiar surroundings. They have maintained their pride and dignity, continued cherished customs, and kept a tribal identity by holding themselves apart. Over the years they have even managed to expand the boundaries of their reservation, acquiring adjacent lands, and becoming in the process the largest Native American tribe, in the size of their reservation and in numbers.

But the record of the hundred-plus years since their return from exile has been so dismal that some have characterized it as a second "Long Walk." The land base was too small for a pastoral people, and overgrazing by livestock ruined reservation rangeland, bringing economic hardship to people untrained for any other way of life. Coupled with this there have been increasing pressures on the Navajo and their land from forces outside the reservation. While the reservation may look like a vast void, in the twenties and thirties the government as well as mining and energy companies began to realize what had been given away. Studies suggested that perhaps one-quarter of the nation's natural-energy resources were located on American Indian lands, making them among the most highly valued real estate in the West, thanks to the nation's voracious appetite for uranium, coal, oil, and natural gas.

The Navajo were of two minds about the development of

their mineral wealth. Clearly the revenues from leases and royalties would bring benefits, and there were limited economic opportunities on the reservation. You raised sheep, or you went off and worked as a farm or railroad laborer. But there were liabilities, too. Traditionalists felt it violated the spiritual interpretation of the meaning and value of their land, and they objected to selling out their historic obligation to protect Mother Earth.

A bitter debate ensued: Was it better to love the pristine land or earn a living from it? In the end the tribe granted long-term leases for coal and other minerals to non-Navajo developers and made commitments that allowed for electrical power production, bringing a steady flow of funds into the tribal treasury. But the Navajo were naive in their negotiations and undersold the rights to their resources. Few of the companies complied with job-training promises. And the amount of environmental pollution generated by development was grossly misjudged. The first astronauts in space said that looking back at the planet, one of the only visible signs of life on earth was the smoke emitted by the Four Corners Power Plant near Shiprock. The 252 tons of soot and 452 tons of smog-causing gases pumped into the air *each day* were almost mistaken for a weather front.

Most people in Farmington learned about the murders from the daily paper, but Rena Benally found out while sitting in a classroom at the San Juan Community College that Monday morning. She was waiting for the instructor to arrive when she looked up and saw a girlfriend standing in the doorway, staring at her with unusual intensity. She watched as her friend approached, took a seat beside her, and continued to look meaningfully at her. Rena was about to ask if something was wrong when her friend dramatically whispered Rena's husband's name: "Benjamin."

Without thinking, Rena spoke in Navajo. "Don't tell me something has happened to him?"

Her friend nodded. She said she had just heard an announcement on "Navajo Hour," a daily broadcast, that the bodies of two Navajo men had been found the previous day, and one had a tattoo of an Indian woman on his arm. "It sounds like Benji," she said.

Rena stared at her in stupefaction.

"If you want . . . I'll drive you to the mortuary."

At the word "mortuary" Rena Benally's eyes widened, she caught her breath, and though she wanted to run out the door, she remained seated, afraid if she tried to stand she would faint.

Rena was used to her husband going into town and not coming home at night. Too drunk on Tokay wine to make his way back, sometimes he would flop at the home of relatives who lived on the edge of Farmington. Or, if he was unable to get that far, he would nest up in a culvert or behind a downtown building. The week before he had spent the night in the Farmington jail—the thirty-eighth alcohol-related arrest on his record. It was the reason she was living apart from her husband at the time. Exasperated with his drinking, his indifference and aimlessness, she had decided to take an independent step in the direction of a career of her own. At thirty-four years of age, with five children to be responsible for, she had moved the family into a tiny apartment in Farmington and enrolled at the community college in an intensive clerk/typist class that would prepare her for a respectable secretarial position. Secretly she had hoped that her ambition would bring him around to taking some initiative of his own. The reality was that it had only made things worse. She had worried that something terrible would befall him if he kept on drinking, but she never imagined it would come to this.

When her breathing had leveled, she whispered, "Okay."

The Lee and Oviatt Funeral Home was a large one-story stucco building that occupied the west side of a small shopping center, across from Sonny's Sporting Goods and the House of Beauty. Already a crowd of people were gathered outside, and as Rena approached they parted for her, forming two lines. Her heart sank as she recognized most of them as relatives of her husband on his father's side. It didn't prove anything, but it made it more likely that her girlfriend had guessed right.

From her left she heard an angry voice hiss in Navajo, "He's dead, and you're the one who killed him."

A flick of her eyes was enough to see the insult came from her husband's aunt, a woman with whom relations had always been strained, and who disapproved strongly when she had moved to town. That was the only response Rena allowed herself to make as she committed her face to blankness and continued to march stiffly down what felt to her like a gauntlet. She was trying her best to put up a brave front, but the truth was she felt extremely fragile and vulnerable, and unprepared for what awaited her on the other side of the glass doors.

Entering the front foyer, she felt as if she had stepped into someone's living room. The decor was designed to create that kind of pleasant, comfortable atmosphere. Matching couches and easy chairs. Globe lamps on the side tables. Artificial bouquets blooming on plant stands. A framed print of Jesus with a beard and flowing hair hanging on a wall, over a lectern on which an open Bible beckoned. In the office straight ahead she saw a group of her husband's relatives sitting around a table. Several looked over their shoulders and turned back without greeting her.

A tall soft-talking Anglo in a dark suit and black cowboy boots walked toward her and asked if he could be of assistance. When Rena identified herself as Mrs. Benjamin Benally and said she had come to see if they had her husband there, the man seemed confused. He said it was his understanding that the relatives of the deceased had already identified the body. Gesturing toward the office, he said they were discussing funeral arrangements.

Rena did not think it was appropriate to comment on family conflicts with an outsider, and with uncharacteristic firmness asserted her rights. If the body of Benjamin Benally was being kept under this roof, as the surviving spouse she demanded to see her husband.

As if hoping to avoid a scene, the man nervously acceded and led her down a narrow gold-carpeted hallway, past a chapel, past an area where a variety of expensive caskets were displayed, to a room that was empty except for a table on which lay a body flat on its back, covered with a white sheet. Rena's breathing quickened as she approached and, taking a deep breath, drew the sheet back.

Shock at what she saw and momentary disbelief that she knew the broken figure delayed an emotional reaction. A perfunctory attempt had been made by attendants to clean him up, but clots of sand and blood matted his singed hair, and little could be done about the crushed cheekbones and flattened nose that shattered the normal planes of the face. In fact, had it not been for the tattoo of an Indian woman on his arm Rena would not have known it was her husband lying there. When the kids would ask him who it was supposed to be, with a wink he would reply, "It's your mother."

Reality struck Rena full force, and old griefs shifted to make way for a fresh pain. She remained standing there in silence for several minutes longer, and then she pulled the sheet up tautly, neatly, as though tucking him in for a final night's sleep. As she walked away an almost terrible control braced her, a dignity that appears in some people when they are confronted with the worst calamity imaginable and somehow rise out of the wreckage stronger than before.

Under normal circumstances the deaths of two Navajo men would have warranted little more than back-page blips in the local paper. Indian fatalities were so common that two more customarily would not have caused much of a stir. But when published accounts poked readers in the eye with graphic details describing the "mutilated" condition of the bodies, the grisly discoveries left the community shaken. People were horrified and disgusted by the crime, and angry that a malign force had opened the town to scandal and fear.

"You almost expect to read about things like this happening in big cities, where crime and maimings are old news," a lifetime resident would comment. "But in Farmington, New Mexico, perverse outbursts of homicidal violence were still relatively rare."

Breaking with the tradition of wry understatement that is characteristic of county sheriffs, Dan Sullivan was quoted as saying out loud what everyone in town was thinking. "The murders themselves aren't all that unusual. We see more than our share of dead Indians. But why burn their genitals off?"

"An all-out manhunt was under way in San Juan County today for the slayers of two men whose mutilated bodies were discovered several miles apart Sunday in Chokecherry Canyon," reported the *Farmington Daily Times* in its Tuesday edition. Citing Sheriff Dan Sullivan as its source, the paper announced that four deputies had been assigned to the case full time and all days off for department personnel were canceled. Pressed for more details about the crime, he said confidentiality allowed him to add only that at this point authorities believed the killings were connected, and they could not tell if the victims had been robbed since most of their clothing was burned. Beyond that, all he would say was that deputies were working round-the-clock to produce a motive or suspect in the brutal slayings, but he doubted any arrests would be made soon.

*   *   *

Though none of it was case-breaking, a substantial amount of information had indeed been collected during the first few days of the investigation:

Early Monday morning Lieutenant Miller contacted Jerry Van Lancker, the resident senior agent at the FBI office in Farmington, and requested his assistance. Although the FBI was not held in high esteem by New Mexico lawmen (agents were perceived as glory-grabbers who would come in and call a press conference after city, county, and state cops had done all the police work leading up to an arrest), Miller was good friends with Van Lancker, who had ten years of investigating crimes on the Navajo Reservation, and access to the best forensic opportunities in the country through the FBI laboratory in Washington, D.C. Not knowing what evidence had been lost, the lieutenant wanted to be sure about anything left.

They found more bloody rocks, more charred fabric, and more tracks that convinced Miller that the individual wearing waffle-stompers had been present at both scenes, but other than a hawk twirling on a thermal, deer droppings, and a jackrabbit they spooked, they encountered no other signs of activity than had been noticed the night before, and nothing that advanced their knowledge about who was behind this squalid business.

"Seen anything like this before?" Miller asked as they traipsed back toward their vehicles.

"Not in my time," the agent replied. "What we generally see are crimes of passion. I'm out drinking with you, you piss me off, I shoot you. Simple as that. We rarely see signs of premeditation, or a lot of sadistic activity, which is what you've got here."

"Any thoughts?"

What he thought was Chokecherry Canyon had done all the talking it was going to. What he said was, "Just that when you finally do apprehend a suspect, you've got a strong case for first-degree murder."

Meanwhile, two other deputies went calling on the Indian bars—Harry's Lounge in Farmington, and the Zia and Turquoise lounges, watering holes along the highway between Farmington and Shiprock that catered almost exclusively to reservation winos. Each place they went they were given the cold shoulder. Seeing uniformed officers come through the door hushed conversations, caused heads to turn—first in their direction to suspiciously check them out, then away in thinly disguised hostility. Owners didn't want to get involved. The help seemed uninterested. And they were greeted with stony silence when they tried to question the patrons about Harvey and Benally.

By the end of the day they established that the two were drinking companions and had been seen together at various times on Saturday. But no one remembered anything unusual, like seeing them getting into a vehicle, either voluntarily, through enticement, or by forcible abduction.

Shake, because he spoke Navajo, was given the job of checking with the victims' families, and talking to friends and neighbors. Any domestic squabbles lately? Feuding or fighting? Not only did his interviews fail to uncover any personal or family conflicts worth looking into further, his instincts and experience, which in the past had proven more valuable than facts, seemed to have dried up on this case. He was as puzzled as anyone.

After checking with the neighboring towns of Cortez, Durango, Dulce, and Cuba to see if they had any outstanding homicides that sounded similar, and turning up nothing, Sheriff Sullivan had better luck with a phone call to the sheriff's office in Gallup, on the south side of the reservation. He was informed that there had been at least three brutal slayings of Navajos over the previous year, all unsolved.

What seemed at first like a development with promise was dismissed, however, after the crime reports arrived. While the Gallup slayings were also characterized by extreme brutality, including mutilation, there was evidence of knife play and none of the victims had been burned. It was a significant enough departure in the method of operation for Sullivan to conclude there was no connection between the slayings.

On Tuesday, while deputies were out on the street talking to Indians hither and yon, following the sheriff's order to interview "every swingin' dick who'll give you the time of day," two phone calls from the outside came which added grist to the investigation. A man called who said he had gone to Chokecherry Canyon on Saturday night to drink beer and shoot his guns in the dark, and he'd noticed several vehicles that he was able to describe as if he'd been there on a stakeout. According to his report, a maroon Pontiac Bonneville of mid-sixties vintage whose high beam on the driver's side wasn't working had passed him going the other way. Passing him from behind had been a black-over-red Chevy with a jacked-up rear end. At a parking area near where Benally's body had been found, a white '64 Ford two-door hardtop had been parked. And driving back to town around 1:45 A.M., he had given a jump-start to a blue Chevy pickup with a six-cylinder motor and a dead battery.

Later that afternoon the preliminary results of the autopsy were phoned in by Dr. Stewart Loeb, a local pathologist under contract with the Office of the Medical Investigator. He confirmed in medical jargon what officials already suspected. Both victims had been blindingly intoxicated at the time of death: Benally's blood-alcohol level measured .444, Harvey's .392, each almost four times the .10 standard above which a person was considered legally drunk. These were brain-deadening levels, sufficient to kill a nonalcoholic, and would have left the victims in a totally helpless state. As best as could be determined they had met their deaths late Saturday or early Sunday. Cause of death, in both cases, had been skull fracture. Both men had been severely beaten and the pattern of burns, the intensity and duration of which indicated at first that there might have been an attempt at cremation, appeared instead to have been "sadistically inflicted with sexual connotations." There was no doubt in Doc Loeb's mind that overtly sexual motivations accounted for much of the torment that had been inflicted on the victims; however, after inspecting both men's rectums, he did not see signs of the kind of disturbance that warranted a semen examination.

Early each morning the deputies working the Indian murders would meet in the sheriff's office in Aztec before heading west toward Farmington, where the investigation was focused. They would stay in radio contact throughout the morning, and then meet for lunch at Van's Cafe, a popular coffee shop in a centrally located plaza. The three deputies, plus the sheriff, undersheriff, and Lieutenant Miller would crowd their bulks into a booth and wash down chicken fried steaks, hot roast-beef sandwiches, and greasy hamburgers with mugs of black coffee while they reviewed the evidence, traded information, talked about what they had run down that morning—and shook their heads over the depressing progress to date.

On Wednesday, after the waitress had filled each of their cups with coffee and taken their lunch orders, after the morning reports had been given and a tense look gripped the sheriff's face as he realized they were running out of persons to question, leads to work, and he didn't know in what direction to go next, now Dan Sullivan once again gave voice to his conviction that this was an Indian-against-Indian crime. His argument was based on a quarter-century of law enforcement in Indian country. Never one to miss a chance to reminisce, he repeated how the Navajo concept of justice worked independently of the white man's laws. "Many's the time I'd hear about a break-in or an assault and I'd go out and ask, 'Want to sign a complaint?' And they'd say, 'Uh-uh, we'll handle it.' And a day or two later there'd be the Begay boy doing work at the Yazzies'. And when I'd ask about it they'd flat-out say, 'I told you we'd handle it.' That's their way. And I'm willing to bet those boys were made to pay dearly for something wrong they done by people who knew them."

Covering a skeptical expression with a drag on his cigarette and a swallow of coffee, Lieutenant Miller squinted across the table at the sheriff and asked, "How's that square with the big bootprints?"

"They grow them bucks big these days," Sullivan retorted. " 'Sides, it's not impossible the suspect was wearing boots too big for him."

Although Miller felt a more logical theory would point to sexual deviates or Indian haters, he had not been able to put an argument together that would dent the sheriff's position. Not that it would do any good anyway. The sheriff appeared to have boiled the case down in his mind and decided that what he thought was more important than what they'd found.

Even if he conceded the sheriff's point that 90 percent of the crimes against Indians were committed by Indians, and even if he did not consider the 12½-D bootprint, there were several disquieting details that just didn't fit Miller's notion of an all-Indian crime.

First of all, it had been his observation that if someone was going to abduct another person with malevolent intentions, he would probably head for an area he was familiar with. South of town was Indian land, but the white suburbs of Farmington were north of town, and this was just a few miles farther out.

Second, while it was true Navajo drunks fought like hell with each other (one, he remembered, had been stomped so viciously by his drinking buddies the hole of a boot toe remained indented in his chest), and when they went at it they would use all manner of weapons (from knives and firearms to axes), nevertheless, to strip their victims, punish their genitals, and crush their heads with rocks was not a Navajo thing to do.

Last, and perhaps most significant, Shake, who knew things

nobody else knew about the Navajo, figured it the same way he did for this reason: "A Navajo wouldn't hang around and mess with somebody's pecker. Once he's dead, hey, there's all kinds of spirits released and it's time to hit the road."

But Miller decided to keep his objections to himself. This wasn't the first time he and the sheriff had parted ways on an investigation, and he had learned to check his differences, to do his job by making his case and working through the under-sheriff, who understood how it was between him and Sullivan.

Surprisingly, it was Shake who spoke up, dissenting in a roundabout way with an Indian story of his own. "You need to understand the tricks an Indian can do. Let's say you've got cattle and an Indian decides he wants to butcher one of your beeves for a feast. That Indian can run a cow in your corral and butcher it, and if you don't know how they do it, you'd never know that they did it. They're pretty clever. They'll cut her throat and gut her. They'll put a tarp down, throw all the dirt and blood and insides on it, and haul it out somewhere and bury it. Then they'll load the carcass in a wagon. But before they leave they'll run the rest of the herd in that corral so when you come along you may know what's happened, and you'd be right, but there's no way in hell you can prove it."

Sullivan looked across the table like he had ordered the same dessert as Shake but ended up with a smaller piece of pie.

Miller kept his chuckle to himself. He understood what Shake meant, and it touched on another aspect of the case that bothered him. The way he figured it, if Indians were behind this, the crime scene would have looked different. No thought apparently had been given by the killers—he was convinced two had bagged the same game—to either covering their tracks or hiding the dead. It would have been simple to drag the bodies off into an arroyo and bury them in a shallow grave. Or wedge them between rocks at a less frequented location and let the magpies and coyotes pick them clean. They might never have been found. Or years from now their bones might have weathered out and if they'd been discovered, taken home by souvenir hunters who mistook them for Anasazi skeletons.

But those who had done it had simply walked away after-ward. Was it carelessness on their part? Miller wondered. Were they just not thinking? Then "heedless" came to mind and that seemed like the better word for it. There was a heedlessness about this crime and he felt there was a revelation contained in such heedlessness—that it was trying to tell him something.

Alone, however, without linkage to any other information, it just wasn't coming through.

As the meeting drew to a close Sullivan ordered two men to go undercover that night. "Dress like bums," he told them. "Work the back alleys, hang out outside the Indian bars, act half-crocked but keep your eyes open."

As the chief criminal investigator for the department, Lieutenant Miller had a free hand to work the case pretty much like he wanted, and he said he intended to make the rounds of the shoe stores in town, see if he could locate the place where the boots that had left the prints had been bought.

The sheriff, who thought Miller was as fixed on the bootprint as the lieutenant thought he was on Indians as perpetrators, snapped, "All right, for Chrissake. Go chase it."

Under the heading "Shoes" in the Yellow Pages the lieutenant found a listing for almost a dozen retail outlets. And it took him the better part of the day to visit them all. He had no idea there were so many shoe stores in town. In each establishment he asked for the manager, explained why he was there, brought out an enlarged photo of the bootprint, and inquired whether they carried a line of footwear that had soles like that. Not a single store did.

Then he started with the men's clothing stores, and the sporting goods stores, and finally the discount chains, where at K mart he found what he was looking for. A brown ankle-high hiking boot with a Vibram sole, one star in the heel, six in front. They even had a size 12½-D on the shelf. Borrowing it, Miller went out to the parking lot and placed it on the trunk of his car where he took Polaroids of it upright and on its side. Then he shot the sole. Holding that photo up beside the one he'd snapped at the scene made an identical pair.

Not that he thought he'd be lucky enough to run into a clerk with a photographic memory who would just happen to remember the names and faces of people who had bought a pair of those boots, but you never knew. "Just thought I'd ask," he said when his question drew slow headshakes from a line of shoe clerks.

Miller felt he was one step closer to the killers now that he knew how one of them was shod. But realistically, he knew how far away that was from actually identifying a suspect. While driving slowly through town, his thoughts took the form of queries:

If Indians weren't suspects, who was? he asked himself. Anglos was the only answer that made sense. There were very few blacks in town, and the Hispanics kept to themselves.

If these were not revenge killings, what could the motives be? That was a question he'd gone round and round on. Was it a couple of sickos and thrill-seekers who got their kicks doing horrible things to alcohol-addled Indians? Could they be dealing with a cult killing? After all, there had been a ritualistic look to the crime scene, and genital destruction and fire were not uncommon dynamics of satanic sacrifices.

Of course, in order to know why he would have to know who. And in either case, with nothing more to go on than had been gathered so far, unless the killing spree continued and the evidence left behind was more revealing, or the guilty parties slipped up and talked to someone who was willing to tip the authorities, all he as an investigator could do was hope for an unexpected development.

But Lieutenant Miller was not a patient man when it came to depending on luck for a break. For something to do, during the first two days of the investigation, he would bump along the oil-and-gas roads that meandered through Chokecherry Canyon on the off chance that the guilty party might return to the scene of the crime. (Arsonists were famous for coming back to watch the fire department work.) Now, unable to go home and hope for something to happen, he went home just long enough to change clothes before heading back out to look at boots.

Dressed in a Western-cut shirt and slacks, he made the bars, the lounges, and the saloons. Although he had not developed a clear picture of the individual he was looking for, on the basis of the print he figured it was probably someone between the ages of twenty and forty—you just didn't see many older fellows wearing that model. And with the image of a specific hiking boot blazed in his mind, he sat in booths drinking coffee and looking at boots. He leaned against walls and listened to country-and-western music at different honky-tonks, watching couples dance and looking at boots. He watched like he had a date with a cleated pair of hiking boots, and some he saw looked close enough to cause him to move up and pretend to drop something for a better view. But at closing time he went home looking as depressed as a man who'd been stood up.

In the days that followed there were certain things that required Rena Benally's personal attention. She filed a formal request for the transfer of her husband's body to a different mortuary as a way of controlling the way the funeral would be handled. And she made an effort to answer questions posed to her by a deputy from the Sheriff's Department: Where were you on the night of the murder? he had asked. Why weren't you two living together? Are you fooling around with another man? He had made her feel as though she had some complicity in the crime, and angrily she had ended the interrogation by ordering him to leave.

After that she retreated to her mother's frame-and-stucco house at the end of a dirt road on the reservation where her own family banded around her like a small tribe, and passed several days mourning privately. Friends would stop by to offer their condolences, but none of it really registered. In a drowsy, expressionless way she would thank them, and then a glazed stare would return to her eyes as she looked off across a landscape of pastel tints and desert mirages where memories seemed to live. You're keeping the wound green, her mother warned, but that didn't matter to her. As if going back over their life together would keep her husband around awhile longer, she sat in a chair and let her thoughts carry her back to the day she met him on Chicken Street in the summer of '66.

There is no such listing on the Farmington city map, and if you ask a white resident for directions you'll probably get a funny look. But any Navajo can tell you where it is: A dusty stretch of road halfway between the main drag and the railroad yard where Indian people used to park their wagons and tie up their horses when they came to town in the early part of this century, it has become a squalid area where the town drunks congregate because the condemned buildings and abandoned vehicles offer a range of shelters. The designation is attributed to an irate Navajo woman who stormed into town in search of her delinquent husband one morning and found him up with the sun, panhandling and hunting soda-pop bottles so he could pay for his next drink. "Like a chicken scratching in the yard and pecking at gravel," was the way she described him, which painted a picture so hilariously perfect that other Navajo wives who had lost their husbands to booze took to calling the area Chicken Street.

Rena had been driving through the part of town one late summer afternoon when her car sputtered to a stop. After coasting to the curb, she was unable to get it started again and sat there in a huff for several minutes before she spied a group of men lounging against a parked automobile a block up the street. Adopting the manner of a woman in distress, she went over and asked if any of them knew anything about cars, that hers had stopped running.

She was used to drawing attention. Navajo men who didn't know her name, but wished they did, would address her on the street as Miss Navajo. After a round of grins passed among these men, one of them said he knew a little something and followed her back to her car, sauntering along beside her in a way that suggested he was as aware of her walk as his own.

Lifting the hood, he poked around the engine for a few minutes before telling her the trouble lay in the carburetor. She had no idea what that meant, and before she could ask he was already disassembling it. As it turned out he was a whiz at mechanical repairs. When he told her to turn the ignition switch the engine not only sprang to life, it ran smoother than ever.

How clearly she remembered the tingle that shimmied through her when he held her gaze after she thanked him. He had high cheekbones that gave his eyes a slight squint, a thatch of black hair combed neatly back and to the side, and she thought he was extremely handsome. A smile parted his lips, making her feel they were sharing the same perceptions of each other "That day," she would recall later with a soft laugh, "he was my knight in shining armor."

It took several weeks for Benjamin Benally to determine her status—that she was a divorced mother of four adolescent children, recently returned to Farmington from San Francisco—and to ask her for a date. They went to a drive-in movie, but it was anything but a private evening for just the two of them. They were accompanied by nephews and nieces. She thought the arrangement slightly unusual, but quickly figured out what was going on when they stopped at a package liquor store on the way to the show. Benjamin, the only grown-up along besides herself, was in effect the bootlegger for his younger relations. They put up the money, he provided the transportation and made the purchase, and that way he got to drink for free.

At the time Rena didn't think there was anything particularly wrong with that. In fact she was swept up in the good-time mood and only later, given the way things turned out, would this recollection loom as significant.

She spent that summer in cloudland. She and Benji (on the tribal rolls he was listed as Herman Dodge Benally, named for an uncle who served as one of the legendary Code Talkers, a special corps that in World War II transmitted military information on the airwaves in a language that befuddled Japanese code-crackers, but everyone knew him as Benjamin) went everywhere together, as if making up for lost years. The history she got from him made her wonder how they could not have met earlier. He too was a member of the Mexican Clan, raised in a hogan beneath the bluffs of the San Juan River, between Farmington and Shiprock. As a boy he also had spent his summers tending his grandparents' sheep. Just as she had attended a mission boarding school during her early years, then transferred to public school, he had gone away to an off-reservation government boarding school in Brigham City, Utah, before enrolling at Central Junior High in Kirtland. And as with many young Navajo growing up during the fifties, he, like she, had been introduced to Christianity by white missionaries.

She had come to the church at an earlier age than he had because both her parents had been missionized before she was born, while he had received a more traditional upbringing. Well before he ever heard of the Old Testament, he knew the Navajo origin myth and could recite tales of the Holy People. Rena traced his love of the outdoors to his fascination with the legends that explained the spectacular natural formations of the American Southwest as the sites of mythological battles.

Benjamin had been fifteen years old when he was noticed by Father Eugene Botelho of the San Juan Episcopal Mission, a religious outpost on the reservation side of the San Juan River, near Farmington. Less of a religious recruiter than most missionaries, Father B., as everyone knew him, would make special efforts on behalf of those young Indians who showed unusual potential, for whom a little help could make a lot of difference. He had invited Benji to live at the mission and attend public school because he felt if an Indian was going to be successful in his general dealings with the non-Indian world, he needed to have a strong source of self-esteem, and Benjamin Benally was exceptionally talented in two areas. He was a natural artist. When he sketched a deer it looked like it was about to leap off the paper. And you could almost say he was a genius on the basketball court. For his age he was only slightly taller than average, but he could out-dribble, out-shoot, and out-rebound players much older and bigger than he. As a junior he was the starting forward for the Broncos of Central

Junior High, and led them to a winning record and top seed in the state tournament.

The magnitude of his talent was all but matched by the size of his heart: The day before the championship game he came down with the flu and was instructed to stay in bed. But he defied the doctor's orders and ended up scoring more individual points than the total amassed by the opposing team.

In an entertaining anecdote he had recounted for Rena the anguish his stardom had caused him. It was the tradition at Central for the boy elected Basketball King to escort the Homecoming Queen to the prom, and when Benji was crowned King his pride was undermined by anxiety. The Homecoming Queen was a beautiful white girl. Not only was he unsure how to behave around her, the only dancing he'd ever done was at Indian ceremonials. Father B. had tried to help him out, rolling back the rug at the vicarage and showing him some of the dance steps he knew, but he was twenty years behind the times. The jitterbug was out, the twist was in—a dance that Father B. had only heard of. When Benji pointed this out, Father B. didn't miss a beat. He called in one of the mission aides and asked her to please show Benjamin how to twist. And in the end it turned out fine. He did learn to dance, he went to the prom, and he had a wonderful time. He even dated the Queen a time or two after that.

When he had finished reminiscing, Rena felt the urge to twist his tail. She said, "Oh. So your childhood sweetheart was a *biligaana* [white]?"

Giving her a trickster's grin, he shook his head. "If you want to know the truth, *you* were my childhood sweetheart. You just didn't know it."

"Go on," she said. But he assured her it was true. That as far back as when she was a little girl pedaling her bike along the irrigation ditches, he had a crush on her.

Sure he was teasing, she put him to the test. "If that's so, what color was my bike?"

He smiled easily. "Blue."

She was speechless. Blue was the correct answer. And it was as if he had just said everything about himself she would ever need to know.

As good as he was with her, he was almost better with her children. In her words, "He had a heart for kids." Rena's children had spent all their lives off-reservation in an urban setting and knew little about Navajo ways. But under Benji's tutelage they learned about traditional spiritual practices. He would take them hiking and fishing in remote areas of the reservation and explain to them during the long drives the kinship he felt with nature. How it formed the basis of the Navajo belief that man was an integral part of an orderly universe who must do his part to maintain harmony and balance with all things, which the Navajo call "walking in beauty." Illness and evil, he told them, were the result of disorder in this relationship. When that happened, the Navajo gods must be petitioned through traditional Navajo ceremonies to restore harmony. And drumming on the dashboard, he would sing a ceremonial chant in a high, quavering register.

The kids would listen to all this as though a spell had been cast over them. Then, when their awe for him was almost palpable, he would snap them out of it with some crazy impulsive antic. Once, he had just finished a story that had everyone gaping at just about the same time he was driving across a bridge that spanned a wide and deep section of an irrigation ditch. Suddenly he stepped on the brakes, leaped out, and plunged into the water—without the slightest warning, without even removing his shoes. Rena and the kids sat there for the longest time, staring at the place where he had disappeared under the surface. And just when they began to worry that something terrible had happened, they heard him calling from way downstream.

He proposed in the fall, in the parking lot of an electronics plant in Shiprock where Rena was working at the time. They were sitting in a car talking, it was a bitterly cold day and the heater wasn't working, and at some point he realized the windows were so fogged they couldn't see out. Leaning over, he made two dots in the dew, spaced for her eyes. As she gazed out he offhandedly said, "What do you say we get married?"

She looked at him, not sure she had heard him right. He repeated himself.

Although they had officially known each other only a few months, it had been long enough for her to know his rightness for her. There was a lack of complication about Benji that seemed to simplify her life. His quick wit and whimsical ways kept things light and easy, which was a welcome change from her previous marriage. There were sides to Benji she still didn't know well—sometimes he would lapse into deep thought, as though searching for answers, from which he would emerge aloof and sullen—but what she did know was she felt love for a man who seemed to love her back, and that was all that mattered. Overjoyed, she jumped out of the car and broadcast her reply to the empty parking lot: "yes, Yes, YES!"

They talked about having a traditional Navajo wedding ceremony, but discarded that option when they encountered resistance to their marriage from his relatives. There were tribal taboos against clan members marrying. In the old days it was as serious as incest. But in their minds it didn't matter because they weren't blood relatives; and besides, they thought of themselves as modern Indians. Flushed with their feelings for each other, the idea that they were lovers who were refusing to let tradition stand in their way added romance to their trip to the tribal headquarters in Window Rock, where they filled out the appropriate papers and came home Mr. and Mrs. Benally.

Recalling that initial disapproval of their relationship from her in-laws brought Rena back to the present, reminding her of the rancor that had been directed toward her at the mortuary. Although this was a tragedy which should have created bonds of sympathy and sorrow, she had been treated with outright animosity. She knew how that worked. When she had initiated a separation from her husband, his relations had gossiped cattily about her disloyalty, some even going so far as to blame Benji's drinking on her. She felt Indian people in general found it easier to fault others for tragedies than to accept the notion of personal responsibility, and she thought in this case it was terribly unfair and unjustified because she knew better than any of them what had gone wrong and that it was out of her hands a long time ago. Nonetheless, it left a bad echo she could not get out of her head.

Much as she would have liked to remain inside a zone of private grief, situations continued to come up that required her involvement. She agreed that the funeral service should be held in the chapel at the San Juan Mission and that her husband should be buried in the mission cemetery. She let one of her sisters handle the choice of casket, making arrangements through the tribe for a moderately priced slate-gray metal casket rather than the cloth-covered pine box that the funeral home customarily provided for Navajos according to a contract with the tribe. But, recalling a favorite expression of Benji's—"I like to wear something light, with a little class"—Rena went to a department store and bought a shiny gold windbreaker the salesclerk assured her was top-of-the-line.

The viewing was held in the funeral parlor Wednesday evening. In her present state of mind Rena was not thinking clearly, and years afterward she would regret the decision to allow the casket to be left open. Not only did it oppose the traditional notion that the living should avoid gazing upon a corpse, it went against her husband's wishes. In one of his morbid moods he had told her that after he was gone he did not want gawkers inspecting what was left.

That was not her only transgression against tradition. According to the old ways, one should never touch a corpse. But when she found herself alone in the chapel with her husband shortly before the mourners filed in, the Navajo fear of personal contact with the dead was overridden by the need to make a farewell gesture of her own. When she thought she had a few minutes in which she would not be interrupted, she walked over to the coffin. Benji looked sharp in his new windbreaker, pressed slacks, and shined shoes. A bright Pendleton blanket wrapped his shoulders. It seemed incongruous for a corpse to be wearing a pair of large black-framed sunglasses, and she didn't like the color of his face, which had been painted in death to look alive again. But she knew what the morticians had had to work with and under the circumstances felt they had probably done their best. His hands were at rest across his chest, arranged so as to show off a new sports watch on his wrist, the gift of an uncle. For some reason she thought to look and yes, it had been wound up.

It was without forethought that she found herself twisting and tugging at the silver ring with the double turquoise setting she wore on her wedding finger. It was a ring he had designed and had made for her and she would never have given it up for any other reason. Now, once she had worked it off, she reached out and slipped it on the little finger of his left hand.

The sound of someone gasping startled her. She glanced up to see her mother-in-law staring at her with a horrified expression. "Don't do that," she reproached sternly, reminding her that any contact with the dead was dangerous, and a dead body, even a loved one, was capable of causing trouble or bringing illness to those who touched it. "You have your children to consider."

But Rena wasn't thinking that way. If she had been, she would not even have allowed her tears to fall into the casket.

As it was, she let them drip hotly from her cheeks to spot the shiny satin lining.

Four days into the investigation, Dan Sullivan began to feel all fifty-seven of his years. His health wasn't what it used to be—a smoking habit that started with roll-your-owns as a kid, the alkali dust he'd kicked up while rounding up cattle in the canyons as a teenager, and all that greasy smoke he'd inhaled barbecuing for pretty near every political organization in the county at one time or another left him gasping if he had to walk a city block—but that wasn't what was bothering him. He was troubled by the effort it took to solve crimes nowadays. His methods had been shaped in the days when everything happened on a local basis, he was acquainted with most everyone in town, and a case could be put together simply by knowing the right person to talk to. That type of law enforcement had gone out of fashion in the fifties, when the oil and gas boom brought hundreds of new people into town daily, but it was still the way the sheriff liked to do business. When forced to hunt up evidence, or consider the possibility of interstate flights, he was at sea.

To make matters worse, the press was nipping at his heels. At Kiwanis and Lions Club meetings, when asked about the media, he was used to saying they were just doing their job and it kept the department on its toes. Were he to be asked now, four days into a murder mystery that had aroused the interest of western papers throughout the Southwest, his position would have been: There are times, by God, when the demands by the media for news ought to be curbed.

Due primarily to front-page coverage, what had started out as a complex crime was threatening to become a political spectacle because he was unable to offer the press any newsworthy disclosures that would give the impression progress was being made. The whole truth was they had two bodies and little else; but naturally he didn't want to go public with that confession. If he offered nothing else soon, however, he knew there were only so many ways they could rewrite "NAVAJO SLAYINGS CONTINUE TO BAFFLE OFFICIALS," the headline in today's paper, before they switched their attention from the investigation to the investigators.

Sullivan was doing his best to keep the upper hand without showing his cards. He had started out bringing newsmen up-to-date on a daily basis, taking phone calls or meeting them over coffee, as his schedule and their deadlines required. He would brief them on developments over the previous twenty-four hours, and do his best to answer their questions. Now, however, his strategy was one of coyness. He would let them know that the investigation was at a sensitive stage, that he was not at liberty to reveal all the details or findings at this time. Laying it out this way—reminding reporters that he had to keep key pieces of incriminating information from the public record in order to give investigators an advantage in their interrogations and, come the time to turn the case over to prosecutors, he didn't want vital evidence and testimony to be challenged on grounds a trial had already been conducted in the press—he left it open to speculation just how close the department was to breaking the case, without raising public expectations.

But the heat of public pressure made the sheriff uncomfortable. From white residents in the county he'd heard statements to the effect that the citizenry was getting nervous, maybe it was coincidental that Indians had been singled out, and anyone could be next. From Indian quarters had come rumblings that the authorities were dragging their feet and putting a minor effort into the investigation because the victims were Navajos.

Dan Sullivan hadn't won every election he'd entered without learning something about public relations. So it was to counter the criticism that was heading his way, as well as with the hope that a cash incentive might provide a much-needed break in the case, that he picked up the phone, dialed the number of the local newspaper, and gave them their story for the next day.

"REWARD OFFERED FOR MURDERERS" read the headline to an article that announced a lack of clues had prompted Sheriff Dan Sullivan to deposit $500 of his own money into a local bank and that it would be awarded to anyone who came forward with information leading to the arrest and conviction of the persons responsible for the multiple murders in Chokecherry Canyon.

A winding dirt footpath connects the San Juan Episcopal Mission to the cemetery where its deceased members lie buried. Most of them died as violently as battlefield casualties. A sample page of the death register lists the causes: knife wound, beating, burning, malnutrition, exposure. Their white wooden crosses rise out of long mounds of dirt, row after row, like a crop the bones of the buried caused to grow. On Thursday, April 25, 1974, Herman Dodge Benally joined their ranks.

Rena Benally would remember very little of the actual funeral. The chapel was filled to capacity, with people standing in the halls. A reverend delivered the eulogy, citing selections from the Old Testament, New Testament, and Gospel. But she would have to consult the guest register afterward to know who all came, and she did not realize a Holy Eucharist had been performed until she was told later.

Everything was observed with half-a-mind for her. What would stand out in her memory was a single moment, after her husband's coffin had been lowered by ropes into a hole in the ground, when she looked around at the other graves that would be keeping his company. A few were well tended—desert grass weeded, sun-faded plastic flowers sprouting out of the raised earth—but most were neglected and leaning in different directions. Many were small and decorated with toys and bore a single name on short crosses: Baby. All were set on a plateau that dropped in a half-mile slope to the San Juan River. If Benji were able to raise up his head and look down, she thought, he would gaze over a landscape that changed from rocks to sand to water, forming a kind of shoreline to the Navajo Reservation.

And just then the sun broke through a cloud cover, blessing the day with light and warmth. She took it as a sign that when death had come to her husband, it had been his time.

As with many missionized Navajo, Rena's observance of burial customs shuffled orthodox Navajo practices with Christian procedures. Her Indianness did not prevent her from praying to God the Father any more than her Christian upbringing stopped her from obeying certain traditional practices. Honoring ritualistic restrictions, for four days after her husband's death, the time it was said it took him to reach the underworld, she had neither showered nor washed her hair. Yet throughout this time she put herself deep into the consolation offered by her Christian faith, drawing strength from God, not questioning, just accepting the purpose of His ways. "I put it all in the Lord's hands," she would say later. "I was angry and hurt and sad, so I let Him handle it."

An internal conflict between the old ways and the new, the Indian ways and the Anglo, came to a head after the funeral when Rena returned to the cinder-block government-built house that she and her husband had shared before she moved to an apartment in Farmington. As she drove up she regarded a black ash heap in the side yard. Without a second thought or closer look she knew what it meant. Her mother-in-law had come out to the house, dragged everything outside that was closely associated with her son—from his bedding to his clothes to his personal effects—and set them afire. It was a traditional custom performed for two reasons: so the deceased's possessions might accompany him on his journey, and to prevent his ghost from returning to watch over them.

What ignited a struggle within Rena was that even though she was familiar with the prescribed mode of behavior for dealing with the belongings of the dead, she was sufficiently acculturated to be able to think differently. She had come out to the house in the hope of salvaging some of her husband's things that had personal meaning.

As she walked through the empty house, noting the work that had been started and never finished—a half-tiled floor, wall partitions that had gotten no farther than the 2×4 studs— her eyes swept the corners and shelves in search of keepsakes that her mother-in-law had overlooked. When she spotted a candy box on top of the refrigerator that contained a collection of memorabilia intended for a scrapbook, she smiled for the first time in a week.

Still abstracted by the rhythms of the reveries that had moved her around in time over the preceding days, Rena seated herself on a kitchen chair and began to sift through the contents. There were a dozen photographs of Benji at different times of his life; notes and documents that validated events in his life. And each one she picked up seemed to float her into a trance. . . .

Bound with a rubber band was a pack of black-and-white snapshots of Benji and several other Indian boys standing with Father Botelho in front of the Statue of Liberty, the Lincoln Memorial, the Washington Monument, and the Liberty Bell. In order to raise funds for his mission activities Father B. would annually drive his Chevy station wagon on an east-coast tour to appeal for aid from church groups. To give donors the opportunity to meet the beneficiaries, as well as to show Indian youths the world outside the reservation, he would take three or four boys from the mission along with him. In an effort to provide them with an inspirational as well as educational experience, he made a point of visiting sites in Washington, D.C., Philadelphia, and New York, where events had taken place that would give them a better understanding of American history, and, he hoped, an uplifted feeling that would elevate their own aspirations. Benji had gone along on one of these trips.

The focus of her eyes turned inward as she thought about how, when she'd met Benji, knowing he had been one of Father B.'s boys had been like a second opinion from a concerned physician whose advice was, Go ahead, follow your heart. She had believed that because he had lived for a time at the San Juan Mission under Father Botelho's tutelage, and been baptized a Christian, their mutual faith not only would be a bond between them, but would help them overcome the difficulties that life presented. Only later, after they had married, had she learned how cynical he had become about the church.

Though it had disturbed Rena, who faithfully attended worship services, not to have her husband sitting beside her, she understood that he had his reasons for staying away. Benji had lived with and worked for two Baptist missionaries during his late teens, going along on visitations and interpreting for them because neither spoke Navajo. What he had seen had turned him against Christianity. It wasn't so much the strict regimen of religious practices they had demanded of him every morning before he was allowed to eat breakfast—such as prostrating himself before them, praying for forgiveness for his sins, and reading the Scriptures aloud. It was the Christian presumption of superiority over the religious beliefs of native cultures. The missionaries had forbidden Navajo members of their congregation to sing their own songs or use their own music in the worship of God because such things were not mentioned in the Bible. Hymns had to be sung in English, even if they were not understood. That was why they wanted Benji along—to interpret the words into Navajo. Spiritual growth to the missionaries was measured by the degree to which Indians renounced their Indian beliefs, he told her once, not their daily walk with the Creator. "I have nothing against Christ," she remembers him saying. "I just wish He would come and talk to the Indians and leave the missionaries at home."

Two other snapshots captured the highlights of his junior year in high school. In one, the Broncos were lined up on a dirt playground in uniform, though the argyle socks and street shoes worn by some suggested it was a post-season photo. The coach was standing to one side; the captain was kneeling in the foreground resting a trophy on his raised knee; and Benji, flanked and fronted by teammates, looked out of a squint at the camera, a smile about to come to his lips. He was the only Indian in the picture.

The other snapshot was taken at the spring prom, and it showed the Basketball King standing awkwardly beside the Homecoming Queen, a very pretty white girl wearing a formal gown with a crown of flowers in her hair. They were posed before a banner which read: Hats Off To The CHAMPS!

Under different circumstances they were the kinds of photos Rena might have arranged in a collage, framed, and hung on a wall so everyone would know that accomplishments highlighted Benji's past. Mitigating that urge was her suspicion that perhaps right there was where things had gone wrong for him. As he had explained it, in the last month of his senior year in high school, after another stellar year on the basketball court, he had been called into the principal's office and told he did not have enough credits to graduate. At first he couldn't believe it. He had never taken his studies very seriously, doing just enough to get by; but he had never flunked a class before and no one had given him any indication he was about to fail an entire grade. When he asked how this could have happened the principal did not say exactly, but left the impression that apparently some of his teachers had promoted him through his sophomore and junior years solely to maintain his athletic eligibility, and that that dispensation had just run out.

It had been too late in the year for him to bring his grades up to a passing level, so in reaction he dropped out of school, taking up with a crowd who wasted their days cruising in cars and looking for good times, which they found in bottles of Tokay wine.

With a sigh she replaced the photos and picked up a brochure for the Allied School of Technology, an industrial trade school in Chicago. According to Benji, he had found the brochure at the tribal office in Shiprock and been hooked by the sales pitch that billed Allied as "The Gateway to Opportunity for thousands of men who have made themselves more useful to American Industry and so, also, to themselves." After filling out the pertinent forms, he had received a grant from the tribe and at twenty years of age had taken the bus to Chicago. She knew where he'd stayed because there was a postcard in the box with a picture of the YMCA Hotel in Chicago on the front. And she knew he'd done well because there was also a copy of a diploma stating that Herman Dodge Benally had completed all the requirements for a mechanical-drafting certificate.

It had been a courageous effort to rise above his circumstances, one that made her proud to recall. But for all the good it had done him he might as well have stayed home and herded sheep. He said that after receiving his diploma he had gone on numerous job interviews for positions he had been trained for at Allied, but knew before he walked out of the office, just from the way the personnel people looked him over, that he wasn't going to be hired. He complained bitterly about how you were told working hard would get you someplace, but in a white man's work situation it didn't matter what kind of effort you made—if you were an Indian it was never good enough.

Some Indians were able to shrug off humiliating experiences of prejudice; others found it fueled their drive to succeed. Benji's response had been to withdraw and return to the reservation, where there were even fewer job opportunities but at least his basic needs would be taken care of. He had gotten by fixing cars for different people, and taking spot jobs painting houses, laying bricks, loading and unloading trucks. But he could never find permanent employment, and when he went into town to find a day job and there was no work available, with idle time on his hands he would meet up with friends and they would go have a drink together.

The thought of his drinking made her stare. It hadn't been so bad at first, and because he was understandably frustrated and discouraged she had started out being accepting. Besides, her instinct was to try to deal with the problem within the traditional context, which maintained that the woman's role was to be supportive of her husband. And he was never abusive when he drank. Sometimes, rather than enter the house drunk, he would crawl into the backseat of the motorless car parked in the dirt behind their house and spend the whole next day there, ashamed to show himself. The only way she knew he was there was that when she set a glass of water on the hood of the car for him in case he was thirsty, the next time she looked out it would be empty.

Many times she tried to talk to him about his drinking, but it was no use. He would cajole her with a silly answer, calling liquor his medicine and explaining he didn't drink to feel good but just to feel normal. Or he would tell her to stop trying to reform him, he was who he was. Or he would sheepishly apologize for being such a disappointment and promise that, okay, he would quit and make it up to her and the kids. But his words were never followed by actions. Town would call to him like an open gate, and the next time she saw him he would be reeking of alcohol and unsteady on his feet; when she reminded him of his promise, guilt would float briefly to the surface of his glazed gaze before sinking beneath a fish-eyed opacity.

When Rena found herself pregnant she thought maybe fatherhood would bring a new maturity to him, that having his own child for whom he would be an example might force him to be more responsible. But the naïveté of that notion hammered at her, between contractions, the night she drove herself to the hospital because he was too drunk to be trusted behind the wheel.

As time passed it got worse. He would go on benders that would last for weeks and was in a drunken state more often than not. There were times when the only way she knew he was still alive was when she would hear that he had stopped in at the home of a relative, intoxicated, rambling about how poorly the world was treating him. Or that he had been jailed again for public drunkenness.

Jail wasn't so bad, he told her once. It kept him out of the rain. Gave him a place to sleep. He was fed. And most of those he shared a cell with were his drinking partners, so in essence jail was their clubhouse.

Once he'd agreed to take part in an alcohol-rehabilitation program, and she had been optimistic that things would change. The counselors tried to get him to take a good look at himself. They told him he did not need to conform to the stereotype of the drunken Indian, that he had more going for him than that. They talked about self-respect, the positive advantages of getting a job. But he benefited very little. He teased them to see how much he could get them to do for him. Would they find him a job? How about a new place closer to town for his family to live in? A car that ran? Groceries? When they tried to make it clear to him that they thought he needed help, and were available if he really wanted help with his drinking and getting his life on a stabler basis, but the rest was up to him, he lost interest.

At some point his descent seemed to become irreversible. Not only did he give up on finding employment, he lost all motivation and abandoned any goals for himself. The only people he felt comfortable with and esteemed by were the other drunks on the street who caged drinks with him, begged money with him, and stole bottles from package liquor stores with him.

It was painful to witness the self-destruction of a loved one, and Rena knew it could not go on forever like this, but she didn't want to think about how these stories ended. Since nothing worldly seemed capable of producing a transformation, she began to pray to God to send her husband a sign that would sober him up. It came one stormy night when he was home alone, sleeping on the couch, and a bolt of lightning struck the ground just outside the window, hurling him to the floor. He was badly shaken. Lightning was a supernatural omen to the Navajo, one of their gods' conveyances. To be the victim of a strike meant he was out of balance and should seek a proper cure—a ceremony and, after consideration of what had been done to offend the powers, a rearrangement of his behavior.

At least that was the conventional interpretation. But stubborn and unrepentant to the last, Benji became even more fatalistic about his lot in life, and used it as an excuse to drink to greater excess.

At the bottom of the box was a yellow newspaper clipping from the *Navajo Times*, a letter to the editor that her husband had written before they had met. It read: "Our Navajo Nation can become a greater and stronger government, able to wield much more in the midst of this Atomic Age, only it must have character and principle. Without these two, we may be temporarily strong, but we can never be great. . . . Where is the Indian known for his ambition and abilities? He was strong in spirit, a symbol of greatness for those who knew him, admired him and respected him. . . . What happened to this Indian, the Navajo Indian?"

As she gathered herself up, closing the box and putting it under her arm, Rena shook her head at the shame and sorrow of so much promise unfulfilled, and thought, Yes, what happened to this Indian?

3

FULL
CONFESSIONS

On Thursday morning the undersheriff called Lieutenant Miller into his office and told him he had just received a phone call from a Farmington woman who said her daughter, a student at Farmington High School, had been told by a girlfriend that she had overheard a boy in school ask another boy if he wanted to see a finger he had taken off a dead Indian.

The lieutenant looked at him, and waited. Not only was it hearsay, factually it didn't coordinate with anything they had. There were no digits missing on either of the bodies.

Brown read his thoughts. "Hey. I'm just repeating what she said."

"Did she mention the reward money?"

"She said she didn't want nothing to do with the reward. She didn't want her name associated in any way. Hello, here's the information, goodbye. That's the way it went."

Doubtful as he was—he thought it was probably some kid who'd read in the papers about the homicides, shooting his mouth off to get attention—Miller said he would check it out.

Built in the late 1950s, the cement-and-glass buildings that made up Farmington High School sprawled over thirty-seven hillside acres north of downtown. The community was growing fast at that time, and a facility to accommodate the children of the Boomers needed room to grow. As a result, a campus-like setting evolved, with different buildings for each department. The student body numbered about 1,800, of which 25 percent were Hispanic, 19 percent Indian, 1 percent black, and the rest Anglo. The school's colors were green and white, its yearbook was called *Naniskad*—Navajo for "roundup"—and its mascot was the scorpion.

Lieutenant Miller was at home around the high school. Before going to work for the sheriff's office he had been a juvenile probation officer for the county, and truant officer for the Farmington school system. But it had been several years since he'd had an occasion to pay a visit, so he was surprised when he walked into the office of the assistant principal, Barry Sigmon, and found himself received as if he were expected.

Sigmon was a stocky, dark-haired man who looked more like a football coach than dean of students, until you knew his position put him in charge of disciplinary matters at the high school. After shaking hands, Sigmon closed the door behind them and said, "Showing up like this, you've saved me a phone call."

Taking a seat at his desk, Sigmon gestured to a chair before he explained. "The corridors are buzzing with disturbing rumors about the statements one of our students is making about Indians. Some say they think he may know something about the murders."

"Is his name Vernon Crawford?" Miller asked.

Sigmon's eyebrows went up. He nodded. "How did you know?"

"We got a phone call said the same. What do you make of it?"

The assistant principal shrugged. "I don't know. Kids will say anything. I find it hard to believe a student could be mixed up in something that heavy. But as soon as I say that, one'll make a liar out of me."

"What have you heard he's saying?"

"Bizarre stuff. Dismemberment. Of Indians."

The lieutenant was silent.

"What can you tell me about the kid?"

Showing Miller his palms, the assistant principal said, "Not much. He's a junior. Neither a scholar nor an athlete. Kind of a loner. As far as I know there are no disciplinary reports. I could think of a lot more likely suspects before Vernon Crawford's name came to me."

Miller thought a minute before asking, "Would there be any way in the world, keeping everything quiet and what-not, that you could find out what kind of shoe this kid wears? And if it's a waffle-stomper, what the sole looks like?"

Sigmon's eyes narrowed. If a high school student was involved, or if it was a matter of clearing one of suspicion, either way he wanted the doubt resolved. "You bet," he said without hesitation.

*   *   *

Sammye Waldroup was the junior-level creative writing teacher at Farmington High in 1974. She was thirty years old but looked younger. Slender, leggy, and pretty enough to draw wolf-whistles in the corridors, she was also popular with her students because she demonstrated a caring about them that went beyond their performance in the classroom. She was new in the school system, which was how she ended up teaching writing. "It was a course nobody else wanted, I had a background in English, so they gave it to me."

It was during the lunch hour that the assistant principal approached Sammye Waldroup and asked her to "do a little detective work for me."

When Barry Sigmon came up to me in the teacher's lounge and said, "I want you to find out what size shoe Vernon Crawford wears. And if he's wearing waffle-stompers, what the bottom looks like," I thought it was a strange request. But I didn't think a lot about it. I figured it probably had something to do with an infraction in the cafeteria, where there had been a series of altercations.

At the same time it bothered me that, of all students, Vernon Crawford was implicated in some sort of trouble. I had been worried about him all year. He was an odd boy, and I felt sorry for him. I also found him slightly frightening.

For some reason he had taken a special liking to me. He brought me a recipe for fry bread once when I told him it was one of my favorite foods. Another time he gave me a yellow butterfly pinned inside a Plexiglas box. For no reason. Just as a gift.

I thought maybe he was drawn to me because, as he told me after class one day, his parents were never around. I tried to give each of my students individual attention. I wanted my class to be a place where everyone could freely express his innermost thoughts. And I would listen to what they said, or wrote, as the case might be, and give them my honest response.

With Vernon Crawford, that was hard to do. He had a habit of doodling on scratch paper during class, and handing these sketches to me afterward as if he were turning in an assignment. Almost all were mildly pornographic renderings of Indians. The women were scantily clad and well endowed. The genitals of the men were . . . oversized.

Almost worse were his short stories. There was sex and mayhem and terror in almost every story he wrote. I'll never forget one of them was about these people who lived in a mansion who committed murder and destroyed the evidence of their crime by cutting up the bodies and feeding them to dinner guests. Vernon referred to the cuts of meat by name. Jamie Roast. Suzie Steak.

I didn't know what to make of them. I think I wanted to believe the class was offering him an outlet for his violent energies, and that drawing and writing them would be a catharsis. When I tried to discuss the issue with fellow teachers, they thought I was making a big deal out of something harmless. And even I couldn't bring myself to believe he would actually enact any of the awful things he was writing.

Ours was the first class after lunch, and as I watched the students file in I saw—and I had never noticed this before—that everyone, everyone except one girl and myself, wore hiking boots. I watched Vernon take his seat and, when he looked up, I smiled at him and said, "My gosh, Vernon, you certainly have big feet."

With an oafish grin he lifted one of his feet into the air and said, "Yep. I bet nobody else in class wears a twelve-and-a-half."

Getting the size was that easy. Finding out what the sole looked like wasn't much more difficult. I assigned an in-class essay, and while the students wrote, I sat at a desk at the front of the room with a blank pad in front of me, and waited for Vernon Crawford to cross one leg over the knee of the other.

Lieutenant Miller spent the rest of that day doing a background check on Vernon Crawford. Moving up and down the halls and around the grounds between classes, he would spot a kid he'd had dealings with before and call him over for a chat. You weren't going to find the names of these kids on the honor roll—a fair number he'd met at the police station in the middle of the night, and lectured their parents on the need for discipline—but with most he felt they had an understanding that allowed him to ask them, "Tell me what you know about Vernon Crawford," and get a straight answer.

The lieutenant conducted his research as if he were planning to write a biographical quickie on the kid—asking for anecdotes and quotes, nipping and tucking questions into his interrogation about Crawford's attitude toward Indians. The character that emerged was goofy and juvenile (what he heard repeated like a refrain was, "He's just . . . weird"), but no one he talked with admitted to having actually seen Crawford produce any Indian fingers for viewing.

By the time he closed his notebook the school day was over, so Miller had to wait until the next morning before he called the assistant principal for an update.

"Any luck?" he asked.

"Come on up," Barry Sigmon said. "I think I have what you're looking for."

Fifteen minutes later the assistant principal reached in his desk drawer, withdrew a sheet of white paper, and handed it across to the lieutenant. The teacher's drawing of the boot sole so perfectly matched the photos of the bootprint from the crime scene, it could have been traced. One four-pointed star in the heel, six of the same in the sole.

To steady his shaking hands, Miller leaned forward, elbows on knees. He had to admit, when he had asked himself what kind of mind could conceive and execute two agonizing deaths by torture, he had never seriously considered the possibility it was a goddamn eleventh-grader. The crime had been so vile, so far beyond anything he had seen before, that even now it was hard to believe.

And yet there was no doubt in his mind that the Crawford kid was involved. And with that conviction came a connection. Could this be the message behind the heedlessness? Was the lack of circumspection that characterized the crime scene— tracks everywhere, bodies brazenly abandoned in a place where they were sure to be found—the heedlessness of adolescence?

The only other person in the sheriff's office who knew the lead Miller was working was Doug Brown. Miller not only wanted confidentiality, he had insisted on it. "Let's don't put this no place where it can be seen," he had said to the undersheriff before heading for the high school. "At least until I've had a chance to look into it a little further."

Behind this request was the memory, not so long before, of having been beaten on a murder case because a Farmington police officer had carelessly leaked information that warned a suspect, allowing him to destroy crucial evidence before he had been picked up. Miller's concern in this situation was that the sheriff, who was feeling the heat from the press, might let it out that they were about to break the case, throwing an alarm that could trigger the same response.

And he had no intention of informing the sheriff of the progress he'd made, even as they sat around the table at Van's that Friday afternoon, swapping news. But when the opportunity presented itself, he was unable to resist the temptation to drop a big hint. At a certain point in the conversation, when Sullivan was worrying out loud about how the headlines looked, the lieutenant made an elaborate show of checking his watch before aiming a glance at the sheriff and saying, "Give me an hour and forty-five minutes, and I'm gonna tell you who killed them Indians."

To this day, Miller recalls Sullivan's response with particular satisfaction: "He snorted and gave me a you-crazy-bastard look. Then he let his mouth overload itself. 'You do,' he said, 'and you got two weeks vacation comin' to you.' 'I'll take it,' I told him."

All Rena Benally knew about the particulars of the crime was what she had read in the newspaper. But she had heard different, dreadful versions from others that, added to her own upsetting visions, had unsettled her sleep with nightmares. And so, when the deputy who had interrogated her contacted her again, this time offering to take her out to the murder scene and to answer all her questions, she went. But she refused to ride in the same vehicle with him, instead following his patrol car out to Chokecherry Canyon in a pickup truck driven by Benji's brother.

When they parked at the edge of a natural rock amphitheater and walked along the rim of a cliff that gave her a good view of a flat sandy area, dotted with the sparse growth of dry-country vegetation, the term "widow's walk" came to mind.

"This is where we think they threw him off," the deputy said, motioning downward.

Rena swept the earth beneath her with her eyes. And as if she believed the sounds of tragedies were somehow recorded in the landscape and could be heard if one listened closely, she strained to hear a distant sound from that night. But the quiet was complete, so she turned to her imagination, and for a dizzying moment it was as if it were happening again. Only she was there like a shadow watching two men lead her husband toward his death. It is dark so she can't make out their faces, but she can hear their quick hard breathing as they walk her husband up the ridge. Two against one makes the scuffle a short one, and with a big shove from behind, the ground gives way beneath and Benji cartwheels through the night with nothing to grasp to break his f a l l . . . .

The ground at the base of the cliff was thoroughly trampled by the investigating authorities, but she knew that among the many prints mussing the sand were her husband's and that was enough for her to feel she could track the trail of his flight. The evidence, backed by the deputy's terse narrative, told of a wild midnight chase as her husband frantically tried to outrun his tormentors, scrambled to avoid their instruments of torture, crawled defenselessly on hands and knees when he could do little else.

I wonder what he said when they were torturing him. Knowing him, I think he was trying to say something or talk to them. And I think they were probably surprised at his English because it was better than mine. . . . Maybe he was trying to talk his way out of whatever he was going through, whatever it was they were trying to make him do. I know they must have been trying to make him do something. What, I don't know, but maybe he wouldn't do what they said and that's the reason they tortured him.

"Here is where we found him," the deputy said.

Pieces of charred fabric peppered the ground beside patches of blood-caked sand. She stared at the depressions left by rocks that were now resting on the floor of the evidence locker at the Sheriff's Department in Aztec, smeared with her husband's blood. Stirring the ground with her foot, she unearthed something that caused her to drop to one knee. She came up holding a fire-blackened section of a pants' zipper in her palm. "I heard he was castrated," she whispered.

The deputy's voice was naturally raspy, but sounded more so when he said, "Mrs. Benally, your husband was so drunk, I don't think he felt much."

But it wasn't alcohol that killed him. Yes, he was probably drunk, but alcohol didn't drive him out here and take his life. He was murdered.

While interviewing classmates about Vernon Crawford, Lieutenant Miller had repeatedly asked for the names of his friends. He doesn't really have any friends, he'd been told. The guy's a loner. He pressed the question: Surely there was someone in school friendly with him? That was when the name Oren Thacker was mentioned. Not that they hung out together, just that they had several classes in common and were sometimes seen in each other's company.

Oren Thacker. Though he did not know the youth, Miller recognized the family name. The father was co-owner of a trucking firm that delivered water to the oil fields, the mother an upstanding lady in the community. Both belonged to the San Juan County Country Club.

Since school was already in session, rather than pull the kid out of class for questioning, Miller had decided to wait until that afternoon. From his sources he had learned that Oren Thacker worked part-time after school pumping gas at a downtown service station. So after lunch at Van's he drove to the station, let the manager know he needed to talk with Thacker when he showed up, then took a seat in his county car beside the undersheriff, who wouldn't have missed this occasion for the world.

Around 3:30, Oren Thacker arrived for work. He looked like a typical sixteen-year-old to the lieutenant: pushing six feet, rangy, with unkempt brown hair. Your paper boy after his voice changed. When he called the youth over and asked him to get in, Thacker did not behave like someone who had something to hide. He seemed more concerned about getting into trouble with his boss than the law.

"It's okay," Miller assured him. "I've already cleared it, and this shouldn't take long."

At that time the sheriff's office had a substation in Farmington—a room in a county building furnished with a desk, two chairs, a typewriter, and a telephone—and that was where they went to talk. Miller did not begin by advising the kid of his rights and coming on like the bad cop. The hand he was playing presumed innocence on Thacker's part.

"I understand you're buddies with Vernon Crawford," he began.

Thacker nodded.

Wasting no words, the lieutenant said, "Then you probably know he's in a heap of trouble."

Something sparked in the back of Thacker's eyes. "No," he mumbled. "I didn't know that."

Miller said, "We hear he's been saying some pretty strange things about Indians. What can you tell us about it?"

There was an overlong pause. Now the boy seemed scared. His eyes were jumpy when he answered, "I didn't hear anything."

Sensing the kid was wrestling with loyalties, Miller spoke gently. "Come on, son. I think you know what I'm getting at."

When the words came they seemed to be choked out at first. But then they flowed in a torrent that gave Miller the impression the kid was almost relieved to tell what he knew. He let him talk for only a few minutes before stopping him and leaving the room to make a phone call. When he had Tom Hynes, the assistant district attorney, on the line, he told him, "Tom. I've got a boy here and the story he's telling is getting heavy. I think you better come down."

VOLUNTARY STATEMENT

OREN THACKER 4/26/74

Q Oren, do you go to school?
A Yes sir, I do.
Q Where?
A At Farmington High School. I'm a junior.
Q How old are you?
A I'm 16.
Q Oren, directing your attention to April 20, 1974, which is a Saturday, did you have an opportunity to see and talk to Vernon Crawford?
A Yes sir, I did.
Q And where were you when you talked to him?
A I was working at the station.
Q Where's that?
A That's at Jerry's Shell, at Main and Vine.
Q Approximately what time did you talk to him?
A I'm not sure, but I think it was 7:00.
Q In the evening?
A Yes sir.
Q Tell us what you talked about.
A Well, he asked me if I wanted to go rolling Indians. And I said, "No, I'm working." He said, "Well, okay then," and he drove off.
Q Was he alone?
A No sir. He was with a friend. A boy.
Q Do you know who that person was?
A Not for sure.
Q Was he in a vehicle?
A Yes sir, he was. In a light blue Galaxie. I don't know the year, but it was an old make.

Q When was the next time you saw Mr. Crawford?

A Next Monday, at school.

Q At that time did you discuss anything regarding the deaths of the two Navajo Indians north of town?

A Yes sir.

Q All right, what caused you to discuss this matter with Mr. Crawford?

A Well, in third period, which is history class, the teacher brought up the subject that there were two Indians that were dead. That had been murdered, brutally murdered. And I got to thinking that it was Vernon Crawford.

Q Would you tell us why you discussed this with Mr. Crawford?

A Like I said, when the teacher told us about it, I kind of wondered if it was him, 'cause that night he asked me if I wanted to go rolling Indians with him. And so it brung to my mind that he might have done it. So at lunch I asked him. During lunch we go to the Tijuana Taco, and on the way down there and back, I asked him and talked to him about it.

Q Tell us how the conversation came up.

A Well, we got in the car, and we went to eat. I asked him then. I said, "Did you kill those Indians?" And he didn't give me an answer. All he said was, "Don't talk about it." And then I started asking, kind of pushing him. And then he told me that they took them out in the hills, and they pushed them off cliffs, and burned them with, you know, hot plastic. And so on.

Q Did he tell you who was with him?

A Yes sir. I recall he said Peter Burke.

Q Are he and Peter Burke friends?

A Yes sir, they are.

Q Oren, what did he specifically say about this incident?

A Well, I started out asking him, you know, where they killed them at. And he said they killed them out Chokecherry. Then I asked him where they picked them up at, and he said they picked them up at the Esquire Bar. They were walking down the sidewalk, and he got out and asked them to get in. This is what he said. And they took them out to the desert, and he said that they pushed them off this cliff and threw rocks on them. And poured hot plastic on one of them. He said that one was about three miles apart from the other one. He said that one, the older one, was kind of big. And he said that was the father, and the younger one was his son.

Q Did he tell you how they burned the Indians?

A Yes sir. He said they got plastic cups and they lit them on fire, and as they melted, the hot plastic just dripped on them.

Q Did he say anything about striking any of them with rocks?

A Yes sir. He said that they were throwing rocks at them.

Q Did he say anything about beating the Indians?

A Yes sir. He said that he kicked them, hit them, and kicked sand on them.

Q Do you know whether or not Mr. Crawford wears waffle-stompers as a habit?

A Yes sir. I remember him telling me once that, you know, they were the best shoes he ever had 'cause they were so comfortable.

Q Oren, did you discuss with him the possibility of him getting caught doing these acts?

A Yes sir. I asked him what he would do if he got caught. And he said, "Well, I'm not gonna get caught 'cause nobody saw me." And I said, "Well, how do you know?" And he said, "There was only one car that drove by, and we had our lights out, and it drove by slow, and we waited for about a half-hour and then we left."

Q Oren, is this statement of your own free will?

A Yes sir, it is.

(The following is part of an answer by Oren Thacker. The tape recorder must not have been working properly, for the question and the first part of the answer are not recorded on the tape.)

. . . liked to, 'cause he'd laugh, and he'd run around saying, "Oh, goody," and all this kind of stuff. He gave me the impression that he just liked it for doing it, instead of for the money.

Q Did he seem to you to be mentally unstable?

A Yes sir, he did. I think he's crazy.

Driving north, away from the police station where Thacker's statement had been tape recorded, toward the address obtained for Peter Burke along the outskirts of town, took Lieutenant Miller along the outskirts of town. The views extended clearly to the Colorado state line, but he saw none of the country passing by his windows. He was too absorbed in thought.

You see people do a lot of cruel things when you're in law enforcement. Finally, you don't put anything past the old boy you've lived next door to all your life. Nothing surprises you anymore. You know anybody is capable of anything. If he's done it, he's done it. And yet it came with a jolt, I can't deny it, to find out that one of the killers who had held this community in terror for almost a week was none other than a kid who grew up here, went to school here, and I knew his mother and he used to play with my son when he was a boy.

Miller would be the arresting officer for Peter Burke because he used to live on the same street as the Burkes, and could recognize the boy by sight.

He parked in the lot outside the Coronado Apartments, a two-story stucco complex on North Dustin Avenue, less than a mile from the high school, and proceeded to apartment #26. His knowledge that both of Burke's parents were dead and an older brother and his wife were now legal guardians made this more difficult for him than it would have been otherwise. He knew they were sure to feel they had failed in providing the proper supervision. He countered this sentiment by reminding himself that, as strange as it was to be arresting a boy he'd known since the boy was a toddler, it didn't begin to compare to the way those Indian men had been treated.

Mitzi Burke, as pert and cute as an A&W carhop and only a few years older than the teenager she was raising, answered the door, according him recognition by way of a warm greeting.

His effort to arrange a balance between friendliness and seriousness felt awkward. "Good evening, Mitzi," he said, removing his Stetson. "Is Peter home by chance? I need to talk to him."

"He's in his room," she replied, and called his name.

When Peter Burke materialized in the hallway leading to a back bedroom, he seemed rougher than Miller remembered. Perhaps it was the way his eyebrows locked at the bridge of his nose, giving his narrow face a sinister scowl. Or it might have been that his dark and flat eyes seemed as devoid of emotional current as blown fuses. He looked like he didn't have a friend in the world and didn't owe anybody anything. When Miller read him the Miranda warning, he reacted as though the words had no particular meaning to him. He did not make a pretense of innocence or ignorance. He did not ask, What's this all about? He listened, and when he was asked if he understood his rights, he said, "Yeah."

Tom Hynes, the ADA, had accompanied Lieutenant Miller,

and he led off the questioning by asking, "Pete. Would you be willing to talk about the murders of the two Indians who were found in Chokecherry Canyon?"

Burke shrugged. "I don't know nothing about it."

Hynes looked at him steadily. "Well, Pete, we just finished talking to someone who told us otherwise."

The boy answered the challenge with a glare.

Miller pointed to the canvas sneakers he was wearing. "You wouldn't happen to own a pair of cowboy boots, would you?"

Burke acted like he hadn't heard the question.

"If you do, I'd like to have a look at them."

When he neither moved nor spoke, Mitzi said, "Go get your boots, Pete."

He didn't budge, so she repeated herself. "Go get your boots, Pete."

When he returned carrying a pair of cowboy boots, Miller relieved him of them and held them up, turning them in front of his face. There appeared to be a bloodstain on the left side of the right boot near the instep. On the other he found a cactus thorn stuck in the leather upper. Like pins in a map placing Peter Burke at the scene of the crime, he thought, as the assistant district attorney advised the youth he was under arrest.

The Crawford family resided in Beckland Hills, a subdivision on the northern outskirts of town whose outer perimeter bordered open range. Undersheriff Brown, accompanied by a Farmington detective, went to the Crawford residence because he and his wife bowled in the same league as Earl and Ida Crawford. Not that he considered them personal friends. Ida, a sharp-featured chain-smoker, was too loud and coarse for his liking, while Earl, a large, soft man who worked for El Paso Natural Gas in camp maintenance, painting company houses, was such a good ol' nice guy he wouldn't holler "Scat!" at the cat. There was no mistaking who the boss was in that outfit, which made them an uncomfortable couple for Brown to be around.

But that wasn't the whole of it. They had two teenage sons, and the older, Dalton, seemed to operate out of an outlaw corner of his psyche. Theft, drugs, you name it. He had been in and out of trouble with the law throughout his teen years. But bad as he was, he had managed to avoid the trouble his kid brother Vernon was into.

Ida answered the undersheriff's knock drying her hands on a

dish towel and wearing the smell of supper cooking on the stove like a strong perfume. She flashed him a smile. "Doug Brown. What a surprise. Come in, come in."

When he stepped inside the front door he saw Vernon sitting on the living-room couch in his stocking feet, watching television. Never having had dealings with this Crawford, he sized him up quickly—big for his age, six foot or better and at least 200 pounds, with fleshy features that were given an animal countenance by a pair of small, close-set, wary eyes. Keeping the boy in the corner of his eye, he turned his attention back to Ida, who had just asked, "What brings you around?"

He could think of no other way to be than blunt. "I've come for your son, Ida."

She followed his eyes. "Vernon?" she exclaimed. "Why? What's this all about?"

"I'm taking him in for the murder of two Indians."

She stared at him for a second, then squinted in disbelief, reacting as any parent in her situation would; as he imagined he would have reacted if the same charge had been made against his own child. "There must be some mistake."

"I wish there were," he said, and meant it. He turned to face the kid. "Let's go."

Vernon Crawford looked at his mother and, as Brown would later describe the scene, "He went to squalling like he'd got his foot caught in a trap. 'Ooh, Mama. Don't let him take me. I don't want to go to jail.' "

Something about the kid's behavior rang false to the undersheriff and, all business, he told Vernon to put his shoes on.

Sniffling, the boy started to slip on a pair of brown ankle-high waffle-stompers.

"Wear something else," Brown said, taking the hiking boots and handing them over to the detective to be tagged as evidence.

There was one other matter.

"Is that Ford out front the car your son drives?" Brown asked.

Ida Crawford, still unable to believe what was happening, nodded.

Turning to the Farmington detective, Brown instructed him to remain with the vehicle until a wrecker could come out and tow it into the yard, then to lock all doors and bring him the key. After that the undersheriff led Vernon Crawford out of the house to the waiting police car. He did not find it odd in the least when, as soon as he placed the kid in the rear seat and he was out of his mother's earshot, he stopped bawling as if someone had clapped a tight grip on his throat.

The interrogation of the two suspects was conducted in separate rooms at the Farmington Police Department by the assistant district attorney for San Juan County, Tom Hynes. A graduate of Farmington High School himself, of Notre Dame where boxing was his sport, and of Georgetown Law School after joining the marines and serving in Vietnam, Hynes was used to getting answers to his questions. But Crawford played dumb. No, he hadn't killed any Indians. The finger story he'd told around school was just a joke, he said. The finger wasn't real. It was a fake rubber finger he'd bought at a novelty store. The kind you wore on Halloween that looked as if it had been smashed with a hammer and turned gangrenous.

Burke also denied everything. "Pete, we know you did it," Hynes would say. To which the kid would shake his head. "I don't know what you're talking about."

Both youths were close-mouthed and uncooperative for close to an hour, when Hynes sensed an incremental weakening in Peter Burke. On a hunch that the boy might loosen up more without a uniformed officer present, he signaled to Lieutenant Miller, *Leave us alone.*

Hynes was sitting on one side of the desk, Burke on the other. When the door had shut behind the lieutenant and his footsteps faded down the hallway, Hynes shook his head. "I don't understand it, Pete. Why in the hell would you guys do something like that?"

He was giving voice to his own confusion as much as he was asking Peter Burke a question, so it came as a complete surprise when he heard the boy reply, "I don't know why we did it."

Without moving his head, the ADA slowly turned his eyes to the youth. He exhaled silently. Then he called Miller back in and said Pete was ready to make a statement. Burke was asked if he wanted to use the restroom first, or have something to drink, or make a phone call, but he shook his head no to each. He did accept one of Miller's Salem cigarettes however, and then in his own words he began to tell them what had happened that Saturday night.

The room, as it turned out, was not equipped with a tape recorder, and neither of the investigators wanted to interrupt

the mood long enough for one to be set up. So notes were taken
on a yellow legal pad. They would read:

8:30—Sat. 4-20-74
Vernon Crawford—Peter Burke
Rear of Esquire
Talked to subjects
Offered ride
Drove to Chokecherry Canyon
Fat one (Dad) fell asleep
Put him in trunk
Carried smaller one out (Son?)
Told him party on other side of hill
Vernon pushed off mountain
Searched subject—burned
Both Peter and Vernon burned
We set match to clothing and it lit
Q. Did little one run when set on fire?
A. Yes! He kept falling down. He would take a couple of
   steps then fall.
No screaming
Hit w/rocks
Bleeding badly
Vernon melted plastic cup in little one's mouth
No gasoline!
No personal effects—they did not have wallets, money, or
anything
Peter took silver ring off little one
Went back for big one
Vernon knew where to go
Told big one friend up hill
Walked up hill—pushed big one off
Both burned big one
Took clothing off before fire
Q. What clothing?
A. All his clothes. Set on fire. Used brush—wood. Then put
   the fire on big one.
Hit w/sticks—did not jab w/sticks
Big one ran—chased, tripped, and burned, hit w/rocks
Drug sand up around face
Little one still alive when we returned second time
So we burned and hit him w/rocks
While burning subj car came by

Put out fire—hid behind tree
Car turned so lights on them
Car stopped for few seconds
Car left—so did we
Q. What were you wearing?
A. Blue jeans, Levi jacket, cowboy boots, T-shirt.
Q. Whose idea was this?
A. Both of ours.
Q. When did you discuss this type of murder?
A. That night. When we were riding around.
Q. Did you try to get other Navajos to go?
A. Yes.
Q. Where?
A. Harry's.
Q. Have you and Vernon ever rolled Navajos before?
A. Yes!
Emotions—No!
Why—No!
Feel good—Yes!
Tell anyone—No!

When Peter Burke finished giving his account of the murder night, Tom Hynes left to inform Vernon Crawford that his partner in crime had just made a full confession, and it was his turn to talk.

When the news was released that two teenage boys had been arrested in connection with the mutilation slayings of two Navajo men, the town as a whole was horrified. Not since the assassination of John F. Kennedy had so many people who had no personal connection to either victim or suspect felt so personally touched by a murder case. Initially the names of the two youths were not released because the suspects were juveniles, just that they were Anglos, fifteen and sixteen years old, and attended Farmington High School, but no doubt was left about their guilt when Undersheriff Brown was quoted as saying, "We have full confessions."

Just in case those confessions might be challenged in court, however, the undersheriff contacted the New Mexico State Police Crime Laboratory and requested their assistance. When the lab team arrived in Farmington they were escorted to the yard where Vernon Crawford's light-blue Ford Galaxie 500 was being kept, which they processed for evidence. An examination and comparison would be almost a week in coming, but the evidence would be overwhelmingly conclusive. The tire tread from Crawford's vehicle would match the photographs taken by Lieutenant Miller. Soil samples from the area where John Harvey was found were identical to sand and gravel retrieved from the vehicle's trunk, as were hair samples taken off a rock picked up at the scene and hairs discovered in the center of the vehicle's trunk. A section of the left side of the rear seat was excised and examined for prints which would be identified as belonging to Herman Dodge Benally.

The role of the Sheriff's Department was nearing a close. Suspects were in custody. Statements had been obtained. Evidence was being processed. Reports had been written. The rest belonged to San Juan County's prosecuting attorneys.

And then, within hours after Lieutenant Miller had typed "This case is considered cleared pending court action" at the bottom of the OFFENSE REPORT, at 3:38 P.M. on Saturday afternoon according to the dispatcher's log, a phone call was received that by now was all too familiar. The body of another naked Navajo man had just been discovered decomposing in a ravine in Chokecherry Canyon.

4

NAVAJO
WARRIORS

When I first met Wilbert Tsosie in the cafeteria of the Farmington jail after the riot in the summer of 1974, I thought he looked all wrong for the role of militant Indian leader. In part because he had the cherubic outline of face and figure one tends to associate with a jocular character, but also because I sensed within him a spiritual sensibility that was inclined toward harmony rather than discord. When I saw him on later occasions his trademark old-fashioned high-crowned black felt hat, mirrored sunglasses, and Levi jacket and jeans gave him an unmistakable paramilitary patination; but my first impression that he was not a born battler for Indian rights remained the strongest. As we became better acquainted and he told me about the experiences that had brought about his political radicalization, I realized that in fact two different hearts beat within him.

A warrior example had been set for him by his father, a decorated World War II veteran who had served with the 65th Armored Field Artillery Battalion, also known as the Thunderbolt Battalion. Before going overseas his father had had a Blessing Way ceremony performed for him for protection, consisting of songs and prayers, and whether it worked or not depends on what you think about the power of ceremony, but among those who came to believe were the men of the Thunderbolt Battalion. They nicknamed him "Chief" and joked at first about the Navajo prayers he mumbled and the corn pollen he carried in a pouch worn around his neck with his dog tags; but his cool under fire and the absolute conviction of his faith made him seem like a good man to stay near. In short order their own thoughts took a superstitious turn: When the Chief went to sleep at night, his fellow GIs would arrange themselves in a circle around him, forming a human wheel with Wilbert's father as the hub of security at the center.

According to Wilbert, although his father survived the war without injury, he was a casualty of another sort. Officially he was a victim of battle trauma, but on the reservation it was perceived as something else. According to Navajo thought, the ghosts of the enemy dead were haunting him and he needed to be purified through an Enemy Way ceremony. But the type of trouble this sing was believed to remedy did not exorcise all his demons, and his father continued to suffer from a condition that periodically put him in a hallucinated state where he would think the war wasn't over and he would grab his guns and start shooting. It got so bad the menfolk would tie him up with ropes so he wouldn't hurt anybody. Excessive drinking seemed to quell the symptoms sometimes, create them at other times.

Because of the problems his father was having, Wilbert, at age seven, was sent to live with his grandfather, who had been trained in the ways of the medicine man. When he wasn't going to school he was herding his grandfather's sheep in the summer pastures near White Rock, deep in the reservation, attending squaw and fire dances, and listening to stories about Navajo history and the Navajo value system.

Wilbert was sixteen before he moved home again. His father was no longer possessed by demons and he had quit drinking, but new tensions divided the household. His dad had completed his turnaround with a conversion to Christianity, and he enthusiastically tried to press his newfound faith on his children. This did not sit well with his teenage son, who had already been indoctrinated into traditional Navajo beliefs, and explains in part Wilbert's dedication to schoolwork: He wanted to graduate from high school (which he did in 1964) so he could go away to college (Ft. Lewis College, in Durango, Colorado).

His major was history, which gave him an above-average understanding of current events. This was a time when students across America were vocalizing their criticisms of national values and traditions, when young whites were resisting American involvement in Vietnam, when the surging ethnicity of the early sixties was arriving in Indian country. No Indian student involved in higher education could be oblivious to these nationalistic stirrings, and each, it seemed, had to decide for himself how to express his Indianness. Wilbert Tsosie's ambitions by now were decidedly mainstream. He wanted to become a lawyer. To some this sounded like he was trying to create a place for himself in the white man's world, but that wasn't at all the way he saw it. He was of the mind that the problems confronting Indian people opened multiple opportunities for educated Indians, and going into law would put him in a strong position to help his own people.

These were his thoughts when he enrolled in a six-week course at the University of Colorado campus in Boulder. It was billed as a summer Indian Youth Leadership program presented by the Clyde Warrior Institute of American Indian Studies, and he went expecting a curriculum that would leave him better informed about Native American rights and treaties, and prepare him to be a more effective member of the Indian community. He watched, he listened, and what he learned was that Clyde Warrior had apparently been set up as a breeding ground for Red Power activists, and its intent was to build a warrior class for the seventies, eighties, and nineties.

In general he agreed with the basic tenets of the Indian-rights movement: that the restoration of dignity and pride in Indian heritage was a good thing; that it was right to reaffirm the tribal way of life, and for Indians to be free of colonialist rule and run their own affairs. He could even see that the historical time had come to address grievances and injustices done to tribes. But going beyond generalities, what he could not bring himself to accept was that militant action was the only way to change the system. What he questioned was the call for dramatic confrontations with the white "power structure." Some of the angry young intellectuals in attendance went so far as to advocate armed resistance and occupation.

Being legal-minded at this time, Wilbert thought the right and proper way of doing things would, in the long run, be the most effective. He believed if things were done in a right and proper manner, justice would prevail. So he was drawn to solutions like affirmative-action programs, voter registration, and increased education.

He was still formulating plans to attend law school when he returned from Colorado and took a position with the Navajo tribe writing grant proposals, one of which resulted in the multimillion-dollar funding of a program to provide working adult Navajos with the opportunity to attend regional universities to obtain teaching certificates. On the basis of his success there he was offered a job with the Equal Employment Opportunity Commission (EEOC) in Farmington to coordinate projects affecting urban Indians. In the belief the experience would be valuable to his general education, and sharing the concept behind the agency—that only through widespread improvement of American Indians' economic opportunities and basic living conditions could long-term racial peace and justice be obtained—he accepted.

As he busied himself getting to know the Indian situation in Farmington, he discovered that not only were the lives of city-dwelling Indians filled with social and economic problems every bit as serious as those on the reservations, but they faced a peculiar set of circumstances. They were cut off from federal services to which they were entitled on the reservation, and they lacked official representation. An estimated 2,000 Navajo, Ute, Apache, Pueblo, and Sioux Indians lived in town, but no one represented their interests. When problems arose that affected the Indian community, the tribes begged off, saying their jurisdiction did not extend beyond the reservation. City officials likewise excused themselves on the grounds that Indian affairs were not their responsibility. Wilbert Tsosie saw that his mandate was to develop programs that would improve the lot of these city-dwelling Indians.

Typical of many conservative western communities, Farmington was suspicious when it wasn't hostile toward federal agencies charged with upgrading the status of minorities; knowing this, Tsosie devised a strategy to deflect the predictable resentment toward "outside interference." He enlisted the support of conservative, business-oriented members of the Indian community in the formation of a local organization that would exist "to establish communication, cooperation, and understanding with non-Indian communities on issues of need on the part of the Indian community, and to plan and work with non-Indian communities to bring forth mutual respect and understanding." The result was the Farmington Intertribal Indian Organization (FIIO).

In the months that followed, Tsosie's balancing act between the cautious and the clever was masterful. At first no one took the organization seriously—neither the city fathers (when he called a meeting to discuss the lack of low-income housing for Indian people they sent a representative of the Parks and Recreation Department) nor the local Indian population (an announced caucus on Indian issues drew an empty hall). It was out of desperation that he undertook an ingenious, self-styled campaign to cultivate media attention.

The way it worked was like this: He would invite, say, a

Navajo leader from Window Rock to come and speak. Then he would draft a press release filled with dramatic quotes attributed to the guest speaker, along the lines of "I am personally very concerned about my people living in Farmington. I am coming to see what I can do for them. Once I too was an urban Indian so I know what it is like." And as a kicker he would add: "Mark my words: In twenty years Farmington will be a Navajo-controlled town."

When the speaker arrived he would have no idea that the wave of publicity that preceded him was due to falsely attributed predictions. Nor did he much care. All he knew was he was playing to a packed house, and whatever had been said to draw such crowds, as long as it wasn't foolish or inflammatory, was fine with him.

Patiently, carefully, Wilbert Tsosie was laying the groundwork for the introduction of more serious concerns facing Indian people. He felt he had reasonable cause to believe the city had violated the 1964 Civil Rights Act by discriminating against American Indians on the basis of race with respect to recruitment, hiring, job assignment, promotional opportunity, training, compensation, and other terms and conditions of employment. The fact of the matter was, he had come to the conclusion that Farmington was a town of habits and prejudices that made it, in his eyes, a racist community.

Nevertheless, he was smart enough to know that if change was to come about, cooperation with the white administration, and not confrontation, would be necessary.

Everything changed with the slayings.

After the previous fiasco Undersheriff Brown had vowed that never again would he allow a crime scene to be handled in such a sloppy manner, and on this Saturday afternoon he made good on that promise. He was the first member of the Sheriff's Department to arrive on the scene, and his instructions to the Farmington patrolman who had responded to the call were, "Nobody, and I mean NOBODY, except Bob Miller and I are to get past. I don't give a damn if Dan Sullivan shows up, even he ain't gettin' in till we're by God through workin' the scene. Got that?"

Just then Lieutenant Miller pulled up. Brown hailed him with the good news. "Hey. Ain't nobody bothered *this* sonofabitch, I'll guarantee it."

Two kids riding dirt bikes on the motorcycle trails that laced the hills near Chokecherry Canyon had found the body. They had noticed buzzards circling in the sky and, thinking maybe a dead deer was attracting their attention, had zoomed into the area, almost crashing into the body.

"Where is it?" Miller asked, and one of the youths aimed a trembling finger toward a striated and eroded ridge.

"Over there."

The two men smelled the body before they saw it. Breathing shallowly through their mouths and fighting back a nausea roused by the sickening stench, they stopped about ten feet away and closed the remaining distance with a squint. The body was lying face up in the nude, badly battered about the head, blistered on the chest, stomach, and legs, and the man's private parts looked like they had been fed to a fire.

"Here we go again," the undersheriff muttered.

After snapping ten Polaroid photographs, Miller began a search of the surrounding area but turned up virtually nothing of relevance to the crime. No physical evidence, no footprints. Which didn't surprise him. By the condition of the body he guessed it had lain exposed to the elements for at least two weeks, and in that time the wind and rain had probably swept the area clean. It was when he widened the radius of his hunt that he came across a campfire approximately 150 feet from the body. Squatting and scooping a handful of charred sand, he spread his fingers far enough apart to let the grains and ash sift through, leaving glittering in his palm several brass rivets from a pair of Levi pants and the kind of pearlized snaps you find on a Western shirt.

Strange, he found himself thinking, how in a single week a scene so bizarre could become so recognizable.

He stood up, continuing in a northwesterly direction, following furrows in the soil that could have been hoed by the heels of a dragged man, but with some attention missing from his eyes as he found himself preoccupied by the question: How many more dead Indians lay rotting in these hills?

One of the beguiling peculiarities of Navajo country is the way a single cloud will sail in from beyond the horizon, drench a lone acre of ground in the middle of a hundred square miles of sagebrush desert in a torrential downpour, and then sail away. Watching it happen is like witnessing a direct response to a rain prayer.

Jackson Lake looks as if it were conjured by one of these godsent cloudbursts. It is an oasis body of water that laps against shifting sands. If you didn't know it was an irrigation reservoir fed by a man-made diversion, you'd swear it was the spawning ground of all mirages, shimmering in sunlight in the outback northwest of Farmington.

A week shy of May a group of Navajos gathered at Jackson Lake for a party to welcome spring. It was too cool for swimming so some stood at the shoreline spin-fishing for stocked trout, while others lounged around a campfire barbecuing hot dogs and playing a traditional game in which an older member of the group tested the younger generation's knowledge of the Plant People. Holding up various samples, he made everyone guess their name and what they had been used for in the old days. He knew so much, he said, because he had accompanied his grandmother herding sheep in springtime when he was young, and while the stock nibbled at needle-and-thread grass—he held up a tuft of tall grass with a feathery top—she would pick wild celery—in his other he produced a small plant that grew almost flat to the ground—to flavor soups and stews.

A pickup truck trailing dust returned from a run to the convenience store for more beer and pop, and the designated driver trudged back toward the group with several six-packs and a newspaper under his arm.

"Snakeweed is a disaster," the plant specialist was saying. "It has a power that grass doesn't. Grass is to be eaten, snakeweed was made to survive. It has taken over the country and it poisons livestock. The only thing it is good for is ant bites and snake bites."

His commentary was interrupted by the exclamation "Oh no!" from a girl who had picked up the newspaper. Everyone looked at her. For some moments she said nothing. When she lifted her eyes they were filled with tears.

Wilbert Tsosie was sitting beside her and, with a leader's preemption, he took the paper out of her hands. Scanning the front page, his eyes went right to the inch-high black headline. Glancing swiftly around he saw the group had become an attentive circle, so he began to read aloud: " 'The mutilated bodies of two Navajo men were found Sunday in a gully about six miles north of Farmington. . . .' "

When he had finished reading, without words people began to break camp. The festive mood had been spoiled. Bad weather could not have doused the group with a deeper depression. No one present knew the murdered men personally, but that didn't matter. The distinction between an individual and the community was an alien concept to a Navajo. An attack on one member of the tribe was an attack on the whole tribe. In the sense that all of The People were related, two of their brothers had been slaughtered.

Back at the Farmington Police Department Peter Burke was hauled into the interrogation room where Tom Hynes put it to him straight: "All right, you little sonofabitch. What's going on here? You told us about two. Where does the third come in?"

Burke acted remarkably unbothered. "You didn't ask about no others."

Hynes glared in disgust. "Well I am now."

Burke spoke with carelessness and insouciance. "We did him a coupla weeks back."

"We—meaning you and Crawford?"

Burke thought a minute, then said, "There was another on that one."

Hynes squinted. "I don't get your meaning."

"Wasn't just me and Crawford."

Reacting with some astonishment, Hynes asked, "There was a third kid with you?"

Burke nodded in the affirmative.

"Who?"

"Oren Thacker."

After taking a statement from Peter Burke on his version of the events on the night in question, a phone call was placed to the Thacker home asking the parents to bring their son to the police station for questioning at 8:30 the following morning. He arrived in the company of his mother and the family attorney, Marvin Baggett, an engaging country lawyer whose twang and yarns belied a shrewd legal intelligence. Having interviewed his client late into the night, he had decided that cooperation from the beginning would look best to the court if the case went to trial, and in the presence of the authorities he wagged a finger and counseled, "I'm gonna tell you something right now. You're in a peck of trouble, young man. Every word you breathe had better be the truth."

Under questioning Thacker admitted that he had taken part in a portion of the crime, but stated that he had not been present when the victim's clothing was burned or when any fires were started. He maintained that he had held a flashlight while Crawford and Burke did the serious beating, and that the Indian had been alive when he had left the scene.

Both Lieutenant Miller and ADA Hynes found Thacker's statement persuasive. Not once had he denied his involvement, and his explanation for why he had not said anything about it before—because he had not been asked, and he assumed the man was alive—made sense. After a brief conference they asked him if he would be willing to submit to a polygraph test. Peering across the room to his attorney, who inclined his head, he said, "Yes sir."

INTERVIEW WITH OREN THACKER

I was introduced to Oren Thacker at the courthouse in Aztec, New Mexico, at about 10:30 A.M. on April 30, 1974. Present were Sheriff's Officers Brown and Miller and Thacker's attorney, Marvin Baggett. I advised Thacker of his rights under the Miranda ruling in the presence of the above-named people. Then I interviewed Thacker alone.

Thacker stated that his birthdate is August 18, 1957, and that he lives with his parents Boyd and Joyce Thacker, at 3599 Sunset Avenue, Farmington, New Mexico. Furthermore, he said he is a junior attending high school and is employed at Jerry's Shell Station at Main and Vine in Farmington, New Mexico.

When asked, he admitted that on a Saturday night about the first week in April he was working at the station when Vernon Crawford came to the station in his car. This was around 9:00 P.M. There was another boy in the car that he said he did not recognize at that time. He quoted Crawford as saying, "Oh boy, we've got an Indian in the trunk."

The two waited in the car until Thacker got off work at about 9:30 P.M., and when he got into the car, he recognized the second boy as Peter Burke. He said he asked Crawford, "Where did you get the Indian?" and was told, "In back of the Esquire."

After leaving the station, Crawford drove downtown around the A&W Root Beer, and then down by the railroad tracks, before suggesting, "Let's take the Indian out in the hills." Both Thacker and Burke agreed that sounded like a good idea. Crawford said he knew a place near his house they could go, and it was on the drive there that he said, "I think we will kill him." According to Thacker, his response was, "If you're going to kill him, you'd better take me home because I don't want any part of it."

Crawford's reply was, "Okay then, I guess we won't kill him."

Crawford had some marijuana and Thacker rolled one cigarette and all three boys smoked it. He stated that the one cigarette was all that was smoked that night. At one point on the drive Thacker said he told Crawford, "Drive so you'll shake him up," and Crawford swerved from one side of the road to the other.

He said they drove about five miles and stopped on a hill. Crawford opened the trunk and Thacker pointed a flashlight at the Indian, who was "way up by the spare tire." He said they all laughed when they saw the Indian in the back of the trunk. He said that next they helped get the Indian out of the trunk and stood him up in back of the car. Crawford searched his pockets and came up with two books of matches, he thinks from the Holiday Inn.

He doesn't say who, he just says "we" decided to undress the Indian, and he helped Crawford take the Indian's clothes off. He said Crawford ripped the underwear off. After he was undressed, the Indian got up and started wandering around and Thacker said, "Look, a streaker," and they all started laughing again.

Crawford then pushed the Indian down and said, "Let's burn his hair." Crawford had a lighter. The Indian was lying on his left side and Crawford started burning his hair on the other side. Crawford then said, "Why don't we burn the hair on his dick," and he set fire to the Indian's pubic hair. All the boys were laughing.

On the way out to the scene, Crawford had mentioned that Peter Burke had some firecrackers that they could throw on the Indian. After Crawford burned the Indian's pubic hair, Peter got out the firecrackers. "Let's put one in his butt," Crawford said and put a firecracker between his "cheeks." When it went off the Indian started groaning. Crawford said to the Indian, "Shut up, nobody can hear you out here."

All the boys started kicking him in the side, but Thacker said, "I didn't kick him as hard as I could have."

Crawford said, "Look, his butt's bleeding," and the Indian had blood on his fingers from his butt. Crawford then lit a firecracker and put it on the Indian's stomach but it just fizzed. Crawford suggested, "Let's put one in his nose," and he put it in his right nostril, but the Indian brushed it out and it fell on the ground and went off.

Thacker said, "I said, 'Let's tie him to a tree,' " and Peter Burke took the laces out of the Indian's boots as Thacker and Crawford dragged the Indian to the top of the hill where they pushed him off and pushed him down the hill with their feet. Crawford jumped on the Indian's butt with both feet and Thacker said he thought that was stupid. Peter brought Crawford the laces and Thacker thinks Crawford tied the Indian's feet. Peter got a stick about a foot long with a knot on the end and hit the Indian on the head several times. The Indian started groaning again. Thacker doesn't know for sure if he was tied, but thinks his feet were tied and his hands were not tied.

Crawford burned the Indian's hair again and then all the boys kicked him again. (Repeatedly, Thacker said, "I didn't kick him as hard as I could.") All the boys then hit the Indian with small branches they pulled from a tree because Crawford told them that it would make the Indian itch.

I asked Thacker if they had built a fire. His first response was, "Not that I remember." He then said that he was sure that they never built a fire and said that they did not burn the Indian's clothes.

Thacker said he walked up the hill then, with the flashlight still in his hand, and he shined it back down on Pete and Crawford. He states that the Indian was still by the tree, and that the Indian was breathing when he left. Crawford then took him home. He arrived home before midnight. He said that he turned on the TV and got something to eat and then went to bed.

On the following Monday Thacker said that he saw Crawford at school and asked him if he had gone back "out there," and Crawford replied, "I went out there the next morning and the Indian finally rounded up all his clothes and had them on. He had a fire built to keep warm, and when he saw me, he ran off holding his side."

E. R. DeLuche

When the results of Oren Thacker's polygraph test were turned over to the investigators, they came with the examiner's own conclusions. Apparently Thacker had "reacted" to a number of relevant questions, particularly when asked about the burning of the Indian's clothes. Meaning: "It is my opinion that Thacker did not give me the whole truth as to his involvement in the incident."

In the course of the interview Thacker stated that since the middle of his sophomore year he had been involved in no fewer than ten, nor more than twenty, "rollings" of Indians, and he willingly supplied the names of six other boys he had "rolled" Indians with. But he swore that on no previous occasion had the level of violence approached a killing power, nor did he have any knowledge of any other bodies. On these last two points he did not react. Meaning: He was telling the truth.

Lieutenant Miller and ADA Hynes had suspected Thacker was giving them a highly selective version of the crime when they were unable to find any corroborating evidence of human activity around the tree he said they tied the Indian to. But there was another discrepancy that impressed them more. On a visit to the scene Thacker had walked them through the events of that night. Here is where we parked. Here is where we stripped him. Here is where we rolled him down the hill. Here is where he was lying when we left him.

"Are you sure?" he was asked regarding this last statement.

"I'm positive," he had replied.

The two lawmen had exchanged glances. The distance between here and where the body had been found was a good 200 feet.

Since Crawford was the one with the means of transportation, and since he had admitted to Thacker he had gone back out to the scene, both Miller and Hynes considered it a likely possibility that Crawford had returned the next day to finish personally what the three had started.

They brought Crawford into the interrogation room and, when he denied returning to the scene, sweated him.

"If you didn't do it, then tell us how the body got over there?" Hynes demanded to know, his voice rising. "How did it happen? HOW THE HELL DID IT HAPPEN?"

Crawford wasn't talking, but the pressure was getting to him. There were times when he shook so badly they thought he might be having a seizure. When it looked as though pushing him any harder might send him over a mental edge, Hynes seethed, "The hell with it. We already have enough for a conviction. Book him on three counts of first-degree murder."

Every day of the week it took investigating authorities to make an arrest in the Indian-murders case, Wilbert Tsosie read the news accounts in the Farmington, Albuquerque, and Gallup papers, looking for reporting differences. The intensity of his interest in the police investigation can be explained only in part by his position as a leader in the local Indian community; a personal suspicion that he already knew who was targeting the Indian race for murder also figured in.

Although it shamed him to remember, while attending Farmington High School, as a way of ingratiating himself to fellow Anglo students he had participated in the harassment of Indian people who came to town to drink. Because he spoke Navajo as well as English, he had taught his Anglo friends to swear in Navajo, and joined in with them when they cursed and insulted the winos wobbling up and down the streets of Farmington.

Some white kids took it further, he'd heard, beating the drunks up and robbing them. He had drawn the line short of that, but now, knowing nothing more than what he'd read in the paper, he was convinced that the Saturday-night sport of mugging intoxicated Indians had probably been taken to lethal extremes by white teenagers.

When, after five days, the authorities had yet to produce a suspect, his suspicions broadened to include the investigating agencies. With each passing day he grew more and more distrustful of the authorities, until he began to wonder if there was some kind of cover-up going on—that because the victims were seen by whites as lowlifes, cretinized by booze, the crimes were not being diligently investigated. Or that they knew who was responsible but were keeping them under wraps, hoping public interest would fade.

When, on the sixth day, New Mexico newspapers carried a front-page article reporting on the arrest of two Anglo suspects, he was stunned and saddened, but he was one of the few people in town who were not surprised.

When the paper came out the following day with news of a third Navajo who had been found in a similar condition, he felt an immediate response from the Indian community was in order. That very evening, while sitting around the kitchen table with friends in the trailer where he was living, he proposed they put their feelings down on paper and distribute handbills around town. The idea was roundly approved, and an unattributed statement was drafted, mimeographed, and by the following afternoon the entire town was papered with fliers that read:

Yesterday, Life was beautiful and free.

Indians were bonded with nature as children with their mother.

Theirs was a way of peace and harmony.
There was no fear and it did not take courage to live.
Yesterday is Gone!!

The life that is so precious to the Indians is becoming a toy to the Whites. A toy that can be tortured, destroyed, and mutilated. It has reached the point where they are physically attacking us!

What will it be like in the future if they continue in this manner? If the white teenagers freely take the lives of Indian people? What will happen when they become adults?

What have we ever done to the Whites to deserve this? They took our land, humiliated us, made us suffer. Why do they do this? Why??? Our sorrow, together with fear, is more than we can bear.

John Earl Harvey, Herman Dodge Benally, and other forgotten Navajos: We will remember you. The Navajos will not vanish. We will remember when we stand united! We will remember when we stand up for our rights! In our grief, we will remember!! In our victories, we will remember! We shall stand together and we will remember. . .

Early the next morning Wilbert was eating breakfast and listening to the radio when the regular programming was interrupted by a news bulletin. Unidentified militant Indians had distributed throughout the town of Farmington unsigned, anonymous leaflets threatening violent disruption, the announcer said in an alarmed tone of voice. The report ended with a quote from a local police official who responded that forewarned was forearmed.

"Quick and all-out action by the San Juan County Sheriff's Department has brought results in the brutal slaying of a third Navajo man," read the news reports published the day after the discovery. But it would be another five days before the victim would be identified, and coming up with his name would be more a matter of luck than forensic professionalism on the part of the Sheriff's Department.

Fingerprints were not rolled at the scene because of the condition of the victim's body. The natural process of decomposition, in concert with two weeks of exposure to the New Mexico sun, left the remains in such an advanced state of decay that it was doubtful a clear set of prints could be obtained.

What was left of the victim had been removed to a mortuary where it was hoped that a Navajo family with a missing member would come forward with a matching description.

For three days Navajo families had streamed through the mortuary, making inquiries. But no jewelry or tattoos adorned the body, the damage to the facial area left it so far from any resemblance to its original state that a positive ID from viewing the remains was not even considered, and no one came in with a relatively similar physical description of a missing person. Faced with another potentially embarrassing situation, Sheriff Sullivan sent a deputy back to the mortuary with the instruction, "Get me a set of prints."

When the deputy showed up at the mortuary and told the funeral director he had come to work on the cadaver, he slammed into a wall of resistance.

"Have you ever smelled decomposed human remains, Deputy?" he was asked.

The deputy just looked at his questioner.

"There is absolutely nothing in this world worse. It is unique unto itself. It not only leaves a lasting impression on the mind, once it gets into a carpet, the drapes, you've got an odor problem for life. There is no way to mask the odor, and the most powerful product in the industry only works to a slight degree. Do you understand what I am saying?"

The deputy had asked for permission, not a lecture, and he was about to say as much when the funeral director told him in no uncertain terms, "If you want to do something to this individual, you are welcome to take him anywhere you like. As long as it is out of this building and off these premises."

When the deputy called Sheriff Sullivan to report on the conversation, he found his boss unsympathetic. "I don't care what you have to do, goddamn it," the sheriff growled. "Get me a set of prints."

An hour later, accompanied by a volunteer member of the Sheriff's Posse, the deputy pulled up to the ramp at the rear of the mortuary in a borrowed panel van. Moving with haste and stealth, the two men retrieved a slim metal casket (sealed with a rubber gasket, it was designed especially for decomposed remains and could fit inside a standard-sized coffin) which they threw into the back like freight that did not require delicate handling.

They headed for the hills north of town, not far from where the body had been found in the first place. At a remote spot where they were shielded by trees yet had a view for miles in all directions so they would not be surprised by unwelcome visitors, they parked. Neither moved for a moment as each reminded himself they were not body snatchers, that this may be dirty work but it was for a good cause; and then the deputy said, "Let's do it."

Slipping on gas masks normally issued in riot situations but donned here to combat the stench, they unloaded their fetid cargo. The instant the casket was opened they knew the gas masks were a useless defense against the stench, but they left them on anyhow, thinking about the contagious diseases that infect decomposing corpses.

There was a heavy-duty vinyl pouch inside, which they unzipped and peeled back to reveal the remains. Both stared momentarily, for the corpse was unnaturally white. Only later would they be informed that it had been dusted with formaldehyde in powder form to inhibit the odor.

To the deputy's credit he had given a good deal of thought to the problem of how to get prints off fingers that for all practical purposes were mummified. A rancher when he wasn't wearing a star on his shirt, he had decided to deal with it through a home remedy. Corn oil. Knowing how well corn oil worked as a leather softener on saddles, he hoped it would work just as well on dried skin.

Both men were nervous and paused frequently to look around. "That was all we needed," the deputy would say when reflecting on the episode. "For the Sheriff's Department to be caught messing with one of the corpses."

It got worse. Quickly he realized a corn-oil massage was not going to do the job. The fingers needed a real soaking before they were going to recover any pliability. And ordering his partner to maintain a full-time lookout, he withdrew his pocket knife and started cutting off the victim's fingertips, which he then marinated in corn oil until they were soft enough to fit snugly into a fingerprinting spoon.

To this day, when asked how long he was out there, the deputy's only reply is, "Too damn long." But as crude as his technique was (had he known what he was doing he could have injected a glycerine solution into the fingertips and they would have plumped up), in the end it worked. Not solely because of the corn oil, but also because of a unique set of circumstances.

The elements involved in decomposition are primarily blood and bacteria. Human blood is alkaline in a living person, but becomes acidic when it is no longer oxygenated, and the natural bacteria that help digestion become a powerful agent in the putrefaction of tissue after death. As it so happened the victim was lying on his back with his hands up when he was found so most of the blood in his upper extremities had settled in his body. Combined with exposure to the sun and wind, the fingers had dehydrated rather than rotted, and for this reason the deputy was able to bring the tissues back to a state where he could roll a decent print. Had the body been left face down, as the other two victims were, he might still be unknown.

On the basis of those prints the victim was identified. His name was David Ignacio, and he was a fifty-two-year-old Navajo from the Huerfano area, about twenty-five miles south of Farmington. And other than a phone call from the medical investigator's office in Albuquerque, where the autopsy was performed, inquiring, "What kind of animal you got up there in San Juan County that nibbles the fingertips off corpses?" there would be no mention of what the Sheriff's Department had gone through and how it had lucked out on the way to an identification.

The day after unsigned handbills bugled Farmington into a state of alert, officials from both the Navajo tribe and the city of Farmington went public with formal statements concerning the killings. Peter MacDonald, chairman of the Navajo Tribal Council, condemned them and expressed the "hope that the speedy conviction of those who are responsible for this outrage will make sure that this will never happen again." Marlo Webb, the mayor of Farmington, for his part conveyed his "deepest sympathy," coupled with incomprehension "that such an action could take place in this community that prides itself as being ever ready to open its heart and arms to those in need of a helping hand. Farmington and its citizens over the years have enjoyed an especially close relationship and friendship with the members of the Navajo Nation."

A cynical smile curled Wilbert Tsosie's lips when he read these statements. He found the tribal chairman's remarks totally lacking in leadership. Three of his people had been horribly murdered and he was handling the matter as diplomatically as a hot campaign issue. As for the mayor's enthusiastic characterization of race relations, it was laughable with unintentional irony. Neither addressed what Tsosie felt to be the most important issue raised by the tragedy: It epitomized the racial hatred that had been building for a long time; the white community should recognize this, the Indian community should refuse to tolerate it, and specific steps should be taken to change it.

This was the thrust of his comments before an emergency meeting of the board of directors of the Farmington Intertribal Indian Organization the following day. And the gist of their response, he would remember with unconcealed sarcasm, was, Okay, Wilbert. You seem to know what's best. Handle it your way. But you're on your own.

The board's timidity created a dilemma for him. In their reluctance to authorize a statement or endorse action that might heighten tensions in town they were remaining true to the conservative organizing principle that Wilbert had originally believed was necessary if they were going to provide effective representation for the Indian community. And yet, in failing to take a strong stand under these circumstances he felt they were proving their inability to deal with the tough realities affecting Indians in Farmington.

He decided to call for a public meeting of the Indian community and measure its reaction. It was held at the Indian Center in Farmington and was attended by a crowd estimated at 300 persons. Their comments, in general, fell into two opposing camps. On the wait-and-see side were those who agreed with Navajo tribal vice-chairman Wilson Skeet, who recommended nonviolence and patience, and urged citizens, "Don't do anything to make the problem worse." And on the ready-to-hit-the-warpath side were those who argued that the murders showed that America's treacheries were not just a matter of historical record, but were continuing today and needed to be met in kind.

If there was one area of agreement it lay in what would constitute justice in this case. Everyone felt that for taking three human lives the slayers should pay with their lives. At the very least they should be put behind bars for the rest of their lives. There was symmetry to that expression of justice, an evenness that would put things back in balance.

Although he wanted to believe that the local courts would see it this way too, Wilbert also knew the wheels of justice had a way of slipping when it came to the American Indian and his rights. And in order to be reassured that the San Juan County prosecutors were taking this case seriously, he paid a visit to the assistant district attorney, Tom Hynes.

The ADA was circumspect in his answers. He assured Wilbert there would be "full application of necessary law."

"What does that mean?" Wilbert asked warily.

"We will prosecute to the full extent allowable."

"Allowable?"

Hynes considered his words. "There are mitigating circumstances that we are required to consider."

As Wilbert found himself thinking about all the legal manipulations and subtleties of law that had subverted due process for Indians in the past, his pulse picked up. "Like what?"

"The major one is the age of the suspects. Before kids this age can be tried as adults they must first be bound over from juvenile to adult court."

"Is that going to happen?"

Hynes paused. "We haven't decided yet if we're going to push for a bind-over. We must look at all the facts and then make a decision."

Tsosie stared. "Looking at the bodies wasn't enough?"

Hynes ignored that remark, glanced at his watch, and suddenly remembered he had a pressing engagement elsewhere.

Walking away from that meeting, Wilbert felt thwarted and powerless. He read the ADA's indefiniteness as a bad sign, but nevertheless he was willing to wait and hope he was wrong.

In the meantime he decided to approach Farmington officials and ask them what steps they intended to take to prevent similar occurrences of this kind of anti-Indian activity in the future.

Marlo Webb was a middle-aged businessman who owned the largest Chevrolet dealership in town. He had dark wavy hair, handsome aquiline features, and spoke with a self-confidence that bordered on arrogance. But he held his peace, listening with a deepening frown as Wilbert accused Farmington of turning a blind eye to a pattern of harassment, intimidation, cruelty, and violence against Indian people, and insisted the mayor take action to make the streets safe for Indians.

Mayor Webb, gazing archly across his desk, asked, "Are you through?"

Wilbert nodded.

Holding up his thumb, the mayor said, "Number one. You must recognize this. You represent no one but yourself. Not the Indian people in this town. Not the Indians on the reservation. You are not an elected official so I have no obligation to listen to what you say."

When Wilbert tried to speak the mayor interrupted him.

"Number two. I have received more calls than I could count from constituents advising me not to deal with you, let alone grant you a meeting. But I did, anyhow. I took an extra step. Just listening to you, I have bent over backwards.''

Wilbert started to protest, but again the mayor cut him off.

''Number three. I have also received a fair number of phone calls from your very own people telling me *they* do not approve of what you are trying to do.''

The mayor went on until he ran out of fingers. But Wilbert had stopped counting because the berating was so belittling and the force of the mayor's argument so overwhelming that he lost track of whatever his justification had been for coming here. By the time the mayor was finished, all Wilbert wanted was to make a swift exit and regroup. When he thought he heard the order ''Now get out of here,'' he pitied himself for a moment before arising with effort and, appalling as it would be to remember later, contritely apologized for taking up the mayor's time.

Waiting in the hall outside were a handful of supporters who had come to show their solidarity. They were people he had felt he was representing whom he now felt he had let down. They had overheard his tongue-lashing and were angry at the manner in which he had been treated, but his humiliation got in the way of any indignation he was capable of mustering, and in a daze he pushed his way through.

Back in his office at the EEOC he was sitting dejectedly at his desk indulging in self-flagellation—he had gone into the meeting unprepared for a debate, his thinking had been fuzzy, he had not been able to think of the right things to say: in short, his performance had stunk—when he sensed a silent presence in the room. He looked up from his desk into the face of a stocky Navajo man, slightly older than he was, who wore horn-rimmed glasses and the patrician air of someone keenly conscious of his heritage. His jeans were tight, his shirt loose, his hair tied up with string in back. A turquoise bracelet banded each wrist and an arrowhead dangled from around his neck. Wilbert found himself staring at the arrowhead. When he was seven, before he had gone off to school, his grandfather had done a Blessing Way sing over him to protect him against evil spirits, and at the end he had been given just such an arrowhead to wear.

What is this? Wilbert asked himself, watching as the man entered his office, took a seat across from him, and, leaning forward, spoke softly. ''I was there this morning. I heard what was said.'' He hesitated. ''You did your best, brother.'' And he held out his hand.

The formal introductions were brief. The stranger said his name was Fred Johnson and that he was deputy director of DNA (Dinebeiina Nehilna Be Agaditahe), the tribal legal services organization based in Shiprock. But a more significant identifying aspect to him was revealed when he asked what clan Tsosie belonged to.

"The People from the Badlands," Wilbert replied.

Fred Johnson smiled. "I guess I was more right than I thought when I called you brother. That's my clan too."

Looking down, Johnson shook his head, laughed lightly, then looked up. "Let's cut the bullshit, brother. It's time to kick ass."

Wilbert wasn't sure what that meant, and Fred Johnson did not elaborate. Instead he invited Wilbert to be his guest at a meeting of the like-minded that evening in Shiprock.

It was not quite dark—the sun was long set but twilight lingered on the bluffs and in the branches of the highest cottonwoods—when Wilbert turned off the highway, following a rough road that straggled along an irrigation ditch to a sandy driveway that curved toward a low, flat-roofed adobe house with cars parked four-deep in front. He didn't know what to expect as he knocked on the front door and was let in by a woman he didn't recognize but who seemed to expect him. People talking loudly filled the rooms inside, mostly men, young and old, and a few he noticed wore knives in their belts and AIM (American Indian Movement) patches on their leather vests.

From the other side of a crowded room he heard himself hailed by Fred Johnson, who introduced him to several people whose names he quickly forgot before Johnson roared for everyone to take a seat.

The way people obeyed, ending conversations abruptly and dropping into chairs, squatting or sitting cross-legged on the floor, acknowledged Fred Johnson as a leader who commanded respect. Wilbert was impressed, and was about to follow suit but Johnson's grip on his arm kept them standing side by side.

"My brother here took the fight to city hall today," Johnson informed the gathering, "and I asked him to come here tonight and tell us about it."

Wilbert had not prepared a speech so he had to improvise. He gave a brief accounting of his background—where he grew up, went to school; his position in Farmington and what he was trying to do—before he recalled his rumpus with the mayor that afternoon. He redeemed himself this time with a few choice gibes now that he'd had a chance to mull over what he should have said, but for the most part it was a moderate speech, and when he could think of nothing else to say he turned to Fred Johnson.

A low murmur of approbation circulated around the room as Fred Johnson took Wilbert's place, thanked him for his words, and like the headliner replacing the warm-up act, proceeded to deliver a fiery, uninhibited diatribe against the town of Farmington that made everything that had come before sound like social pleasantries. He mixed Navajo and English with soaring eloquence and biting humor, and Wilbert listened in awe, amazed at the way Johnson was capable of expressing radical notions in a way that was as inspirational as it was passionate.

Johnson's attack on the city was based on its discriminatory treatment of native peoples: "Navajos are not considered human beings in that town. We're Farmington's niggers. The only Indian Farmington ever cared about is the Indian on the back of a nickel."

And he linked the murders to racist attitudes: "Those murders were not simply the act of three crazy kids. They reflect prejudices that have long been ignored. We have the right to live freely and without fear. It's time we stood up and united in a common cause to confront the enemy."

It was an electrifying speech, and the ignited crowd roared with approval when he called for rallies, for demonstrations, and for marches that would "bring that honkie town to its knees."

"Come here, Wilbert," Johnson bellowed. And when Wilbert stood beside him, Johnson threw his arm around his shoulders and challenged the crowd. "My brother's with me. Are you?"

From all corners men jumped to their feet and vowed their support. World War II vets cried out, "I fought for this country, but I'll fight for the Navajo Nation if it comes to that." Others shouted, "I'm with you. I'll fight the white man in Farmington right now."

Seizing the moment, Fred Johnson tore his long hair free of its tie, shook it in the way warriors used to before going into battle, and began to howl. "HEE-YAH!"

5

DAYS OF RAGE

In order to be certain there were no more bodies baking in the desert, no more students involved, investigators searched the immediate areas around all three murder scenes (though with so much wide-open space and so many canyons and arroyos it was impossible to be thorough) and the youths were given lie-detector tests before criminal charges were filed. Because of restrictions on the release of information in juvenile cases, all the public was apprised of were the facts of the motions, with no details, supporting arguments, or background considerations to fill in its understanding of what was happening. And so everyone knew that on Monday, April 29, in San Juan County District Children's Court, a district court referee ordered Vernon Crawford and Peter Burke held in custody and they were taken to a separate juvenile facility in the Aztec, New Mexico, jail until the matter could be heard before a district court judge. And that on Tuesday a petition of delinquency alleging murder was filed against Vernon Crawford and Peter Burke, charging them with three counts of murder each; which was followed on Wednesday with another petition, charging Oren Thacker with one count of murder for his role in the death of David Ignacio.

What was less well known, and would later cause confusion and turmoil, was the thought behind the course of events that was initiated next.

Under the laws of the state of New Mexico, a juvenile could not be charged with a capital offense because, according to the Juvenile Code, a juvenile could not commit a crime, he could only commit an act of delinquency, unless he was transferred from children's court into adult court. The significance of the bind-over process, as it was called, lay in the severity of sentencing. If a juvenile was tried and convicted in the juvenile court system for murder, the maximum penalty he could receive was two years' confinement in the New Mexico Boys School. A conviction in adult court for the same offense, on the other hand, could mean life imprisonment in the state penitentiary.

In order for a youth's juvenile status to be amended two requirements had to be met: He had to be at least sixteen years of age, and prosecutors had to successfully argue that the juvenile was not amenable to treatment or rehabilitation within the existing juvenile facilities and programs. It was the policy of the state to try and rehabilitate juveniles who commit vicious crimes, rather than punish them.

ADA Hynes would recall his internal considerations for me many years after the decision had been made. "You're talking about an incredibly complex problem that I don't know will ever be answered satisfactorily: What do you do when children commit incredibly heinous crimes? You want to punish a kid for this. You want to think that by the age of sixteen he knows right from wrong and he knew it was wrong to put another human being through living hell. And then take his life. If any case screamed for punishment, this one did. And yet you send them to prison and you know what's going to happen there. They're going to be put through a living hell of their own. They're going to be sodomized by older, tougher inmates; they're going to be turned into hamburger, and what concept of justice does that serve? And regardless, Burke, who was in on three of the murders, goes to the Boys School because there's an absolute bar against trying a fifteen-year-old as an adult. So I don't know. And lucky for me, I didn't have the final say."

In the end, Hynes filed a motion that put the matter in the hands of the court. He submitted the pertinent papers requesting the transfer of Vernon Crawford and Oren Thacker to adult court, knowing it would set in motion a series of actions that would leave the outcome up to the discretion of the judge in the case.

On Wednesday afternoon, Judge Frank Zinn, a former state attorney general and the current district court judge from McKinley County, flew in from Gallup to preside. A silver-haired man whose heavy black-framed glasses gave him a stern, commanding presence, Zinn brought a reputation as neither liberal nor conservative but extremely intelligent, unafraid to rule though often unpredictable in his rulings. His first ruling in this case was entirely expected. After considering the prosecutor's request, he issued an order authorizing the transportation of all three youths to the Children's Detention Home in Albuquerque for psychological examinations that would help him decide to what extent, and in what fashion, he would hold them accountable for their crimes.

To hear Wilbert Tsosie accuse Farmington of being a racist community harboring long-standing prejudices against Indians that were epitomized in the murder of three Navajos had come as a shock to Mayor Marlo Webb, and after scoffing at the charge and withering the messenger, he had put the outrageous meeting out of mind. He was in the second month of his first term as mayor of Farmington and had more pressing matters to tend to. Having carried eight of the city's ten polling districts on the slogan "You can't run a city on promises," he was feeling a personal obligation, as well as public pressure, to deal immediately with priority problems confronting the city, of which there were many more important than addressing the speculations of a community activist who saw racism lurking behind every unfortunate incident that befell Indians.

At Webb's inauguration the oath had been administered by the retiring mayor who, along with a gavel, had presented him with a giant bottle of aspirin. At the time he had laughed along with everyone else, thinking it was a big joke, but now, just eight weeks in office, he was beginning to realize how appropriate a parting gesture it had been. History was indeed catching up with Farmington, but it had little to do with Indian issues. The management of city affairs and planning for orderly growth loomed as his formidable foes, as Farmington struggled to avoid the disruptive cycles endemic to all western boom-towns.

In addition to the big issues there was a full plate of minor matters requiring his involvement: a recommendation the city add a zoo to its present recreational facilities; a debate over whether to use pesticides or plant minnows in the breeding grounds of mosquitoes; a proposed ordinance that would make it unlawful for anyone to intentionally possess one ounce or less of marijuana within the city limits; and how to deal with the increased incidence of drunken citizens on the streets.

Now *there* was an issue that the Indians should take up if they wanted to improve life for the Navajo, he thought. Drunken Indians were a major problem and had been for over a century. The recognition that alcohol and Indians were a volatile mix had led Congress to pass an Indian Prohibition Act as early as 1832. Of course laws forbidding the sale of liquor to Indians had been no more effective in Indian country in the 1800s than they would be for everyone in the 1920s, and the bootleg traffic of alcohol to Navajos would be big business, especially in the springtime when they sold their wool and blankets and in the fall when their lambs were brought to market. And in part it had been the inability to control illegal liquor sales, along with a movement started by Indian veterans who had not been subject to discriminatory liquor laws during their service in World War II, that caused Indian prohibition laws to be repealed in the early 1950s. After that, it had been legal for intoxicating beverages to be sold to Navajos, but only outside the borders of the reservation. The tribe had refused to legalize liquor within its borders, which meant if a Navajo wanted to drink he went to the reservation bordertowns.

Listening to Wilbert Tsosie complain about white attitudes toward Navajos, the mayor had found himself wanting to say, What about our grievances with your people? What about all the Navajo binge drinkers who pass out in the doorways of our downtown businesses, whom shop clerks have to step over in the morning? What about the criminally high number of auto accidents caused by inebriated Indians?

In his memory Webb carried a snapshot of an angry businessman who had showed up at a city council meeting with a gunnysack full of liquor bottles, which he emptied on the chamber floor, saying he was sick and tired of having to clean up after these people. And written on the backside was the text of a conversation he'd had with a Navajo tribal official he had approached to discuss solutions to the problem. It had been a waste of time. The tribal line had been: "They're not drinking on the reservation. You're selling them liquor, you cure them." In other words, it was up to the bordertowns to figure out how to clean up the mess.

While the mayor had felt an annoyed impatience with Wilbert Tsosie, and sincerely did not believe that the city of Farmington should in any way be held responsible for the murders, he nonetheless had been stunned when he first read about them in the paper, and appalled when two Farmington youths were arrested. He was still acquainting himself with the different divisions of government and had yet to establish close relations with the police department, but he had called over and requested a briefing, at which he had been assured that this was a one-time deal. The boys had picked up the drunk Indians, taken them out into the hills to roll them, and apparently gotten carried away.

Feeling reasonably assured that the authorities had done their jobs and the guilty parties were under arrest, he had decided that as the figurehead of the community it was his responsibility to speak on behalf of all Farmington citizens, and he drafted a personal letter which he sent to Peter MacDonald, chairman of the Navajo Tribal Council. In it he cast the crimes as totally uncharacteristic of the friendly relationship Farmington enjoyed with the Navajo people. "The entire community is shocked by and abhors this violent, brutal, and senseless taking of human lives," he had written. He finished by pledging "continuing efforts directed towards eliminating any barriers that exist between our people and solving any problems that might be keeping the Navajo people from fulfilling their rightful place as citizens of this community and of this great nation."

The statement intentionally played up the good-neighbor angle and tried to divorce the murders from the context of normal community relations. And if it came off as sanctimonious bunk to Wilbert Tsosie, in all fairness to the mayor, as the top administrator of the local government, damage control in matters like this was part of the job. While his regret and dismay were genuine enough, he was cognizant of the fact that this could not help but reflect poorly on the town. It certainly was not going to help the current push to attract industrial development to Farmington for the city to become the dateline on a lurid multiple-murder case committed by the sons of three of its citizens.

"How in the hell can we expect outside businesses to come and set up shop when they hear about this bullshit?" Jimmy Drake, a flinty Oklahoma oilman newly elected to the city council, lamented at the prospect of negative publicity. "This shoots you in the foot."

Although the mayor might have phrased it differently, he agreed.

Once the perpetrators were apprehended, however, he felt that with less media coverage and waning public interest the story would recede into the background, becoming a tragic and unfortunate incident, the sooner put behind the better. Which was why Marlo Webb couldn't believe his ears when he picked up the phone several days after summarily dismissing Wilbert

Tsosie to be informed that Tsosie had just applied for a parade permit and was planning to memorialize the slain Indians with a march through the streets of downtown Farmington.

It was the week after she buried her husband that Rena heard there was going to be a meeting at the San Juan Mission to make plans for a memorial march to respectfully remember the men who had been murdered, and show sympathy and support for the families of the victims. She attended, and listening to the speeches made her thoughtful, especially when she heard Wilbert Tsosie, speaking on behalf of the Farmington Inter-tribal Indian Organization, explain the importance of "standing up for ourselves." Though he spoke for a long time, it was the words he directed to those in mourning that she would remember: "It is unfortunate this happened to your loved ones, but the next time it could be any of us. We must do something to let the people of Farmington know that we will no longer put up with the mistreatment of Navajo brothers and sisters. If we do nothing and remain silent and accept this without protesting, then what kind of future are we creating for our children?"

Until then she had not thought of her husband's death in terms larger than personal tragedy. As she heard the brutal murders become a political call to arms, the three victims elevated to symbols of white abuse of Indians in Farmington, her loss took on new significance, supplying her with a meaning that had been missing. Maybe this had not been a senseless killing after all. Maybe there was a reason all this had happened. Maybe Benji, a man who would be remembered by most people for the way he died, not the way he lived, would be given a measure of redemption if his death did something for his people.

For this reason Rena decided that it was right for her to participate in the memorial march through downtown Farmington on the upcoming Saturday.

The parade was scheduled to start at 2 P.M. but she arrived early, bringing along her children. Someone had prepared blank placards on which slogans were being written, and when she was handed one, for a long moment she did not know what to write. Others were waging a war of words—"WHITE RACISM MUST GO"; "JUSTICE BETTER PREVAIL"—but Rena did not feel she knew enough about issues on that scale to add to what was already being said. All her life she had had experiences that made her feel unwelcome in Farmington, but she had given very little thought to the problems facing Indian people as a whole, and even now her involvement was not of her own initiative. From nothing she had done she had been thrust into the tumult of the outside world.

Another reason she was having trouble making up her mind about what she should say was that while others seemed almost to be making a martyr to racism of her husband, she felt a certain ambivalence toward him. Sometimes, when she thought about the way he let himself go, how he just gave up, bringing misery to himself and to those who loved him, she would get angry. It was so unnecessary. Then she would reverse herself and remember the shared moments of peace and happiness together. For all his flaws and faults she had felt love for him, which was why it had been so difficult for her to leave him.

She looked at her youngest, Benjamin Jr., and that gave her an idea. Although at five years of age he was too young to understand what was going on, he knew something was wrong. He had asked her repeatedly, "Where's my dad? What happened to Dad?" Grabbing a black Magic Marker, Rena wrote a message that spoke for herself, her son, her family. And no sooner had she finished writing than one of the leaders asked her if she and Benjamin Jr. would be willing to lead the march.

On the parade permit, in the space where the number of participants was to be written, Wilbert Tsosie had estimated no more than 300. His thinking was based on the fact that this represented the largest turnout they had drawn at any of their meetings at the Indian Center; the event had been hastily planned and poorly organized; and a march was a daring departure—he was asking Indians to do what no Indians in Farmington had ever done before. His most optimistic hopes would not have approached the figure of between 3,000 and 4,000 as the size of the march was reported by the Associated Press. And striding at the head of the parade were Rena and her son.

It was the hardest thing she had ever done. All along the route she was taunted by white hecklers who stood on the sidewalks jeering, hissing, and imitating machine guns, making her feel as though she were walking through enemy territory. That impression was strengthened when she turned a corner and saw a line of helmeted riot police who had been placed on alert. But keeping her eyes straight ahead, she refused to be intimidated, drawing strength and courage from the unity of spirit she felt with the column of marchers that stretched behind her for eight blocks.

Down Lake Avenue, onto Main Street, east to Allen Street, south to Broadway, and back to Lake, they marched. And those who observed it would remark on its eeriness: The only sound coming from the marchers was the shuffle of feet on the pavement. The rage, the rhetoric, the violence—that would come soon enough. Today was a day of solemn and respectful remembrance that was given heartbreaking poignance by the presence of a mother and her five-year-old boy who toted a sign almost as big as he was: HERMAN D. BENALLY SR. WAS MY FATHER.

For an evaluation to determine whether they should be bound over for trial as adults or treated within the juvenile justice system, on May 1 Vernon Crawford, Peter Burke, and Oren Thacker were transported to the Children's Detention Home in Albuquerque. It was the closest appropriate juvenile facility, and where they would be kept until the psychological testing and psychiatric interviews could be scheduled.

D-Home, as it was referred to by those who were employed as well as confined there, was a rundown one-story cinder-block building laid out in wings. The long dark hallways were lined with metal doors it took a key to open. Wire mesh laced windows that lightened not brightened rooms bare of everything but metal bunks stacked on top of each other and chained to walls decorated with graffiti: notes to God and obscene sayings written in gothic script; crosses and lightning bolts drawn in 3-D so they appeared to be chiseled into the concrete. You couldn't heat D-Home in the winter, couldn't cool it down in the summer, and no amount of wax could bring a luster to the floors because, as the staff was wont to say, "You can't shine shit." Two years from now a film crew would use the facility as a setting in the film *Born Innocent*, in which a runaway girl is incarcerated and brutalized in a notorious juvenile home. Very few changes were necessary to fashion D-Home into the juvenile dungeon it already was.

It was policy at the facility to separate people involved in the same offense, so the boys were split up and assigned to different rooms. But whenever they entered the routines of D-Home—attending a daily academic session, taking meals in the cafeteria, watching television, and playing pool and Ping-Pong in the rec room—they kept each other company, which only made sense when you took into account they were from out of town, knew only one another, and found security in solidarity.

At the time, most of the other juveniles in custody were petty offenders: runaways, tire-slashers, glue-sniffers, residential burglars. Altogether they were a scruffy, rough-looking lot, most of them raised on the streets and branded with crude ballpoint-pen tattoos. If you had walked around and on the basis of physical appearances tried to single out the most violent kids, the last ones you would have picked would have been Vernon Crawford, Peter Burke, and Oren Thacker. And yet they were the only ones charged with Murder One.

Though none of the three played the role of tough guy or commanded an aura of leadership, the big-time crimes they were accused of inspired a perverse kind of respect, even awe, among the other delinquents. Complete strangers tried to buddy up to them, to get them talking about what they'd done: *Hey bro, you really off them Injuns? Why for? How'd you do it? What's it like?*

A familiar phenomenon was at work: the attempt to associate with those seen as possessing power in hopes some of it will rub off. But it was all strange and surprising to the boys. They weren't sure how to respond. They didn't get the message. And noting their discomfort with their exalted status, the staff allowed them to have access to the rec room separately, and in time even let them room together.

Juveniles generally went through five distinct phases during the course of their confinement. When they were first brought in they couldn't seem to believe this was really happening to them. There was a detached quality to their attitudes and interactions, as if they were watching themselves perform in a movie. A form of denial was at work that collapsed with the onset of the second stage, when it hit home they were locked up behind bars. They can no longer escape the realization they have committed a crime and there will be consequences. As reality strikes them, so does depression, and they walk around in a shocked kind of stupor. In the third stage they begin to take an interest in how the system works, what is expected of them, and how they must fit in if they are going to get along. Comes the fourth stage and they are resolved to the fact that they will be doing time in an institution, and they begin the adaptation process, which turns, in the fifth stage, to the search for ways to manipulate people and rules and adapt the system to themselves. These three youths never reached the third stage while they were in D-Home. They moved beyond the this-can't-be-happening-to-me stage, but never got out of the daze that settled over them when they realized this was not a dream they would wake up from.

If the surrounding environs were bleak and gloomy, the attitude of the staff at D-Home at least partially negated the downbeat atmosphere. A core of caring, committed people worked there, most of whom would still be employed in the juvenile justice system fifteen years later. In contrast to the public reaction in the outside world, where the horror these three youths had perpetrated rendered them feckless and contemptible without any redeeming virtues, the response of the staff was more empathetic. They were able to get to know the youths on a more personal level, so at times it was hard for them to believe that these were the same people they were reading about in the paper who were responsible for atrocious crimes.

During their stay at D-Home none of the boys was what could be called a behavior problem, but Ed Sullivan, the D-Home counselor at the time, was called in to assist one of the boys who was having personal troubles. Primarily an adjustment counselor, there to help the kids who were having difficulty abiding by the institution's rules or having interpersonal conflicts with other residents, Sullivan remembers that his assistance was solicited when Vernon Crawford began to suffer from extreme nightmares at night and, during the day, hallucinations, both visual and aural.

There was no question in Sullivan's mind what he was seeing. "One of the things you learn as you go is when someone is hallucinating. If they're hearing voices in their head they'll tilt to one side as if they're listening. When they're seeing things that aren't really there, they react as if something is going on right in front of them. There was no doubt what was happening. The boy was hallucinating."

In his conversations with Crawford about the hallucinations, Sullivan was told about "this little guy who rode around on his shoulder, who talked to him and told him what to do. It was a grandparent, he said; his grandmother."

Knowing that hallucinations were frightening experiences, Sullivan tried to help Crawford deal with the fear that accompanied them. He did this by helping him to accept the fact that even though these strange things were occurring, they were not, in fact, real. They could not hurt him. And he could learn to live with them. Sullivan did not try to determine the source of the hallucinations. "That would be a therapist's function, not a counselor's, and certainly not a D-Home counselor."

As for the nightmares, these were not simply bad dreams that disturbed Crawford's sleep; he woke up screaming, night after night. Whether the source was connected to this business of conversing with an imaginary person, or related to images imprinted on the murder nights, the staff didn't know. Nor did they feel it was their place to probe the workings of his subconscious. That would come with the psychological evaluations. They were his stewards while he was in their custody, however, and acting in his behalf, as well as considering the other juveniles in detention, after a while they began to let Crawford stay up to all hours, sometimes all night, watching TV, helping them mop floors, in hopes he would get so tired that he would eventually be able to sleep soundly.

It was during one of these all-nighters that the unit supervisor for the girl's ward, Sue Furney, got the scare of her life. Although it was against the rules to sleep on duty, everyone did it in those days, and one night in the wee hours of the morning she stretched out on a couch in the lounge just off the kitchen for a short nap. Someone shaking her woke her. At first she thought it was her boss rousing her because a juvenile was being admitted; but when she opened her eyes she saw Vernon Crawford standing over her with a long-bladed bread knife in his hand.

Because she knew who he was and what he'd done, she thought, *This is it. It's all over with.*

She waited, and when he made no threatening moves she calmed herself enough to ask him what he wanted. As it turned out, her counterpart on the boy's ward had Crawford up with him and they were in the kitchen making sandwiches, and he'd sent the kid in to see if Sue wanted anything to eat. Not knowing his intentions at the time, only what he was capable of, she had assumed the worst.

Afterward, they talked about it. Crawford knew the reason she had experienced a moment of panic and he seemed to feel bad that this was going to be everybody's first reaction to him. For her part, after that conversation, Sue came to like him, even feel safe around him. That said, the whole thing left her so rattled it was the last time she *ever* fell asleep on the job at D-Home.

Peter Burke was a different story altogether. Dark-haired,

with stone eyes and a voice as empty of emotion as his face was of expression, he had "the look": what those in this business could recognize immediately as an ineffable something that let them know they were dealing with an unpredictable hardcase, capable of anything, and to keep a close watch on this one.

"He was the cold mother of that crew," Sue Furney would recall. "I wear a lot of Indian jewelry. You know, turquoise-and-silver rings and bracelets. When he went through on the line one day, the first time I had any contact with him, he looked at my hands and smirked, 'You like Indians, huh?' I wasn't old enough to get in his face about it, look him in the eye, and say, 'Yeah, what's it to you?' Now I wouldn't allow him to intimidate me. Keeping an upper hand builds respect around here. But back then, well, I was young and I remember being scared to the quick of that kid."

Oren Thacker would be remembered as "the third kid," and little more. In manner and appearance he seemed like such a normal teenager it made the staff who didn't know better wonder at first what he was doing at D-Home. He exhibited none of the peculiarities of Crawford, nor the morose silences of Burke. What would stand out in memory was the romance he brewed with a young female runaway, and the depression she went into after he left.

Although D-Home was 200 miles away from Farmington and the three youths received little news about the repercussions their acts were having in their hometown, they were aware that the Indian community was taking their crimes personally. There was a circular drive in front of the main entrance to the facility, with an island in the middle, and each morning a band of Indians showed up to walk round and round that drive. They carried no placards, and none of them shouted slogans or demands or threats. In fact they were quiet for demonstrators, in a haunting way. They just walked in circles, to no apparent beat, although it took on the aspect of some sort of dance for justice. And they gave no indication of why they were there, other than the long stares they cast in the direction of the wing where the three boys were being kept.

They were ominous, forbidding, unpredictable reminders that there was a lot riding on the outcome of this case. And the rumor spread that some were armed and came back at night with high-powered rifles to watch the windows through scopes, waiting for a clear shot. Whether this was true or not it made the staff nervous enough to move the three from room to room, so if someone placed them in a particular cell during the day, a sharpshooter could not come back and know where he could pick them off at night.

The eyes of the nation should be on northwestern New Mexico, U.S.A., where at least ten brutal murders of Native Americans took place in the last year. A box of monstrous secrets has been opened, and no one knows how many more rotting, burned, knifed, castrated, smashed Indian corpses are still to be found. When the third Navajo body was discovered in April near Farmington, too mutilated to be identified, 60 Indians reportedly called the funeral home to see if perhaps it was the body of a missing relative. Are there 59 more corpses in those hills?

El Grito newsletter
June 1974

Even though suspects had been arrested and charged with the murders of Herman Benally, John Harvey, and David Ignacio, the dark suspicion that there were additional bodies in the area prompted Wilbert Tsosie to establish a Missing Persons Bureau through the FIIO, and to complain to the authorities about what he felt was the lack of an exhaustive search of Chokecherry Canyon. That those investigating the crimes said they had no reason to believe other bodies existed satisfied neither Tsosie nor the activist Navajos who had attended the meeting in Shiprock. Among them was Larry Anderson, a Navajo from Fort Defiance, Arizona, just north of Window Rock, who was also national treasurer of AIM. Acting on behalf of his organization, he called a press conference at which he hinted at the possibility that the hills and arroyos around Chokecherry Canyon were a veritable graveyard for slain Navajos, before announcing plans for a massive search of the area. ''INDIANS HUNT VICTIMS OF DESERT TORTURERS'' would grab the headlines of the *National Star*, a grocery-store tabloid, in its next edition, quoting an ''angry Navajo scout'' as saying, ''Right now, only God knows how many more bodies are out there.''

The morning of the announced search a caravan of close to thirty pickups, the cabs as well as the beds loaded with Navajos, showed up at the sheriff's office in Aztec, where they were

met by a dubious Lieutenant Miller, assigned the task of showing the "search party" the crime scenes. Miller thought the
whole thing was a public relations ploy intended to embarrass
the department and would not have put it past some of those
involved to plant something out there for the others to find. But
on the slim chance they might come across something unexpected, after leading them out to the crime scenes he decided
to hang around for most of the day.

On foot, a few on horseback, the searchers fanned out. But
the operation was not well planned, there was nothing systematic about the coverage, and while the purpose of the search
was serious, it had somewhat of a picnic atmosphere, with
Navajo women tending bonfires on which they cooked fry
bread and heated coffee for the searchers, some of whom were
school-age kids taking advantage of the occasion to play
hookey.

Wilbert Tsosie showed up around midday, not in an official
capacity (this was AIM's show), just to check on the progress.
Nothing of interest had been found yet, he was informed, other
than a discarded Polaroid tear sheet that had been picked up
near where Herman Benally had been killed. The latent negative image showed a naked man, face down in the dust, body
and legs uncomfortably twisted, head positioned beside a huge
rock which was presumed to be one of the murder weapons.
The tantalizing find had brought a renewed zeal to the efforts of
the searchers, who spread out in ever-widening circles.

It was late in the afternoon when two men crested a ridge a
mile or so away from where the two bodies had been found and
spotted something suspicious. Walking closer, they stopped
before a scattering of traditional ritual items. Strewn across a
rippling bed of sand were a mask, kilt, and rattle, material
objects associated with the Yeibichai (Night Way) ceremony,
a sacred healing sing in which masked dancers personifying
mythic figures performed.

The fear and paranoia that many Indians were feeling at this
time were apparent in the ensuing discussion of what these
things meant. Hadn't the murdered men been stripped before
they were killed? Maybe the owner of these things suffered the
same fate.

In no time, the worst-case scenario was consensually accepted. White teenagers must have gone to the reservation,
kidnapped a Yei dancer at a fair, and here was evidence that the
full extent of the carnage had yet to be revealed.

As one, the group turned to the sandhills rolling around them, and within minutes the area was aswarm with people poking under bushes, turning over rocks, and digging into riverbeds, each convinced that a buried body or bleached set of bones was about to be unearthed.

The vicinity was thoroughly explored by the time it was too dark to see anymore, and nothing out of the ordinary was reported. Nevertheless, the suspicion was strong enough on the part of everyone present that the items proved the commission of a crime that a designated group drove to the local radio station that broadcast "Navajo Hour" as a regular programming feature, told the station manager what they had found, and asked him to carry the story. He agreed, and a report was aired that basically said: Just as we feared, it looks like the Indian body count is higher than three. This is what we found; this is where we found it. Anyone with information please contact us.

A reaction was quick in coming, and it was as unwelcome as it was unexpected. A day later a group of Navajo people, accompanied by a medicine man, showed up, took one look at the Yeibichai garb, and proceeded to chastise the finders for their ignorance. The garments belonged to a Yei dancer who had become ill during a Yeibichai ceremony. As custom dictated, his ceremonial garb had been left behind, and for anyone to tamper with the material was tantamount to disturbing a sacred site.

Once they were aware that they had committed a serious tribal transgression, the members of the search party offered to return the ritual clothing immediately. Not so fast, they were cautioned. That wasn't the way it was done. Not only were the mask, kilt, and rattle holy and powerful, they endangered anyone not associated with the ceremony who handled them. In order to ward off the danger and place themselves in harmony with the beings which were the source of power, certain things must be done. The formula for correction required a purification rite. All those who came into contact with the material needed to make amends to the Holy People. Then and only then could the dancer's costume be respectfully returned.

If the search for additional bodies had produced a blunder, the May 4 memorial march was an unqualified triumph. The vision of all those Indians, young and old, male and female, amassed in a common front, clogging Farmington's main streets that Saturday left Wilbert Tsosie feeling exhilarated and vindicated. The fact of the matter was his public statement of purpose— that this was a march to respectfully remember the men who had been slain and show sympathy and support for their families—had been an expurgated version of his private intentions. He wanted to rattle the sensibilities of Mr. and Mrs. Farmington. He wanted to shake awake the white community to the news it could no longer count on passive acquiescence from Indian people. He wanted to remind Farmington that Indians could, if organized, be a social force of significant proportions. If nothing else happened, if every Indian who marched went home afterward and was never heard from again, Wilbert Tsosie thought it had all been worth the sight of Farmington's downtown merchants nervously watching the marchers pass by from behind the locked doors of their closed businesses.

Of course it did not stop there. Emboldened by the astonishing turnout, Wilbert was led to believe that maybe this was just the beginning. That the resentment and anger felt by so many Indians for so long but suppressed by fear and hopelessness was ready to surface at last.

Until now Indians had never challenged the existing inequities between Indians and whites in San Juan County. Blame it on the desire of the traditional and pastoral Navajo to live simply and in harmony with the land, or on an unfamiliarity with the civil-rights struggles of racial minorities elsewhere in the country—whatever the case—until now they had been a silent group, enduring the denials, limits, and indignities that had been imposed upon them as if stoicism were a supreme virtue. The defining response of Indians to racial hostility and humiliating experiences of prejudice had been to withdraw. But if Wilbert was reading the mood of his people right, the murders had tapped a deep emotion and out of hiding had come a righteous fury. Enough innocent Navajo blood has spilled on New Mexico soil! This legacy of violence against Navajos must stop!

The step from a call for justice to an examination of the conditions which had bred violence was a short one. Wilbert felt the town had allowed a climate to flourish which dehumanized Indian people. The way he saw it, the murders were the logical, horrible consequence of common local prejudices, the feeling that Indians were not as good as whites. Such attitudes took an insidious toll in the long run; in full extension they could kill, and in this case they had.

Something about Wilbert had changed. It wasn't physical—he was still a rotund man with a huge girth. But there was a sureness about him that had not been there before—a resolve that showed in the calm but defiant tone of his voice, and the broad new scope of his thinking. He knew his own history up to this point, and as he thought about what had happened in Chokecherry Canyon, he found himself reflecting on other Indian tragedies that were remembered in history. This was 1974, making it 110 years after the Sand Creek Massacre, and 110 years after the start of the Long Walk by the Navajo to Fort Sumner. What if the Chokecherry Massacre were to be remembered as a tragedy that became a turning point in the Navajo's long walk with the white man? What if it became the event that brought about a sweeping reassessment of cultural attitudes in San Juan County? What if it was the spark that ignited a full-blown Indian-rights movement within the Navajo Nation?

It was a tall order, but a worthwhile one, and one that came with a sense of historical inevitability about it. Wilbert would not have thought in this way a couple of days ago, but right now anything seemed possible.

Already he was thinking ahead. He knew if he was to have any chance of accomplishing this turning point he would not be able to work through the FIIO. These ideas and objectives were too radical. A new organization would have to be formed that would not sidestep the difficult issue of Indian/Anglo relations, that would make the business of decisive social change *its* business.

He gave a good deal of thought to what he should name this new organization. He was confident he could gain the endorsement of at least five existing groups (the Farmington Intertribal Indian Organization, the American Indian Movement, the Farmington chapter of the NAACP, the San Juan County Human Rights Committee, and the University of New Mexico Kiva Club), and he wanted a name that would epitomize the fact that this was a unified struggle of diverse human-interest groups. The answer came from a book about World War II belonging to his father that referred to the "coalition" of military forces formed under the generalship of Eisenhower before the famous D-Day invasion of Normandy. That his father had fought in that battle added a poignance to Wilbert's decision to use the term "coalition."

The rest was easy. Revolutionary movements at that time were referring to themselves as "liberation movements," and the people the organization was representing were Navajo. When he put it all together, the Coalition for Navajo Liberation conveyed the message and carried the punch he wanted.

Still, something was missing. Tsosie felt they needed a graphic or logo which pictorially represented what the Coalition stood for. He talked it over with others and they came up with symbols from Navajo history and mythology. The Navajo word for "human being" translates, literally, as "the one that has five fingers." In Navajo mythology the twin war gods who traveled across old Navajoland slaying the monsters were armed with swords of lightning. And so the symbol of the Coalition for Navajo Liberation became a human hand flanked by two bolts of lightning.

All that remained for the organization to become official was a press release or a press conference, but Wilbert went that idea one better. Feeling a strong follow-up was important to build on the momentum begun by the memorial march, he decided on baptism by fire. The Coalition for Navajo Liberation would sponsor a second march through the city's downtown business community—only this time instead of a respectful memorial to "fallen brothers," it would be a protest demonstration that would put Farmington on notice that the Days of Rage had come to the Southwest.

WE ARE MARCHING FOR OUR RIGHTS TO BE RE-SPECTED AS HUMAN BEINGS. HISTORY REVEALS THAT THE WHITEMAN HAS ROBBED, DEGRADED, ABUSED, BRUTALIZED, INSULTED AND KILLED THE NAVAJO PEOPLE. SINCE THE TIME THE BLUE EYED DEVILS SET FOOT ON THIS CONTINENT, THE NATIVE SONS AND DAUGHTERS, THE TRUE LAND-LORDS, WERE FORCED TO ACCEPT THAT THEY ARE LESS THAN HUMAN BEINGS. THE IDEA THAT

THEY ARE SECOND CLASS CITIZENS WAS JAMMED DOWN THEIR THROATS. THE WHITES HAVE TAKEN OVER THIS CONTINENT WITHOUT THE CONSENT OF THE INDIANS. IN THIS REGARD, THEY, THE WHITEMAN (THE ENEMY), ARE THIEVES. THEY HAVE ROBBED THE INDIANS OF THEIR CULTURAL WEALTH, THEIR LAND, MINERAL RESOURCES, WATER RIGHTS, AND POLLUTED OUR PRECIOUS CLEAN AIR. . . . THE ENEMY, KNOWING THAT THE INDIAN WAS A NUISANCE AND STOOD IN THE WAY OF "PROGRESS," HAS CONSPIRED AND SCHEMED IN THE KILLING OF THE INDIAN RACE. HISTORY EXPLAINS THAT IN THE SO-CALLED "WINNING OF THE WEST" INDIANS WERE DEALT WITH ONLY THROUGH THE BARREL SIGHT OF A GUN. . . . BE-CAUSE OF THE BRUTALITIES AND THE ATROCITIES AMERIKA HAS COMMITTED, AND BECAUSE FAR-MINGTON CONTINUES TO COMMIT RACISM AND IGNORES OUR SITUATION, *WE, THE INDIAN PEO-PLE, MUST UNITE*. THE COALITION FOR NAVAJO LIBERATION WILL FIGHT FOR ALL NAVAJO PEO-PLE. THE COALITION WILL NOT STAND FOR WHITE AGGRESSION. THE COALITION WILL FIGHT WHITE RACISM. THE COALITION WILL SPARK OFF A REV-OLUTION TO OVERTHROW WHITE AGGRESSION.

JOIN THE COALITION'S FIGHT FOR FREEDOM. ALL THE POWER TO THE PEOPLE

2

THUNDER
IN
NAVAJOLAND

6

THE CUSTER
OF FARMINGTON

You can skip a stone across the San Juan River, which is all that separates the city limits of Farmington from Navajo country, but for the first half of this century there was not a lot of daily contact between cultures in this area of the reservation. Most Navajo lived great distances from town, roads were unpaved, and horse-drawn wagons were the primary means of transportation, which limited travel; but Navajo life also remained traditional and old-fashioned because the *Dineh* were an independent and aloof people who seemed still to be undecided as to whether or not they wanted to join the rest of the world.

When they came to town, following routes marked by cairns and roads that forded washes, it was usually to buy, sell, and trade for goods and services they could not get at the trading posts. Their stays were usually brief. If they remained overnight they kept to themselves, camping on the south side of town among the cottonwoods along the river, where the townfolk would hear them drumming and singing, and the night air was fragrant with the smoke of their fires. When the time came to return, when the business that had brought them to town had been transacted, they would trundle out of town as if they couldn't wait to get back to the familiar sights and sounds of their home ground.

People who have lived here a long time do not recall there being much friction between Indians and whites during those days. To hear the old-timers talk, locals had an abiding respect for the Navajo because they were tough and enduring, like a desert plant that can grow where all else has given up. "You have to take your hat off to them people," a lifetime resident told me. "They can survive on little or nothin'."

Those who lived among the Navajo also found them trust-worthy in a unique way. Dan Sullivan: ''My grandmother used to say, 'If you can't trust an Indian, you can't trust nobody.' We had campsites all over this country. Cow camps, sheep camps, right in the middle of Indian land, and we never lost so much as a cup of flour. Oh, if they were hungry and ran out, sure, they'd help themselves to some. But they never took all your flour. They'd take enough to last 'till they could make a trip to the trading post. And when they got theirs they'd pop back up with yours.'' The Navajo's credit rating back then gave rise to the saying: If an Indian tells you he'll bring you two sheep in the morning, you can go to the bank and draw money on it.

This is not to say that whites were so impressed they recip-rocated in kind and were as good as their word in *their* dealings with Navajos. Far from it. Many traders and storekeepers took advantage of the Navajo's ignorance of commercial practices by inflating prices, charging outrageous interest rates, under-paying for rugs, livestock, and Navajo labor, and selling pawn before the expiration of the redemption period. While misun-derstandings were to be expected in almost any cross-cultural situation, the deception of local Indians was a fairly common business practice, which generated bad feelings and resentment among the Navajo, but little outright protest.

There was not a lot of anxiety about hostility and violence from Navajos on the part of whites during this period. The lesson of the Long Walk seemed to have taken the fight out of the Navajo for good. There even appeared to be a comforting complacency to the ritual of relations that had evolved over the years. By conforming unthinkingly to the realities of the ex-isting social structure Navajos might have to put up with pa-ternalism and exploitation, but that beat all the other alternatives available to Indians in this country at that time.

With the arrival of the Boomers in the 1950s a boisterous element was added to the already unbalanced equation. As a type, roughnecks were provincial and bigoted and had a great deal of difficulty making mental accommodations for the differences among people. They were unfamiliar with Navajo customs and life-styles, and were the kind of people who laughed at the way Indians dressed, talked, and ate. They were a rootless, transient lot—few came to settle; they came for the work and when that was gone they weren't far behind—so their attachment to the land and sense of community shared no common ground with the tribal identification with Mother Earth. Often looked down on as "oil-field trash," they tended to do unto others what was done unto them. Most came from West Texas and Oklahoma and brought their bias against "coloreds" with them. Their dislike of Indians was, in part, an extension of how they felt about blacks: They were a bunch of lazy, shiftless, ne'er-do-wells who came from inferior stock. You heard them say things like, "Indians're just niggers, less well done."

The way Dan Sullivan, who was chief of police in Farmington then, tells it, this was when most of the white crimes against Indians started. "The Boomers didn't like Indians and that's all there was to it. On their way out to the oil and gas wells—most were located on leased Navajo land—they would make a sport out of shooting holes in the Indians' water tanks, or think nothing of swerving off the dirt roads and plowing a lane through an Indian's cornfield. Little things like that kept the Indians agitated, but they rarely retaliated. They knew there was no way they were gonna win a fight with an Anglo in Farmington. If one started to get the best of a white, he'd have to deal with three or four of his pals. Oh, once in a while they'd get back. Some buckaroo's car might mysteriously catch fire one night and he'd swear up and down it was an Indian who did it. And he was probably right. But it wasn't nothing I could land at someone's door."

Worsening an already tense situation, it was along about here that Indians were given the legal right to drink.

Everyone seems to agree that the Navajo tribe deserves credit for its ability over the centuries to make adjustments and adaptations to the changing environment, incorporating those elements which were beneficial to its well-being and survival. And just as unanimous is the opinion that if there is one element that has been accepted that has been detrimental, it is *firewater*. As far back as 1880 the Navajo agent would lament, "The crying evil that most besets these people is whiskey." Seventy-five years later that observation would be just as true.

Some would say that terminating Indian prohibition laws didn't change anything, it only put a few bootleggers out of business. But talk to those in charge of law enforcement in the reservation bordertowns at this time and you hear a different story. Most greeted the change in the law with optimism. Prohibition had caused them all kinds of problems. Since Indians knew if they were caught with a bottle it would be confiscated, as soon as they bought a quart of wine or whiskey they would disappear into the alleys, empty buildings, and train yards, where they would up-end the contraband as quickly as possible. Fast-guzzling like that, it wasn't long before they passed out, making death from exposure a significant statistical fatality during the winter months. Now that an Indian could go into a bar and drink, officers hoped they would not have the same problem with their passing out and freezing in the gutters.

But by this time the drinking pattern was ingrained, not the least because it was cheaper to buy booze by the bottle than by the glass. If anything, the problem was exacerbated. As the bordertowns became the watering holes for Indians with a thirst for liquor, at any time of day or night they could be found weaving down the street, slumped against buildings, or huddled in a dark corner in a drunken stupor, where they were fair game for foul play as well as foul weather.

The sixties were a time when the eighteenth-century concept of the Noble Savage—which portrayed the American Indian as innately brave and honorable, living in harmony with nature and at one with the world, a spiritually superior being—was enjoying a comeback. This was due in large measure to revisionist historians who wrote about the cruelties and inequities meted out to native peoples during the western settlement in a fashion which so pricked white America's conscience that it suddenly became fashionable to champion Indian causes. To a generation discontented with urban-industrial life, the Indian—not just for his religious and ecological ideals and values, but for his ability to survive a tragic history of conquest and oppression with these ideals intact—epitomized the modern-day anti-hero. Where once his culture seemed destined to disappear under the dominance of white civilization, now it was revered as the antidote.

But people in Farmington on the whole were indifferent to the trend that was taking place elsewhere in the nation. They were unwilling or unable to share that benevolent and frankly admiring view of the Indian and his way of life, because they felt they knew better.

To their way of thinking, easterners had always been soft on Indians. It was easy for those out of harm's way to dwell on the noble, not the savage, part. Those on the front lines—from the pioneers and settlers who braved Indian resistance to expand the national domain to the white residents of reservation bordertowns who dealt with them on a daily basis—possessed the actuality of personal experience. In their minds that gave them an advantageous illumination, a more hard-edged realism about Indians. Until you've worked with and lived around them, they say, your opinion is a tourist's. You might not know, for example, that the Indian is not the same person he had been a hundred years ago. That he is often admired for things he no longer is.

Don't try to tell Red Crampton about the Noble Red Man. For years, before he opened his Shell station on Main Street for business on Monday mornings, Red had to roust the Navajos sleeping off their drunks in the lot out back, and clean up the mess they'd made. It was hard for him not to think of all Indians as dirty stupid people when most of the ones he saw were passed out in a pile of empty bottles with blue flies buzzing around their bloated faces. Some, he had to poke with a boot toe to see if they were still alive.

This has been going on for a long time. Before it was legal for Indians to drink, a mom-and-pop grocery store across the street would order several cases of vanilla extract each week and sell it all to Indians who drank it for its alcohol content. When prohibition for Indians ended, the problem moved to another part of town, near the package liquor stores. But then a Safeway was built next door and the problem came back. The law said you couldn't sell liquor on Sundays, but there was no law against buying Listerine mouthwash or Aqua Velva aftershave or Aqua Net hairspray, which were better than 20 percent alcohol, and drinking it. By the trash you'd think there were a lot of sweet-smelling, well-groomed people walking around town. . . .

Not only did people in Farmington gripe about attitudes toward Indians they thought were "colorized" by romantic myths and sentimentality, underlying their own perspective was a deep resentment of—in their opinion—misguided governmental policies and patronage. The town was mired in an economic slump during the sixties; many residents had to struggle to maintain a decent standard of living, often going from paycheck to paycheck worrying if they could meet the mortgage, pay their bills. In the oil business you could be in the money one day, on the street the next, so you rarely achieved security. And out of the taxes paid on their hard-earned income the government was giving the Indians all these freebies. Indians got direct welfare payments. They got free medical services. They got free housing and education. All without having to put out any effort. They didn't have to work for it. It was available to them just because they were Indians.

"They're like a kid living with his parents," explained one unsympathetic local, "demanding all the comforts and benefits of home, wanting us to give them all these things they can't buy for themselves. But with your kids you can say, 'Okay, I'll keep you clothed and fed until you're eighteen. Then you're on your own. It's up to you to get a job and take care of yourself.' The goddamn Indians—they're eighty years old and still living at home."

Welfare for Indians went against the philosophical grain of Farmington, where the frontier work ethic of self-reliance prevailed, the virtues of hard labor and entrepreneurship were admired, and people were encouraged to look after themselves, not *to* the government. Brigham Young was frequently cited as the authority on what happened to the recipients of government handouts: "My experience has taught me, and it has become a principle with me, that it is never any benefit to give out and out to man or woman, money, food, clothing, or anything else, when there is anything on earth for them to do. This is my principle and I try to act upon it. To pursue a contrary course would ruin any community in the world and make them idlers."

Whenever that advice was recalled in Farmington, it wasn't just Mormons who uttered a resounding "Amen!"

Other than to celebrate certain holidays, and on the occasion of the annual Sheriff's Posse Parade, Farmington was not used to public processions down its thoroughfares. Having been spared the social turmoil of the sixties—there had been no street demonstrations protesting the Vietnam War in Farmington, no rebellious youths waving placards and chanting anti-American slogans to raise the blood pressure of local conservatives—to the townspeople, marching as a mode of publicizing discontent was something that happened only on the evening news.

But like it or not, images that had tramped across the TV screens had come to town, images that could not be changed by switching to another channel.

When the Indians had first applied for a parade permit to conduct a memorial march, Mayor Webb's reaction had been No, not in this town. He had subsequently softened his position and decided to let them march—in part because no one could think of grounds for denial other than it had never been done before, and in part because the mayor did feel he had a moral responsibility to respond to the killings. But when they requested a second permit with the idea of using city streets as a platform for protest, he had no intention of letting that happen and said as much at a meeting with his inner circle of advisers convened to discuss the request.

Seconding his opinion was the city manager, C. M. "Woody" Woodbury, a retired major general in the New Mexico National Guard, the commanding officer of a tank battalion in World War II, and a four-time recipient of the Silver Star. This thing should be stopped early, before the dissidents get to feeling their muscle, Woodbury insisted. He went on to say that his years of experience convinced him that civil disturbances were nourished by the permissiveness and restraint of authorities. "Let them continue to march and it will only get worse," summed up his point of view.

The city attorney represented the only dissenting voice, but his position was also the most informed. He pointed out that there were constitutional questions at stake, and public groups that had not yet acted in a socially disruptive manner were, in fact, legally entitled to march.

Mayor Webb countered: Although the first march had been peaceful and without incident, it had generated a considerable amount of anxiety. To allow Indians to march once again, particularly when their announced intention was to "protest," could be interpreted as putting the town in a dangerous position.

Chief of Police Roy Kerr, a veteran lawman who had attained national recognition when a *Life* magazine article credited him with cleaning up vice conditions in Tacoma, Washington, when it was known as a "sin spot" in the early fifties, then cited the advantage to letting the Indians march. "It would make it easier for us to control the situation. On the permit we stipulate the route, set the parameters, and that way we know where they are at all times, Meanwhile my men will be standing by, and at the slightest sign of trouble, we're ready to roll."

Kerr's opinion held sway. With the conditions that the parade applicants and participants expressly agree to conduct themselves in an orderly and law-abiding manner, that no one carry any weapons, firearms, firecrackers, or explosives, and that in case of emergency or civil disorder the participants would peacefully disband upon order of the police, the permit was approved.

The second march was held on Saturday, May 11, and everything about this march was different. It began in Shiprock, where hundreds of people gathered early in the morning for a rally along the San Juan River. Led by two police cruisers, the crowd began to walk the twenty-odd miles to Farmington, stopping twice along the route for protests at the Zia and Turquoise bars, the roadside honky-tonks sitting along Highway 550, which more or less drew the northern perimeter of the reservation. There, Fred Johnson urged a boycott of the bars, and in a pathetic illustration of the problem, even though it was midday the Turquoise doors were locked (for the first time in recent memory), so the audience for the exhortations was a small band of six puzzled, red-eyed Indians who had been hovering around the bar since it had closed down the night before.

It was mid-afternoon by the time the marchers arrived in Farmington, and the size of the original group had swelled considerably. The Farmington newspaper would put the number at 250, the Coalition leaders at 4,000. Perhaps the most accurate gauge is a rooftop police photo that shows a mass of people filling both lanes of a downtown street from sidewalk to sidewalk for seven blocks behind a banner that reads: MARCH FOR NAVAJO LIBERATION.

In stark contrast to the march the previous Saturday in which the participants walked silently, the tone of this march was raucous, the messages written on many of the signs outright threatening. "And they kept coming," a Farmington police officer would remember, watching the protestors pour with the raging fluidity of a flash flood down one empty street after another, changing direction several times before turning on Airport Road and surging up the hill to Farmington City Hall.

There, under the watchful eye of police sharpshooters perched on the bluffs and squinting through their scopes, the Coalition leaders stepped up onto a flatbed trailer and called for social and economic equality, an end to prejudice and racism, justice in the case of the three murders, and a quick response to a list of ten demands they were hereby presenting to Farmington city officials. Those demands began with an immediate open meeting with the Indian community and went on to demand greater sensitivity toward Indians, expanded employment opportunities, and participation by Indians in all aspects of community decision-making.

What seemed like a thousand fists stabbed the air when Wilbert Tsosie thrust the petition in the direction of Mayor Marlo Webb, who to the surprise of many not only had shown up at the rally but mounted the flatbed to receive it. Putting on a brave face, the mayor had to wait for the booing and catcalls to subside before he could address the crowd. When finally given a chance to speak, he said, "There is no way I can answer all these demands today, and it would be improper to try to do so. But on behalf of the citizens of Farmington, I accept them with a view toward looking into them."

There would be those who would think the mayor intended to say no more; that he felt this alone was a major concession, and were it not for an ominous grumble from the young bucks in the crowd he would not have realized the inadequacy of his response, glanced down at the paper in his hand in confusion and dismay, read the first demand calling for an immediate open meeting with the mayor and the city council at which Indian people would be allowed to voice their grievances and concerns, and saved himself embarrassment or worse by announcing then and there a public meeting would be held two days hence, on Monday evening. The mayor denies this. But there is little disagreement that he seemed visibly relieved when the announcement was applauded and he beat a hasty retreat.

Monday evening the remarkable happened. An estimated 300 people, the majority of them Navajo, packed into the auditorium at the county fairgrounds, and for six hours a lengthy stream of speakers, some talking in Navajo, others in the "foreign tongue," hurled insult upon complaint at the six members of the Farmington City Council and at Marlo Webb. There was a fair amount of blustering, as some Indians seized on the chance to sass authority figures and flaunt their contempt for protocol, interrupting, jeering, and, when it was their turn, expressing themselves in language liberally sprinkled with expletives. But a number of issues important to the Indian community were also identified—and presented in this sensational context, they could not be ignored. Included in the litany of alleged abuses was the systematic harassment, mistreatment, and discrimination by police, merchants, schools, hospitals, and other area institutions.

And then Wilbert Tsosie, like a Grand Inquisitor, stepped up and damned the town itself. "Every day Indian people face hostility, disrespect, and abuse—on the streets, in the schools, and in restaurants and shops. There is no regard for our human rights, no concern for our human dignity. It was this attitude that led to the fanatic murders of three of our people."

None of this went over well with the mayor. When he agreed to set up this meeting he had been thinking as a businessman. He had decided he would handle gripes from minority groups the same way he did customers in the car business, where he dealt daily with disgruntled people who were unhappy because their new car sprang an oil leak or their radiator overheated: Let them sound off.

But over the course of six hours his patience was sorely tested. At first he had tried to be congenial with the hostile crowd. In response to a Navajo request for police protection, he had scanned the faces in the auditorium and half-jokingly responded, "Maybe we're the ones who need protection."

Larry Anderson of AIM had leaped to his feet to remind the mayor, "Navajos are the ones being murdered, and they want protection."

The mayor tightened, found it difficult to restrain sarcasm after that, got caught up in some testy back-and-forth exchanges, and almost lost it when Fred Johnson was deliberately blasphemous and Wilbert Tsosie warned him that if reforms were not forthcoming, "We're gonna turn this town upside down."

At the very start of the evening, the mayor had said he and the council members had come to the meeting to listen, not to act. But those in attendance were wanting something concrete to come out of all the talk. For this to be more than just an exercise, specific actions had to follow.

As much to appease that sentiment as to act in accordance with the responsibilities of his position, Webb announced that later in the week he would appoint a fact-finding committee to examine in greater detail the matters brought before the council this evening.

It was 1:30 in the morning by the time the parley was adjourned, and even though his composure had slowly unraveled over the course of the evening, when he reflected on the meeting as a whole, Mayor Webb felt that, overall, it had gone remarkably well. To arrive at this conclusion he ignored what he thought were examples of inflammatory rhetoric and unrealistic demands and saw the events just ended as part of a strategy that had begun with the issuance of a second parade permit. The Indians had marched and it had gone without incident. Not only that, they had been allowed to have a pow-wow in front of city hall. In a gesture of conciliation and in keeping with their first demand he had essentially called a town meeting. After an exhaustive griping session he had agreed to appoint a committee to study the problem and come up with recommendations. What more could be expected of a reasonable city administrator?

Driving home that night, the mayor found himself thinking that maybe the worst was over. Maybe, now that the air was cleared, the tension that had obviously been building in the Indian community would lessen. Maybe Farmington had just avoided a long hot summer.

The meeting at the fairgrounds did little to appease Wilbert Tsosie. He thought it probably gave Navajo people the feeling they could express their feelings and some good might actually come out of it, but beyond that it had accomplished nothing. He had no faith in the kind of fact-finding committee the mayor was going to appoint, imagining it would most likely be composed of a handpicked group of so-called leading citizens who knew nothing about Indian affairs. And when Webb had explicitly designated a commission recently formed by Tribal Chairman Peter MacDonald as the group he intended to report to and work with, Wilbert felt the mayor had revealed his insidious intentions. No mention had been made of the Coalition for Navajo Liberation, which said to Tsosie that the mayor was refusing to accord it recognition as a legitimate negotiating body.

Wilbert did not discount the possibility that the entire meeting had been a well-staged play designed to calm the natives while pulling public support out from under the Coalition, and when an editorial that blasted the CNL appeared two days later in the Farmington newspaper, he felt his opinion was confirmed.

SELF-APPOINTED LEADERS

The manner in which a number of recently self-appointed spokesmen for the Navajo people have been conducting themselves is not representative of the overwhelming majority of responsible Indians residing in San Juan County.

Violence and the threat of violence have never accomplished a single thing for the benefit of any minority group. These spokesmen place unreasonable demands on the duly-elected officials of a community with the full knowledge that those demands cannot and will not be met. . . .

The people of Farmington have elected city officials who are legally responsible for the administration of city affairs. . . . The voters of this city did not elect representatives of the Farmington Intertribal Indian Organization. They did not elect spokesmen for the American Indian Movement. . . .

For those organizations to attempt to usurp the right of the people of Farmington to elect our community leaders is ridiculous.

Attempts to polarize various racial or ethnic elements of an area in the name of "human rights" are hypocrisy. Efforts to incite those elements to commit violence or illegal acts should be recognized for what they are—that is, to widen the gap which divides individual human beings and to bring about discord among the American people.

The Navajo people have well-qualified representatives who have been elected according to law. We think they are far more representative of the people than those who attempt to seize authority by playing on the emotions of a vociferous minority.

With all due respect, Wilbert expected no better from the *Farmington Daily Times*. The lack of what he felt to be fair and objective reporting of "Indian issues" had been a long-standing complaint of his. Legitimate news was relegated to back pages when Indians were the subject. There was no attempt to write with depth and social awareness about the realities of the "Navajo neighbors." He agreed with Fred Johnson, who had dubbed the paper "the white racist Bible of Farmington."

He also thought the editorial erred in its assessment of the number of people the Coalition represented. He felt that just as whites had their silent majority who rarely spoke out publicly on issues because they felt powerless and didn't think their voice would make a difference, so did Navajos. But it would be a mistake to think that just because they didn't speak their minds that meant they were content. If white people only knew how deeply resentful the Navajo people were toward them, they would sleep a lot less easily at night.

Wilbert had other grounds for dismissing the charges. Having considered the potential for a backlash from the traditional Indian community, he had already sought out tribal councilmen from the region, chapter officials, and conservative Navajo business people, who he expected would frown on militant activities, to explain his position. To his surprise he found that many of them felt at least as strongly as he did about the need to rearrange relations with the white community. Even if they were not comfortable marching, they made him feel that though it might not be their style, they were in sympathy with his objectives.

The next Saturday, for the third week in a row, a thousand-plus demonstrators crammed into downtown Farmington. Speeches made during two stops along the parade route were both shrill and acrimonious. In front of a Main Street liquor establishment Fred Johnson declared "war on the bars" and accused their owners of being "criminal profiteers."

The white man had created a thirst for liquor in the Indian, he said. He profited from the Navajo weakness for alcohol. He engaged in illegal activities: selling booze to obviously intoxicated Indians, and to minors. And he refused to provide the resources for a single alcohol rehabilitation program.

At the marchers' second stop, in front of Marlo Webb's Smoak Chevrolet dealership, a hot-eyed intellectual by the name of John Redhouse spoke, and he stirred the crowd with what sounded to many like a call to arms.

Later Redhouse would explain himself this way: "I felt in self-defense we should arm ourselves. We were being watched by armed cops. Police brutality was a pattern out there. So I felt we should be ready, and not allow ourselves to be helpless victims any longer. I wanted white Farmington to know we would retaliate with force if threatened with force."

But the quotes that made the paper sounded a lot more aggressive: "If law enforcement agencies do not bring the three murderers to justice, then we must be prepared to take the law into our own hands . . . and retaliate against the subjects, their families, and the racist white community of Farmington."

Wearing red-and-green armbands, the colors of the Coalition, regional members of AIM were serving as parade marshals, walking on either side of the marchers and breaking up arguments with white hecklers before they got out of hand. Ostensibly there to provide security and crowd control, they looked like a militia that would provide the first line of defense if the parade were attacked. They were also the most vocal respondents when their commander, Larry Anderson, pledged the support of AIM, telling the crowd that he had been in contact by phone with its leaders Russell Means and Dennis Banks, who stood solidly behind the Navajo people and had ordered representatives of AIM chapters in the Southwest to come to Farmington to assist local Indians in their fight. He said that more members of his organization were camped near Shiprock at this very minute and were prepared to move into Farmington for a direct confrontation if such action was required.

In spite of surveillance techniques that had all the subtlety of watchtower guards glassing a prison yard, the Coalition was not intimidated and their rallies and marches continued to turn out impressive numbers of people. Perhaps the most important individual to swell their ranks was John Redhouse. Compared to Fred Johnson—a one-man show, audacious and passionate, given to outrageous but emotionally powerful speeches and a rhetoric of extremity—Redhouse was the epitome of rational poise and calibrated steadiness. He stood six feet tall, weighed close to 200 pounds, wore his hair at shoulder length, and looked at you through wire-rimmed glasses that seemed to emit a concentrated beam of intensity. Farmington-raised, honorably discharged from the army, he was currently enrolled at the University of New Mexico in Albuquerque where he was a member of the Kiva Club, an Indian student organization. A sharp and serious young man who saw current conditions in Indian country as a continuation of the Indian wars, his commitment to social justice for Navajos had taken him the previous year to Gallup, New Mexico, where he was involved in organizing a protest against the commercialization and exploitation of Indian culture and religion at the annual Intertribal Ceremonial. He had come blazing back into town when he read about the developments in Farmington.

Redhouse varied the rhythms of the Coalition leadership, and in the days following the third march, when he met with Tsosie and Johnson to brainstorm about activities to fan the growing mood of self-assertion and defiance in Farmington Indians, it was his recommendation that they expand their disruptions of business-as-usual to include an economic boycott. The campaign would be directed at the Farmington business community, which profited from Navajo dollars yet treated Navajo customers scornfully and only hired a token few.

"If we wanted to," he reminded his fellow leaders, "we could conduct a boycott so strong the city would go broke."

The idea of calling for a blanket boycott had a certain appeal to Wilbert Tsosie, except he didn't believe it would work. "What alternative do we provide people with, then? If we ask them not to shop in Farmington because it's Navajo money that makes this town rich, where do we tell them to go? Gallup? Things are no better there. Besides, people aren't going to drive hundreds of miles to shop someplace else."

Redhouse maintained that the call for a well-coordinated boycott of Farmington, even if it could not be pulled off, had value "in a rhetorical sense, as part of consciousness-raising. What we need to look at, and begin to move toward, is the internal economic development of the Navajo Nation. Because it is still a colony of the bordertowns. A colony of the corporations ripping off our resources. We need to develop an economic system that provides for our own goods and services, so we don't have to depend on places like Farmington or Gallup, where our people are exploited."

In the end a tactical compromise was arranged. The Coalition would raise the specter of an economic boycott as leverage for discussions with city officials. But to show it wasn't bluffing, it would begin to target specific businesses about which they had received complaints of racial discrimination.

Most of the business people they contacted pled innocent, of course; and some, like the store manager at Safeway, refused to talk with them. But when they warned that they would come back again in far greater numbers if things did not change, a letter from Safeway headquarters informing them it was not company policy to discriminate but a concerted effort would be made to hire more minorities, including Navajos, let them know their point had been made.

At Sambo's Restaurant, where there had been reports that Navajos were refused service, they were rudely turned away and responded as promised the very next day. They returned to conduct a sit-in, occupying every table, booth, and counter seat in the place, and sat there the entire afternoon. Nobody ordered anything but water. There were no raised voices, no combative arguments with the help. The only time anybody even addressed the glowering waitresses was to raise an empty glass and ask for "More water, here."

Meanwhile, the police had been called and were watching in the windows, apparently under orders not to do anything unless an incident was provoked. Finally, around six in the evening, Coalition leaders and the faithful filed out the door, and before the summer was over Sambo's would change managers, and Navajo girls in orange-and-white uniforms were taking orders from customers.

Working with limited resources, the Coalition had no choice but to think creatively, and sometimes their antics were humorous as well as poignant. Take the way they protested appropriation of city funds for the construction of an animal shelter. For two years Tsosie had lobbied the city to build a decent Indian Center. The old one, built in the sixties as a place where Indians who came to town could rest and find washrooms that were often denied them in city gas stations and restaurants, was a shabby, rundown facility. As Tsosie pointed out, an estimated 30 percent of the retail business in Farmington came from Navajo consumers, all of whom paid sales tax, and they deserved better accommodations. He'd been told, "We're not going to build a clubhouse for you and your cronies," so when the city council rejected the proposal once again, citing "priorities," and proceeded to approve $40,000 for an animal shelter, at the next council meeting Coalition members showed up at city hall with their pets, filling the chamber with yapping dogs and mewling cats. When asked the meaning of this, they replied, "It appears you care more about dogs than Indians, even though we are human beings. So they have just as much right to be here, maybe more, than we do."

Other ideas never got beyond the scheming stage, such as the plan to sew a thousand sheets together and drape them over a rocky ridge near Hogback, just east of Shiprock, with a Coalition slogan printed across the expanse. Tsosie got the idea after reading a magazine article about an artist who had wrapped an island off the coast of Florida with a pink plastic ribbon. They called it "art," but it made news and he figured if *that* captured the attention of the national media, so would his banner. And it might have worked if he'd been able to raise the money to buy the number of sheets it would take, and find enough people willing to stitch a thousand together. As for how they would get the material up the side of the ridge, the thinking never got that far.

The most dramatic performance by the Coalition, one that a journalist from the *National Observer* would describe as touched by "the kind of publicity genius that marked Southern campaigns of a decade ago,'' was staged at the city dump on Thursday afternoon, May 23. Billed as a press conference, reporters from local, regional, and national publications gathered along with several hundred Navajo Indians to watch the burning of a rag-stuffed effigy of Mayor Marlo Webb, hanging by its neck from a crooked cedar post, with an American flag stuck upside down in the Styrofoam head.

''If all our peaceful legal methods fail, then Farmington will go up in flames—physically and literally,'' John Redhouse vowed.

Drawing the string on a six-foot bow, Fred Johnson proclaimed ''The fight has just begun,'' before he sent an arrow whistling into the mayor's likeness, symbolically assassinating the man that the Coalition had dubbed ''the Custer of Farmington.''

Twice before in this century peaceful coexistence between Anglos and Navajos had been threatened: once, back in 1913, when a Navajo medicine man practicing plural marriage fled prosecution and holed up on top of Beautiful Mountain with his three wives and nine armed braves, where they were surrounded by U.S. Cavalry troops; and again in the 1930s, when the government's solution to the overgrazing problem on the reservation was a mandatory stock-reduction plan, provoking bitter resentment and approaching, but never reaching, outright revolt.

Neither situation bore an instructive resemblance to the conflict Mayor Webb found himself confronted with, however, and the escalation of activism after the meeting left him edgy and impatient. He realized he had been wrong about the way it had gone. The bloodletting had created a blood thirst. Things were getting worse.

Curdling everything he was feeling was a righteous indignation, because he felt an honest attempt had been made. He truly believed he had done all within reason and his power to respond responsibly to the situation. He had tried his best to establish a dialogue with the dissidents and bring those who wanted their voices to be heard into the political process. But they had rejected his plea to stop the marching until solutions were arrived at, and refused his appeal that hereafter they express their opinions on city affairs and social problems through normal channels. All they did was reiterate their demands. They wouldn't listen to reason, and they accused him of making excuses when he tried to point out that some of their demands were too nebulous to respond to.

For example: When they said they wanted to be recognized and respected as human beings, he had no idea how to begin to meet such a demand. It sounded to him like what they wanted was a change in attitude, but that was not something that could be passed like a law. That occurred over time, not overnight or upon demand.

And when they did have specifics, either they were complaints against individuals without evidence to corroborate their statements and no charges had been filed at the time, or they were unhappy with policies and practices over which the city had no jurisdiction and was not authorized to address.

Privately, Mayor Webb thought that most of what came from the Coalition was the turgid cant of revolutionaries who claim that behind their militancy is a commitment to enfranchise a needy class, when the truth was they were doing it for personal notoriety, media exposure, and a grab for power. He disagreed with just about everything they said, and in particular objected to the idea that the town should pick up the tab for the murders. Nor did he believe local businesses were guilty of discrimination against Navajos. That wouldn't make sense for the very good reason that most businesses in Farmington counted on Navajos for their economic well-being, and it would be against their interests to alienate the very people their livelihood depended on. If you didn't treat a customer right, he would take his money someplace else.

By appointing a fact-finding commission and promising that once it brought its conclusions and recommendations to him they would "receive prompt and proper attention at the appropriate government units," he felt he was showing a clear willingness to work for the improvement of interracial relations. The commission, he hoped, would provide a mechanism that would enhance communication and provide solutions.

But that had not been good enough for the Indians. When he announced his appointments to the thirteen-man "Navajo Relations Committee" at the end of the week, they had booed his selection of chairman, Everett Kennedy, executive vice-president of the Citizens Bank in Farmington. They had criticized the fact that he had not appointed any Coalition members to the committee, and that he intended to work with the legally elected officials of the Navajo tribe; and again, the next Saturday, they had marched, tying up downtown traffic and disrupting normal weekend activity.

Feeling that each and every effort he had made had been rebuffed by the Coalition leaders, who had shown nothing but contempt for the political process and displayed an arrogant disregard for decency, the mayor decided that further consideration of their viewpoint would be unproductive, and he would no longer conduct discussions with anyone associated with the Coalition for Navajo Liberation. He then issued a statement to the press in which he said, "Although we are vitally concerned with improving relations between red and white, we can no longer deal with men who seek violence instead of friendship, and who represent only a small militant portion of the Navajo community."

In addition to concluding that Coalition leaders were not truly interested in sitting down to reason and counsel together and that he was dealing with troublemakers trying to capitalize on a tragedy by exploiting emotions generated by the murders, the mayor felt he had good reason to believe this was not a grass-roots movement supported by real Farmington Navajos. It had been his observation that most of the protestors who were marching had come in off the reservation, which said to him that the local Indians must therefore be content. As for the leadership of the Coalition, Fred Johnson's base of operations was Shiprock, and John Redhouse had been living in Albuquerque for years and only returned when the parading started.

On those grounds alone Webb felt he was justified in disregarding their demands. They were asking for representation for the reservation Navajo, and his responsibility was to the citizens of Farmington—people living within the city limits and having an ongoing relationship with the community.

But the point was dwarfed by a larger issue: the presence of people who claimed an affiliation with the American Indian Movement. Larry Anderson was reputed to be the national treasurer. At the second march the national chairman of AIM, John Trudell, who had been active in the Indian takeover of Alcatraz, had shown up. And there were others who boasted of their membership. Maybe they weren't, and were just saying so because they thought it gave them status, but it furthered the impression that AIM was working behind the scenes.

"And those were the ones we were most fearful of," the mayor would remember thinking. "They had a known history of violence, and some of them gave you the distinct impression they'd just as soon cut your throat as look at you."

Nor was AIM the only non-town subversive organization suspected of showing an interest in inciting civil unrest. At a meeting with the local FBI agent who was monitoring events closely, Webb was informed that a background check of a local priest, one of the few whites marching with the Indians, had turned up information out of his past that identified him as a "communist sympathizer."

Whether it was AIM, the communists, or whomever, Webb felt he had heard and seen enough to convince him that he was dealing with something fomented by outside agitators. These were not the Navajo people he knew. These were people from elsewhere, expressing what sounded to him like imported ideas.

As sure of that fact as he was, neither Webb nor his inner circle of advisers knew what they were dealing with, or what to expect next. Rumors had come off the street that a caravan carrying a thousand armed braves summoned by AIM were on the way from South Dakota, conjuring images of insurrection that flashed strobe-like in the mayor's head—automobiles flipped over and set afire; shadowy figures fleeing ransacked businesses through smashed windows; nights crackling with gunfire; charred blocks patrolled by armed National Guardsmen.

At the time, the intelligence gathered by law-enforcement agencies on militant activities on the reservation was woeful. The FBI claimed to have infiltrated AIM in South Dakota, but in Navajoland, other than reports filed by undercover agents who had attended the publicized Coalition meetings, there was no reliable inside information. So when the authorities were unable to give the mayor the assurances he wanted, he placed a call to Governor Bruce King.

After conveying the seriousness of the situation, Webb expressed his concern that the Farmington Police Department did not have the personnel, the training, or the experience to handle all the scenarios, and he brought up the possibility of mobilizing the National Guard.

After a round of discussions among top state officials, Mayor Webb was told such a mobilization might be provocative and there was not a clear need at this point. Nonetheless, the potential for violence was high enough that the Northern Zone

Tactical Team of the New Mexico State Police, who were practiced at handling prison riots, *would* be deployed to Farmington on the upcoming weekends the Indians marched. Working out of the Guard armory, they would assemble in full battle dress in a parking lot off Main Street where idling buses would move them in immediately after the first torch was thrown, the first shots fired.

As a final safety measure a document was sent which in effect gave the mayor the power to impose martial law. He kept it in his desk drawer and all it would take was his signature at the bottom and the National Guard would immediately be called up to clear the streets of people, make mass arrests if necessary, and enforce a curfew.

Once he felt that the city of Farmington was in a position to protect itself against social disruption, the mayor found himself considering personal precautions. He had received numerous threats, to his face and over the phone, and he took them seriously. Also, in the back of his mind was an incident, less than a year old, that had put city officials in bordertowns all around the Navajo Reservation on notice. Two young Indians active in the Gallup protests had resorted to desperate measures and kidnapped its mayor at gunpoint. Fortunately the mayor had escaped by throwing himself through a plate-glass window, just before the shooting started. One of the Indians survived. The other was celebrated as a martyr whose sacrifice showed the white world that Indians were prepared to die for their cause.

Knowing that the Coalition had touted the kid killed in the fracas as a folk hero, Marlo Webb took no chances. Each morning when he dressed for work he armed himself with a snub-nosed .38 with a two-inch barrel that fit comfortably in a shoulder holster under his arm.

7

IDENTIFYING
THE MALICE

In 1974 Dr. Walter Winslow was probably the best-known psychiatrist in the state of New Mexico. The slight, light-haired, bespectacled director of the Bernalillo County Mental Health Center and chairman of the Department of Psychiatry at the University of New Mexico had traveled extensively around the state lecturing at community mental health meetings on general psychiatry and drug abuse, and had testified before the state legislature and various courts in forensic settings, so it was not surprising that in a case this big the San Juan County District Attorney's Office came to him for assistance in evaluating the three youths charged in the multiple Navajo murders.

After he was briefed on the facts of the case and the surrounding circumstances, Winslow was intrigued. A fifty-year-old father of eight, he had run a large pediatric practice in Vancouver, British Columbia, for five years before he had decided to specialize in psychiatry, so he had a long-standing interest in the diseases of children. But after listening to Assistant District Attorney Byron Caton's appeal, Dr. Winslow was not convinced he was the right man for the job. Yes, the case sounded fascinating. Yes, he enjoyed forensic evaluations, likening them to the drama of the operating room where exciting things happened, decisions had to be made, and the stakes were high. But he had only been to Farmington on three or four occasions, passing through on his way to ski Colorado and once to lecture. And since he was only marginally acquainted with the cultural dynamics at work within that reservation bordertown, he wondered if a psychiatrist living in the area might not provide more expert testimony.

He was informed that this matter had been given thoughtful consideration, and it was the consensus of all persons involved in the case that the boys ought to be evaluated by someone who was not a member of the community.

Dr. Winslow pondered the situation a moment longer, then agreed to put together a team and come to Farmington and conduct the evaluations. The assistant district attorney indicated that he appreciated the offer, but that too had been considered and everyone felt it would probably be best for all concerned if the entire process took place out of town. Arrangements would be made to transfer the three boys to the Children's Detention Home in Albuquerque, just minutes away from the university campus, to make it easier for him.

For the same reason Dr. Winslow thought it would be better for someone acquainted with the cultural milieu in Farmington to conduct the evaluations, a close examination of the social patterns and racial attitudes of the youth in that community seemed to me to be a critically informative line of inquiry. And so each time I visited Farmington I would try and locate an eyewitness or participant to the "rolling" of Indians in the early seventies. In all I spoke with more than a dozen.

One or two never opened up. They would listen to my spiel with sullen expressions, and then reveal the only reason they agreed to meet with me was to find out "Who gave you my name?"

I suspected one guy of hotdogging for the writer. He referred to rolling Indians as the next best thing to sex and said the authorities ought to have pinned medals on the three boys, not prosecuted them.

Most finally warmed to the conversation, however, and reminisced with candor about those days, admitting to a slight embarrassment, even shame, about their acts now, though to be honest at the time it had been fun.

And then along came the definitive interview:

That was what we did on Friday and Saturday nights: Drive around lookin' for drunk Indians to roll. "Subs," we called 'em, as in subhumans. They weren't hard to find, they were everywhere. Lyin' in the alleys shit-faced. Weavin' down the side streets lookin' for a place to flop. Staggerin' along the highway on their way back to the rez. GodDAMN, you'd say. Let's kick some Indian ass.

Maybe it don't make a lot of sense to other people, but it might if they grew up in Farmington or Gallup or Winslow, where this kind of thing went on all the time. And it wasn't just a few who did it. My big brother did it before me, my little one after. I remember goin' through my older brother's desk and findin' a bunch of belt buckles. "Where'd you get these, Johnny?" I asked. "Off Indians," he said. Called 'em his "trophy buckles."

The first I got involved was in the eighth grade. The Allen Theatre was the only picture show in town, and a coupla doors down was Harry's bar, where most all the Indians went to drink when they came to town. So what we'd do, see, is when our parents took us to the theater, instead of letting them park and buy our tickets, we'd say, Just let us out here and give us the money. Right? Then we'd act like we were gonna go in—stand in line, hang around the lobby for a few minutes—and when they drove off we'd come back out and go around to the alley behind Harry's where the REAL show was goin' on. And I mean you'd see everything. Once I saw two bucks get into a knife fight. Another time I watched a couple get it on right there on the pavement.

They had no self-respect and we had no respect for them either. About all they were good for was buyin' booze. We'd give one five bucks to get us a coupla quarts of beer from Harry's, tell him he could buy himself a bottle of wine with the leftover change, and hell, an Indian'll do anything for a bottle of wine.

Sometimes they'd go in and we'd never see them again. They'd sneak out another door and what could you do? But mostly they were good for it, and we'd get our beer, down it before the cops came, and then go up and down the alleys lookin' to get even for the ones that run out on us. Like I say, they'd be lyin' all over the place. So we'd find one off by himself and we'd smack him around, go through his pockets, take his belt and boots—that's where most of them keep their money, in their boots. Not that any of them had much money. And it wasn't money we were doin' it for. I mean, we never sat around the house and said, "Let's go rob somebody." It wasn't like that at all. It wasn't like it was even committing a crime. We did it for the kick, man. I mean, they were just Indians.

All this was before we were able to drive ourselves. Once we got a set of wheels under us, hey, the game changed. We were still underaged so we would still have to find an Indian to buy us booze. But now we'd say, Buy yourself a bottle and let's go drinking together. Or, Let's go to a party up Chokecherry. Then, once we had him alone we'd repossess, in a manner of speaking. Kick him out and keep the booze for ourselves. See what I'm sayin'?

It really was a big game, and it could be funny if you were in a certain frame of mind. We'd do things like cruise the Bisti Highway, catch one walking across the bridge, and once he realized he was surrounded and he couldn't get away, he had a choice. Jump in the river or face the music: Rock 'n' Roll. . . . One time we pulled up beside a pickup fulla Indians at a stoplight and I called, "Hey buddy, hey buddy," to the driver. Then, when he rolled down his window, I tossed this tear-gas canister into the cab. Psssh. Merry Christmas. We took off and about died laughin' when we looked back and saw all them Indians unload. . . . Another time my friend and I were out cruisin' and we had a blackjack we were gonna try out. You know, one of them spring-loaded jobs? We went outsida town and found this drunk old Indian walkin' home. Okay, Gaylon, my friend says. I'll pull up beside him, you open the door and lay him out. So he brakes and I jump out and the guy turns around and we look each other in the face and I notice two things right away. One, he was not old. And two, he was not drunk. Well, I took a coupla swings at him, but it was to keep him off me long enough to get back to the car and we booked it outta there. . . . One guy name of Jimmy developed the best way of rollin' Indians. He'd play sick, roll on the sidewalk moanin', knees cocked up, and soon an Indian would come over to see what was wrong. 'Cause they're good-hearted people, basically. And when the guy leaned over, Jimmy would kick out and plain flatten him.

I know guys who think they killed some. In those days we used to have keggers. You know, beer busts, out in the hills. We had different places: the Grove, this stand of cottonwoods by the river; the Pit, a big hole in the ground up Chokecherry Canyon; the Steps, where these old Anasazi steps went up the side of a cliff. A big brother would be our connection, we'd put out the word there's gonna be a kegger, charge two bucks a head for a good time and all the beer you could drink, maybe a hundred, two hundred kids would show up, and hey, you could make it pay. I heard there was a kegger at the Steps one time, a coupla Indians happened to pass by, and a bunch took 'em up the steps and pushed 'em off the cliff. That's a long fall.

Not many are gonna walk away they go off that cliff. But there wasn't anything about it in the newspaper, so no one thought much about it afterwards.

I never killed one. Least I don't think so. I know there was one time we threw one in the back of a pickup and were takin' him out into the hills to do a number on him, and he come to and jumped out. Musta known what he was headed for and figured that was better. I don't know why. We was doin' about fifty, sixty. We could see him bouncin' down the road behind us. We didn't go back and check him out, so I don't know how bad he was hurt. But it wouldn't have surprised me if he was history.

Rolling drunk Indians had been a time-honored, if unsavory, tradition among Farmington teenagers for a number of years, almost a rite of passage. According to one youth who felt the peer pressure to do it when he was sixteen, "If someone came out and said, 'Let's roll an Indian,' and you said 'No thanks,' you were chicken. So it was kind of like your manhood was involved. It was a step forward. Like Indians had a way of proving their manhood—going out and killing a buffalo or enemy or whatever. Well, in Farmington, New Mexico, you weren't a man until you rolled an Indian."

Even if he was overstating the case, no one argues that there did not flourish during this time a brutal form of nightlife for those teens whose sporting inclinations included, in addition to blowing up mailboxes, mooning, and soaping windows, the darker frolic of beating up drunk Indians. It was seen as the macho thing to do, and first-person reports from those involved, looking back on those days years later, also make it clear that in 1973 and 1974, things got out of hand.

"It just got more vicious and more vicious, and seemed to build on itself," recalls one who was in a position to know. "A bunch of guys would go out and their story would be, 'Score one for us. We found an Indian and broke his arms with an axe handle.' Then another bunch would go out and try to outdo them. Come back with, 'Oh yeah? Well, we stoned a guy.' And it kept getting bigger and bigger, one trying to outdo the other, like they were going after bragging rights."

Those in charge of law and order then will acknowledge that the streets of Farmington turned mean during this period, and blame a lot of it on dope, which was everywhere. But those who were doing the drugs as well as the rolling deny it. "A lot of us were smoking marijuana, but that was no big deal. I know kids who got high before they went to school and church. Anybody who knows what they're talking about knows grass will put you to sleep before it'll get you out looking for trouble. People in this country would like to blame it on drugs, but that's because this is anti-grass country. You know, 'Boys couldn't be normal who smoke dope.' But it wasn't a drug thing.''

Accounts for why it got so rough during this period vary. Some cite a general rise in frustration that needed an outlet, and the Indians made convenient scapegoats: "You had pent-up anger you wanted to get out of your system, what better way to let it out? In the shape they were in they couldn't fight back. Ready-made victims is what they were.'' Some point to specific grievances with Indian people that galled them: "It really pissed us off to see them driving around in new pickups, knowing they bought them with government money, when we had to scratch and borrow for some old clunker.'' Others, however, turned it around and blamed a controversial new law so unpopular even the police were refusing to diligently enforce it. Less than a year earlier, simple drunkenness had been decriminalized. Instead of arresting hapless indigents, police were supposed to escort them to a treatment facility, or place them under protective custody until they dried out. The fact that Farmington did not have at the time a detox center, and some Indians now saw the city jail as a safe, semi-permanent shelter, explains why many local officers chose to ignore the "drunk Indian" problem, or at best would escort inebriated Indians to the reservation border, swat them across their behinds with a night stick, and send them home in an ungainly lope—thereby provoking the youth to justify their activities: "You don't take care of it, we will.'' But the final outrage for many was the killing of Kevin Arnold.

On a December evening in 1973, a popular Farmington High School graduate named Kevin Arnold was driving home from a date in his new red Corvette. Beside him sat his twenty-year-old fiancée. As he passed through an intersection another car, driven by an intoxicated Navajo teenager who was speeding to elude Farmington police, slammed into him broadside. The impact knocked the sports car into a mobile home. City firemen called to the scene were forced to cut through the car with a saw to extract the two bodies. Although the Navajo youth was charged with vehicular homicide he never served time, an injustice many understood to have occurred because he was the son of a ranking officer on the Navajo Tribal Police force. Many would believe that the resentment felt by friends of Kevin Arnold at Farmington High accounted for the increased level of violence toward the southside drunks.

"When that goddamn Indian got off, things escalated. That was the momentum that rolled the ball right there. It was total anger after that."

And after that, at interscholastic sporting events, whenever an Indian went down to defeat at the hands of an Anglo athlete, you could hear "Remember Arnold" called out like a battle cry. And in the south part of town where the Indians hung out, the heretofore antics-of-adolescence turned predatory.

Weapons came into play: lead pipes and baseball bats. One kid drove barn nails through a softball, attached it to a chain fixed to a handle, and would swing it like a gladiator.

Taking out more than one at a time became the challenge. Unofficially the record stood at six, and it went like this: On an unseasonably warm spring night, a half-dozen Navajo sat side by side on a long pipe that ran along an alley near the hospital, passing bottles, chatting quietly, nodding to themselves. There were no streetlights back there so everything was shades of black, and you know they were feeling no pain, so none of them noticed the pickup with its lights doused purring softly as it crept down the alley toward them. At a signal none of them heard, there was an explosion of light and sound. Tires screamed, a V-8 roared, and, blinded by the headlights, the men simply turned their heads. They never saw the Louisville Slugger held out to the side by a figure crouching in the bed of the pickup, until it hit them. The whole row was mowed down, one after the other, *bam-bam-bam.*

"We went six for six that night" went the joke, as if they were keeping track of a batting average. But in this game the only time someone struck out was when others got there first. You'd hear stories about that. How a bunch were cruising the alleys for Indians and all the ones they could find were already stretched out bleeding on the pavement.

Still, according to those who ran and rolled with Crawford, Burke, and Thacker, there was a radical difference between those who thought beating up Indians was a good time and what was done to the Indians who were taken up Chokecherry Canyon.

*   *   *

After deciding that the three youths should be assessed individually, Dr. Winslow approached several of his colleagues in the department. He enlisted the support of Dr. Richard Rada, an assistant professor of psychiatry with an interest in legal-forensic work who had written about men and rape, and assigned him Oren Thacker. Dr. Benjamin Cummins, a child psychiatrist, was given Peter Burke. Dr. Alex Quenk, an associate professor of psychology and a certified clinical psychologist, was brought in to administer a battery of psychological tests on each of the youths. And Dr. Winslow chose Vernon Crawford as his subject.

By their very nature, psychiatric investigations that are undertaken in a forensic setting rarely produce the same kinds of deep revelations that come with a long-term, trusting, therapeutic relationship. Dr. Winslow: "The stage is set differently. You begin by saying, I'm Dr. So-and-so, but I want you to understand I am not here as a treating physician. I'm not here to help you through your problems. I've been sent here by the court, and by your lawyer, to understand what happened. I'm evaluating you for their benefit, not yours directly. Whatever you say can be used in court because what you tell me is not confidential. I'll make inferences from whatever you say, and I hope what I can say will help you, but I don't know that. You have to tell them that, even juveniles. If you don't, the court could throw your entire testimony out. So naturally there is more guardedness in the conversations. They don't tell you as much."

Dr. Winslow planned to meet with Vernon Crawford on at least three separate occasions, but had only spoken with him once before something very strange happened. It was a Saturday evening and he was at home when he received a phone call from Crawford's parents who said they were in Albuquerque and wanted to come over and talk to him. He didn't think it was a good idea, and to put them off suggested they call his office on Monday if they wanted to schedule an appointment. But they insisted, saying they had information that would be of help to him in understanding their son and what had happened. Still not sure it was the right thing to do, he reluctantly gave them his address.

This was the first time he had spoken with the Crawfords directly, and after they arrived at his house and made get-acquainted talk for about ten minutes, the father asked him, "Tell us, do you really think our son did this?"

It was not a question Dr. Winslow expected to be asked, and wondering if he had made a big mistake allowing this meeting to take place, he exhaled slowly. "He said he did it. He described doing it to me. So I have to assume that he did it."

The mother spoke up. "That's not what we meant. We mean . . . do you think our son might have been . . . demon-possessed?"

Dr. Winslow stared at each of them for a moment. Obviously they were very serious. He looked down. Not a believer in demons, he had a little trouble with that one, but he treated it as a possible explanation, though not one that was appropriate in this case.

"I don't really think so. There didn't seem to be a change in his consciousness when he described the event, and from what I know about demon possession, it comes from another world. Right?"

They stared at him steadily. "We think he was." And they went on to say that they had heard some kids in Farmington High School were involved in devil worship, and they believed that somehow their son had gotten caught up in it. They were certain that the devil had gained control of their son and that he, not Vernon, had done those things.

Much later, reflecting on that moment, Dr. Winslow would admit to a very odd feeling because, "When they told me this, it was such a . . . they believed it so strongly. They were convinced of it and they intensely wanted corroboration from me. I think that's what surprised me most—less the idea of demon possession than the parents' fervent belief that this kid was possessed by some evil spirit who had done these evil things."

Not wanting to shatter them with sarcasm or skepticism, or to encourage this line of thinking, Winslow shook his head and said, "I just don't think so. There has been no evidence of his desire to dissociate himself from his actions. He did not say to me, 'I didn't do it, I was told to do it.' He has not told me he was possessed. He has never mentioned Satanism. He has not even said, 'To do this I must have been out of my head.' If you had not come here and told me this, I would never have thought of it."

"We just wanted you to know that's what we think," the parents said, and left.

Thinking about the meeting afterward, Winslow felt he understood what was probably going on with the parents. It had been apparent from things they'd said that they were funda-mentalist Christians who believed in good and evil spirits. They were people for whom the devil was not a concept but a real being, out there, who could show up and take over human beings and make them do things they wouldn't normally do. And they were desperate for an understanding of what had gone wrong with their son. This was the perfect explanation for them. It simplified their ability to account for how their son could have done this, which must have been difficult; and in removing responsibility from him, it also put the unfortunate events outside the family.

In his initial meetings with Vernon Crawford, Dr. Winslow avoided focusing too sharply on what he suspected would be the emotionally charged material, instead prompting the boy to tell his story in his own words, all the while watching out of the corners of his eyes for subtexts. In his presence Crawford was never hallucinatory or irrational, and in fact tried to make a case for himself as a victim of circumstance. He represented the killings as an activity that everyone did that had simply gotten out of hand. And he engaged in a certain amount of finger-pointing, claiming that Peter Burke was behind it all, that he hadn't intended for it to go that far and when he tried to call it quits Burke had made fun of him.

Throughout the early stages of the interview Winslow had the feeling that Crawford was talking for the record. Not nec-essarily in a way that made it seem he was playing Hustle-the-Shrink as that he appeared to be speaking from a state of denial. So anxious was he to cover himself that it became almost predictable, the way he would say one thing that would leave you thinking just the opposite was probably true.

Take the nightmares and hallucinations: Crawford didn't tell Dr. Winslow about them, and when asked, the youth played them down.

"Sleeping okay, Vernon?"

"Yeah, pretty good."

"Sure about that?"

"Oh, sometimes I wake up and feel kinda funny. Bad dreams, you know. But then I go back to sleep."

The staff at D-Home said he woke up screaming on a nightly basis and appeared to be hearing inner voices.

When Dr. Winslow began to probe into Crawford's child-hood and home life for events that would provide insights into his underlying personality structure, the boy became elusive and ambiguous. He admitted that his older brother was a doper and that was how he got started smoking pot, but he voiced no complaints about his relationship with his parents, and denied Winslow access to the private quarters of his deepest feelings. Nor, in this context, was Winslow able to motivate a genuine interest and concern on Crawford's part in self-understanding.

In particular, Winslow wanted to explore Crawford's sexual attitudes. The particulars of the crimes suggested they were committed by someone in whom sexuality and aggression were intertwined and distorted. Often, when a victim is beaten, tortured, and sexually abused in the way the Indians were—when physical aggression becomes eroticized, in other words—it means the offender intended to hurt the person in the same way he was victimized. In this regard the victim symbolizes everything the offender has come to hate about himself and becomes an object of punishment. This is not necessarily so: Sadistic impulses could also be a matter of genetics, or the expression of other deviant obsessions. But extrapolations and intuition told Dr. Winslow that sex was an area of conflict for Vernon Crawford that had a strong bearing on his particular psychopathological variant.

Crawford was extremely uncomfortable with this direction of questioning. Asked about masturbatory practices and early sex play, and whether his experiences had been pleasurable or painful and what form they had taken, Crawford became embarrassed and agitated, forcing Dr. Winslow to make a lot of inferences if he was going to diagnose the precise psychology behind Vernon Crawford's behavior—inferences he might entertain in his own mind, but inferences that were too speculative to put into a report. There was no question that a person who frequently seeks artificial sources of gratification and thrills from the sadistic brutalization of other human beings has severe problems, and Winslow might think that the classic kinds of experiences that would cause or contribute to this kind of abnormal character development included sexual abuse, but without more intimate information, he would be speculating.

When the time came to write up his evaluation, some of the key phrases that Dr. Winslow found himself using were ''an underdeveloped personality with sadistic traits,'' ''marked emotional immaturity,'' and ''an inclination to act out hostile and sexual impulses that most teenagers do not have.'' While he did not assign a specific diagnosis to Crawford's condition, he did feel that the youth was well en route to a full-blown recognizable illness.

"Schizophrenia usually doesn't show up until a certain part of the brain maturates. So when you're sixteen years old it's hard to tell whether this is the normal chaos of adolescence and he's just having a few weird thoughts, more strange perhaps than average but not enough to warrant a psychotic diagnosis. Or, you're seeing something much more serious, like schizophrenia. But I suspected that was what I was seeing."

The Crawford family resided in Beckland Hills, a working-class subdivision on the northern outskirts of Farmington. The trim look-alike houses and crew-cut lawns gave the neighborhood a 1950s suburban ambience, but the backyards of the farthest houses bordered on open range that stretched all the way to the Colorado state line.

Few, if any, of the men who lived there were college educated, but they made good money working in the oil fields, for gas companies, or at one of the power plants. They came from all over—Oklahoma, Kansas, Minnesota—and were the outdoorsy types: Boats and snowmobiles shared the garage with their pickup trucks. Many belonged to the Elks Club, where they went on weekends to smoke and drink and dance. In summer they watched their sons play baseball. This is a big Connie Mack town; the Connie Mack World Series is held here.

As for the women, they were raised to be content as homemakers. Besides, their husbands didn't want their wives working outside the home—something to do with male pride, ego, and where a woman belonged. Each morning they would put on makeup before they cleaned house, and when their favorite soaps were over they would shop for groceries. All the women smoked heavily—Winston and Marlboro—and were perpetually running out of cigarettes, which sent them dashing across the street to borrow two or three from their neighbor. Often they stayed for coffee and to chat, but were sure to be home by the time their husbands returned. If they weren't happy they rarely realized it until after the children left home.

On paper, Earl Crawford conformed to the community profile. During the week he worked for El Paso Natural Gas in camp maintenance, painting company houses, and he struck out for the Colorado mountains in his RV on weekends and on vacations. But in person there was something about him that did not support the image of the roughneck at home in the out-of-doors. Although he was a burly man he had rounded shoulders and a slightly stooped posture, and there was a softness about him that seemed more than flesh deep. Certain character subtleties also marked him as different than you'd expect. His speech and manner were timorous; on occasion his face would take on an open-mouthed expression that looked almost simple-minded; and yet there was also something evasive and sly about him that showed most in his eyes. They rarely met another's in direct contact, constantly darting from side to side with a fretfulness that could be taken for a nervous disposition, or the tic of a guilty conscience. It was as though he carried the burden of a secret in his past, something hush-hush, and the fear of discovery left him permanently jittery.

Ida Crawford, in contrast, was a stout and brash Oklahoma woman with a coarseness about her that was captured in the way she smoked her cigarettes. Once lit, they stayed in her mouth and she talked and laughed around them until she used them to light another. Without a peep from Earl, Ida sold Fuller Brush products and did well enough in sales to become the area manager.

In a neighborhood where most of the residents thought alike and asked little of one another except company, it did not go unnoticed that the Crawfords kept to themselves. Earl wasn't much for palling around with other men; and when he did go, say, on a hunting trip, rather than share a bunk in the cabin he stayed by himself in his own trailer. Nor did Ida mix with other women. On an individual basis each displayed a certain civic-mindedness—he was a volunteer on the Sheriff's Posse and she was a member of the volunteer fire department—and together they bowled in a coed league, but they were neither an outgoing nor a sociable couple.

And they exhibited a wariness about those living around them. One neighbor whose backyard abutted theirs characterized it as a "strange watchfulness. Not like they were voyeurs. More as if they were paranoid about being watched themselves."

Enough people would also speak about the parents' approach to discipline within the household to make it worth mentioning. Apparently *her* hand ruled, and she would light into *him* if he tried to correct the kids. Not only that, it was rare for Ida to be troubled by the thought that her kids might be in the wrong. After an altercation involving one of the Crawford boys, a next-door mother tried to talk to her about this. She came away thinking "Protective, maternal instincts are one thing. But the way that woman just flat-out said, 'My kids wouldn't do that'—well, as time showed, she was flat-out wrong."

Vernon had an older brother by four years, named Dalton, and by just about every account he was a nasty, brutish kid. "A cruel turkey," in the words of a peer. "He liked to kill animals, just to kill them, especially if somebody liked them. One time he found a snake and he was throwing it up in the air with a stick. I told him I'd trade him my old chemistry set for it, just to get him to let it go. He laughed and said 'No deal' and beat it to death."

With smaller kids he was just as rough, bullying them into carrying his schoolbooks home from the bus or shagging flies for him when he wanted to practice hitting baseballs at the park. He sported homemade tattoos when he was just a kid—an eagle and a snake—and when he was barely in his teens he was already selling joints at the local 7-Eleven for a dollar. The greatest shock for those acquainted with the two Crawford boys, when it was announced that one of them had been arrested for murdering Indians, was which boy stood accused. They thought the authorities must have had it wrong. They expected as much of Dalton, but not "Vern the Nerd," as everyone called the other.

Most boys who hold on to their baby fat throughout elementary school tend to hang back, and some of Vernon's reserve was probably in reaction to the wild energies that drove his older brother. But even though he was pudgy and reticent he was always game. For the youth of Beckland Hills, the wilderness to the north was their playground, and Vernon would happily trap lizards, climb the sandstone bluffs, build forts, and play war. Opposing armies would be made up of three or four kids to a side, Saturday morning would be spent digging trenches in the sand, the rest of the weekend was a continual round of raids, and Vernon was a reliable infantryman.

Then for unknown reasons Vernon turned strange. Something—some event, some experience, some development—seemed to transform him from a regular kid into the neighborhood sissy. No one knew what to attribute it to, but everyone noticed the change. His grade-school teachers reported "immature behavior" and "childish talk" in class. His neighborhood friends noticed he suddenly became uncharacteristically withdrawn, lacking in self-confidence, and subject to mood shifts that were inappropriate to the circumstances. He no longer appeared to enjoy the usual activities, and when he did engage in them his emotional overreactions to certain situations earned him the label "crybaby." If he scratched an elbow or knee in the normal course of roughhousing, he would quit and go home, complaining that everyone was out to get him. Popped on the shoulder, even in jest, he was apt to burst into tears.

Not surprisingly, his popularity in the neighborhood diminished; and the disaffection apparently was mutual because now, rather than finding pleasure in a game of catch or camping out with kids his own age, Vernon could be found playing with trucks in the dirt with the younger children in the subdivision.

While a number of the neighbors noticed Vernon's affinity for children, none associated it with a problem, and nothing out of the ordinary was reported to them by the kids. The only insight into what might have been going on with Vernon would come from his father.

"Possibly it came from me, because I'm this way with kids. I love to get close to them. When I was working for the company as a painter, we'd go into people's homes and they'd have little kids, and it was a challenge to me to get close to those kids. If I'm with a kid and he shys and backs away from me, I want to overcome his resistance and I'll do what I can to get him to come, let me hug him, pick him up. And I'll keep trying until I win him over, get him to be friendly with me. It gives me a good feeling to get a strange kid to come to me, you know, and let me hold him. I don't know why."

Nor did Vernon give an accounting for his feeling for kids. And before long it no longer stood out as so unusual, coinciding as it did with a growing eccentricity in other areas.

Accounts of Vernon's odd behavior from classmates in junior high school put him on the fringe when it came to the normal antics of adolescence. His idea of a joke was to ask classmates if they wanted to see a human finger he'd found, and when they expressed curiosity he would hold out a little box that contained what appeared to be a bloody amputated finger on a bed of cotton, but was actually his own Mercurochrome-dabbed finger stuck through a hole in the bottom of the box.

This fascination with mutilation themes and body parts soon caught the attention of his teachers.

Jackie Nielsen was his eighth-grade art instructor and she

remembers that she first suspected he was a disturbed young boy when he handed her a drawing of naked Indians one day after class. She was savvy enough to know this was an age when many youths were experiencing first-time sexual urges, which they often fantasized about in art. What made these drawings troubling to her was the violence also expressed: The Indians were being drawn-and-quartered by hot rods blasting toward the four corners of the page.

Unsure about how she should interpret these artworks, Ms. Nielsen tried to talk to Vernon to determine what was going on in his mind. She came away with the distinct impression that something drastic had happened at home and his behavior was a statement to his parents as well as others, but he refused to say what was bothering him specifically.

After school one day she shared her concerns with Vernon's English teacher, Judy Turner, who told her she too was observing abnormal tendencies.

I had Vernon in English when he was in junior high school, and if I would give the students an essay to write or a paragraph after reading a story, about 90 percent of the time his stories were very sad, very depressing, and very sadistic.

We had a mystery unit, and sometimes I would assign an art project to go with it; a diorama or something like that. His diorama was a bed with a decapitated head in it, and the body hanging in the corner. Now a lot of kids will do spooky, scary things, especially around Halloween. They'll do little caskets, or even a hanging body. But not a decapitated one. Those are the kinds of things he would come up with.

And periodically he would be extremely volatile. We might be talking about a particular topic and he would get emotional and upset and react unusually and violently to whatever it was we were talking about. As if he himself were personally involved or thinking about something that was associated with the topic. Let me give you an example. One time the class was discussing friendship, and how it was important to have friends we could talk to, confide in. And that seemed to disturb him. He'd say he didn't have any friends. Or he'd say, "A lot of people will talk to you, but they're not really your friend." Another time we talked about families, about closeness between sisters and brothers and doing things together, that sort of thing. He didn't like that at all either. "Families aren't like that," he'd say. And it wouldn't be just in the course of a discussion. He'd be sitting there very calm and very placid, and I would think he wasn't even listening to what we were saying, and then he would just interrupt. It wouldn't be his turn, he wouldn't ask if he could comment, or whatever. He'd just blurt it out, as if it were simmering inside him and finally boiled over. Then, after class, it was "I'm sorry, Mrs. Turner, I shouldn't have said that." I would try to talk with him about what it was that was bothering him, but he didn't want to talk about it.

I don't think he had any particular hate for Indians. I remember him sitting in class beside a boy who was part Anglo and part Indian, and he had some hostilities because he wasn't accepted by either group. But Vernon didn't object. It didn't seem to matter if he sat next to an Indian or Mexican or whatever. And it did to some. They'd come right out and say, "I don't want to sit beside him." And we would talk about different cultures and their beliefs and that never seemed to have an effect on Vernon. At least not in my class.

Deep down I knew when he was doing this stuff that . . . well, it was probably a cry for help. But I didn't know how to help. It's real hard for a teacher to go to a parent and say, "I think there's something wrong with your child." Parents almost always stick up for their kids—say "Who are you to say that? Mind your own business." Today we have a law that requires us to do that, and we are protected by law. Then we weren't.

I can recall when we wrote about feelings, if we equated them to a color, his were always black. And he would talk about the devil a lot. In his stories the devil would play a big part in the direction the character would take. He would tell the character to . . . burn a house down, for instance. In one it was take a girl out into the country and . . . he didn't talk about rape, just "hurt" her is what he would say. Lord forbid, I didn't want to know how. I didn't want to get into that. I was afraid he'd tell me, then what would I do?

By the time Vernon Crawford entered Farmington High School his strangeness was almost legendary. A crooked smirk tugged at one corner of his thick-lipped mouth, and when he was moved to laughter he would shake with whooping convulsions that left him breathless. "It was a crazy laugh," remembers a classmate. "You hear it on TV all the time, on horror shows. At first, just like on TV, it was funny. Until it gets to the point you recognize it's someone who has serious problems. Then it's scary." There were people who, quite frankly, couldn't stand to be around him just because of his laugh. Add to that a taste in clothes that rejected the typical jeans and T-shirt for dark and gloomy patterns, a case of acne so bad it looked catching, and a hairstyle all his own (unwashed, combed from the crown forward, with a flip at the end to keep it out of his eyes), and it was small wonder no one wanted to sit beside Vernon Crawford in class, and he was always eating by himself in the lunchroom.

A classmate remembers: "There were different in-groups back then. You had the hippies, the long-hairs, who drove vans, Volkswagen buses, pieces of shit primarily, whatever would run, and smoked cigarettes and pot. You had the jocks, who were the apples of Mother and Daddy's eye, had 'Vettes and Camaros and hung out in front of the cafeteria, near the gym entrance. And you had the goat-ropers, your cowboys, with their pickups, hats, and snuff tins in the back pocket of their jeans. It was really a cliquey place, though I don't suppose it was much different from any other high school in America back then. Anyway, if you weren't in you were out, and Vernon Crawford was as far out as you get. There was something funny about him, and he did nothing to hide it. Whatever it was, nobody I knew wanted anything to do with him."

Anecdotes accounting for his lack in popularity abound.

He would carry pranks beyond the point where they were funny to anybody but himself. Once he pushed two girls into a small closet, locked the door, and said he wasn't going to let them out. They laughed, sure that he was kidding, and waited for him to open the door. Time passed—two hours before a teacher heard them calling for help.

He had a morbid sense of humor. Girls would blanch and recoil when he would shake a Baggie in front of them full of something gushy and ask them if they wanted to see his collection of deer brains and dog hearts. And he would get a big laugh out of their revulsion.

An effeminacy became more pronounced. Another classmate remembers: "Looking back on him now, I almost want to say he had what have come to be known as gay qualities. His voice was pitched high and had a lilt to it. I can still see him in this one swimming class we had together. He was always cold; way colder than anybody else, it seemed. And a real woos about getting wet. He'd tippy-toe around the edge of the pool, dip a big toe in, shiver, and hold his elbows. No one else did that. No one.''

The list of oddities goes on; but nothing else he did compares to the thrill he seemed to get from rolling Navajos.

According to those who knew Vernon during this period, it was when he turned sixteen, passed his driver's test, and was given the use of a Ford Galaxie by his father that things changed for the even worse. The fact that he had access to an automobile and others didn't gave him a sudden popularity. Enjoying his new status, he would cruise Main with a carful of kids. Or he and a couple of boys would go to the bowling alley to try and pick up girls (although he never seemed to be interested in girls, he just supplied the ride). And riding around the south side of town, whenever Vernon spotted a drunk Indian he would pull up beside him, someone would jump out and grab a hat, and he would be the getaway driver.

Soon he was crashing parties (because he was rarely invited), not to listen to music or dance, but to see if he could get someone to go downtown with him and hassle drunk Indians.

"We don't think so. You've got the wrong place, Vernon," was the customary response from those disgusted with his recruitment efforts, which averaged 90 to 95 percent of the party. Now and then, however, someone would say Why not? and follow him out.

"He wasn't into physical harm, yet," one who went along remembers. "Just giving them a hard time."

That soon changed. Once he got a taste of it, he developed an appetite. By the time he was a junior he lived for Friday and Saturday nights, when he would head for the alleys behind Harry's Lounge and the Esquire liquor store on a search-and-destroy mission. Now he was no longer content just giving them a hard time or hunting for souvenirs. Something else was going on. Doing violent things to defenseless drunks excited him in a peculiar way, and he would attack them savagely, with no other apparent intent than to inflict pain.

According to some of those who went along with him on these escapades, this escalation led to his stuffing them in the trunk of his car and taking them out into the hills. He had to keep an eye out for cops on patrol downtown, but in the canyons north of the city he could be unrestrained in what he wanted to do. Which was to raise the violence to a higher level. Once he tied one to a tree and proceeded to beat and kick him mercilessly. Another time he tied one with a rope to the back of his car and dragged him around the desert.

Remembers one classmate: "I was with Vernon one time when he pulled up beside an intoxicated Indian and said, 'Let's go to the caves and drink some beer.' The guy misunderstood him. Thought he was saying, 'I'll give you some cake and beer.' And that sounded good enough to him to get in the car. You'd think the guy would have been smarter than that. Surely he knew enough to beware of white teenagers on weekends. Nevertheless, he got in the car and, I think there were four or five of us, we squeezed together to make room. So we go out into the hills, pushed him out of the car, knocked him down, and were beating up on him, but he offered no resistance. He just lay there, curled up, playing possum, which took the fun out of it. So what does Vernon do? He says to us, 'Get back in the car. I'll run over him.' 'Nothing doing,' I said. And I walked home that night."

It was evident to most of those who accompanied Vernon that his desire to hurt people came from some source other than their own for accompanying him. They might get their punches in, but when they backed off he would step up the beating. He took things a lot further than they were comfortable going, getting a thrill out of hurting people, requiring ever more extreme experiences to satisfy himself, and often taking the abuse in a different direction than anyone else was inclined to go.

Another classmate recalls that Vernon seemed to get some kind of sexual charge out of what he was doing: taking their clothes off and aiming his attacks at the genitals; the adrenaline rush of danger and excitement building to a discharge of raw, aggressive energy; and afterward, driving home, an expression of exquisite pleasure: "Man, that was good."

No one else did that. No one. And sensing that this was leading to something worse, most pulled back, making up excuses the next time he invited them to go cruising.

The world saw two Vernon Crawfords during this period. He struck many who met him as a contained youth, exceptionally polite to adults, diffident even, who may have had his idiosyncrasies, but then most students during the seventies seemed to be marching out of step. And in contrast to those whose rebellious attitudes put them in constant conflict with school authorities, Vernon, on the surface, appeared to have a social conscience. He was a volunteer in the Future Teachers of America program. Several mornings each week he would go to an elementary school on the other side of town where he worked as a teacher's aide to second-graders. Furthermore, on a questionnaire handed out to all students, in the space for club memberships, while he belonged to none, he wrote he would be interested in joining any club where he could go around town helping people.

And yet those who spent more time around him would voice the common refrain: "He was on a weird trip." He would sit under a sunlamp until his face blistered with second-degree burns, listen to rock-and-roll music on headphones with the volume cranked up as loud as it could go. And, baring sharp teeth in a malicious grin, he would brag in the school corridors about degenerate things he had done to drunken Indians over the previous weekend. Some of his boasts were so outrageous his listeners would think he was putting them on, making up stories. To back them up he would invite disbelievers to his locker, where he claimed to have a collection of Indian fingers, taken the way GIs in Vietnam took Vietcong ears. There, he would sometimes pull the old finger-in-a-box routine, or bring out a swollen and bloody finger that looked very real, but in truth was rubber and had been purchased in an Albuquerque novelty store.

Few people at the time seem to have given a great deal of thought to what was going on with Vernon Crawford. It was easier to dismiss his tasteless statements and actions as a desperate means of gaining attention; and any reaction would be a form of reward. Those few who spent time with him blamed it on drugs. Apparently it was nothing for him to drink (beer) and smoke (pot) himself silly. "I used to blow grass with him on the way to school when we were in junior high," recalls a kid from the neighborhood. Another tells of going to the Crawford house to listen to music, and Vernon sneaking into his parents' medicine cabinet, shaking a handful of pills out of a bottle, and swallowing the lot. But not even they would go so far as to try and explain his crimes as those of a drug-addled kook who went grossly out of control when he got high.

Only one person in authority, it seemed, recognized there was something dreadfully wrong with Vernon, and that was his high school history teacher, Bea Bleakeley.

I must confess Vernon was a boy who did not appeal to me a lot. He was sort of . . . smarmy. I really can't—well, he always tried so hard to be so nice to me, no matter what I said. He watered my plants and would want to be helpful in all sorts of ways. Butter would melt in his mouth he was so sweet. He reminded me of . . . remember the TV show "Leave It to Beaver"? Remember Eddie Haskell? And I guess what put me off was I never felt it was a true niceness. It rang false. There was so much sincerity it struck me as insincere, in a creepy sickening way.

He was never an outstanding student, but over the course of that year he got steadily worse. Deteriorated, really, as far as his work, attendance, attitude. At first I attributed it to drugs, but I have to say he was more abnormal than drugs would explain. So I went down to the office, to the vice-principal, and said I was concerned about this boy. I found his responses disturbing, and I thought he needed psychiatric help. I was told they would keep an eye on him, which I took to mean my job was to teach, not play counselor.

I really feel like I missed the boat with Vernon. I sensed strangeness and oddness. I sensed dis-ease within his soul. Frustration and unhappiness. But I never saw anger or violence. When I heard he was going to be arrested after school—one of the teachers at lunch that day told me Vernon had been bragging and the police were going to pick him up—I felt Vernon was the kind who would say he did it when he didn't. And to me this was even sicker in a way. That he would get a perverse pleasure, some secret joy, out of saying all these grisly things just to make people think he did it. To me it takes a really weird person to claim they've done something like he did when they haven't, and I thought he was twisted enough to get a big kick out of the attention it would bring him.

I had him the very last hour the day I heard they were going to arrest him. It was a Friday and there weren't many kids in class, and I was always carrying things from the classroom to my car, back and forth. On this particular day I'd parked way at the end of the parking lot. I didn't want to have to lug what I had all that way by myself, so I said, "Would anybody like to help me carry these things to my car?" And guess who jumped up? Sweet Vernon, who would do anything for me. My heart sank. I still did not believe he'd done it, but I did think if I'd heard who was going to be arrested, he might have heard.

Countless times I'd given kids the keys to my car with instructions and never worried about it. But I didn't dare hand Vernon the keys because I thought he might take off. In case he panicked I didn't want to be the one to give him a way to get away. So I said I would come too.

I wasn't the least bit nervous. I felt no personal threat whatsoever from Vernon. Maybe he didn't feel hostility toward me and that's why I didn't pick it up. Maybe it was because he was always currying my favor and I was feeling guilty because I didn't like him. And even though I'd been told what he was going to be arrested for, I still didn't believe he'd done it. I thought once the police checked him out they'd find he was lying and I'd see him in class Monday.

I don't know how I missed the violence. Unless . . . you know what I'm reminded of? Remember that scene in Psycho, *at the end, when Anthony Perkins says, "You know me. I wouldn't hurt a fly"?*

Vernon and I walked all the way down that deserted parking lot together, and back, and that was the last time I ever saw him.

Dr. Ben Cummins met only once with Peter Burke because the way the Juvenile Code read a youth had to be at least sixteen years of age before he could even be considered for a bind-over for adult trial. At fifteen, Peter Burke's offense was automatically classified as an act of delinquency, and no matter what an evaluation turned up, he was going to be treated the same as if he had been caught stealing hubcaps.

Putting a finer point on the irony, based on the little he saw and heard, Dr. Cummins suspected that this boy might well have been the most incorrigible of the lot. It didn't seem to matter to Peter Burke that he had killed people.

A file containing sketchy biographical information was supplied prior to the interview that let Dr. Cummins know family history alone could explain a lot of the way Peter Burke turned out. Just the outline—the death of his father in an oil fire when the boy was small, a mother who apparently drank herself to death—made it easy to imagine how someone roughed up by that kind of a history could go wrong.

But it was not an inevitable connection. Research indicated there were people who, having had similar experiences in their past, might just as logically have developed a strong sense of altruism. Even those whose reaction was manifested in hateful feelings and hostility, while they might sometimes feel like striking out at someone who angered them, that didn't mean they would do it. The fact that Peter Burke had a twin brother who started out at the same place, only thirteen minutes later, and who the record indicated was a decent kid, appeared to argue that circumstance alone could not adequately explain why Peter Burke had ended up an antisocial, deviant rogue by the time he was fifteen.

So for Dr. Cummins, the real issue to be explored was what separated this youth? What were the inner workings that coerced him to step over a line that was statistically rare and follow a murderous behavior pattern?

But that was something which would be learned only if Burke was willing to cooperate, which he was not. Dr. Cummins was unable to open him even a little bit. Burke spoke with long pauses between sentences, and sometimes didn't even bother to answer when asked a question. He was uncommunicative in a way that made Cummins's attempts at conversation as off-putting as a police interrogation. Not that Cummins really expected him to be able to explain what he'd felt that made him want to do what he'd done. He doubted if Burke's self-awareness included that information. That was true of most adolescents: They weren't in touch with their feelings; they acted without thinking much about their actions or the consequences, leaving it to others to deduce from their behavior what was going on with them.

If he'd had to guess, Dr. Cummins felt some of the psychodynamics of the crime were probably related to the fact that the boy had lost his parents to fire and alcohol. And he felt Peter Burke had probably veered off on a course by the time he was eleven or twelve that would be extremely difficult to turn around. It was unlikely this was something he was just going to grow out of. Indeed, the youth exhibited many of the usual symptoms that applied to a standard psychiatric diagnosis of the sociopathic personality: He was in constant conflict with society, exhibited no loyalty or concern for others, ignored social codes and values and acted only in response to his own desires and impulses, learned little from experience, and remained untouched by punishment.

Two family photos immortalize Ted and Doreen Burke. In one, Ted, tall and handsome, poses beside a tanker truck wearing a leather jacket and a white-toothed grin, looking like a World War II flyboy just returned from a mission that has made him a hero. In the other, Doreen, brown curls floating on the shoulders of a tight gray sweater, smiles shyly, like a 1940s sorority girl waiting to be asked to dance. You get the impression that each was the other's photographer and they had a game going—

that as soon as she snapped his photo he saluted the camera with a beer, and when she heard the shutter click her nose wrinkled with laughter.

If you look at their lives starting with their romantic beginnings (he was a Missouri farmboy football player, she a piano-playing uptown girl, and over parental objections they had eloped to California) and follow them through the day they moved into a new three-bedroom brick house (in Sunset Heights, a new development situated on a leveled hill with luminous views to the west) to the birth of twins (whom they named after the Apostles Peter and Paul, as an expression of thanks), the Burkes were almost a fifties poster couple. But it was all downhill from there.

The twins were still in kindergarten when Ted, employed by a gasoline distributor, was unloading volatiles from a diesel truck and a spark set off an explosion. With clothes aflame he staggered toward a nearby irrigation ditch where he was found by a passerby. Burn victims don't always look so bad at first, but as the damage continues its relentless course the disfigurement and pain get worse. He was burned over 50 percent of his body, severely around the face and chest, and had taken a lot of heat and gas into his lungs. He lingered for almost two weeks, conscious much of the time, though it would have been better for him, and easier on his wife, if he weren't.

His death devastated Doreen, who acted as if she had been stripped of her purpose in life and, after that, to all appearances, seemed incapable of facing life without him unless she had a drink in her hand. As the Doreen all her friends thought they knew disappeared in an alcoholic slide, a slovenly irresponsible drunkard took her place. To this day, women who knew Doreen when her husband was alive will turn with a start whenever they pass someone wearing White Shoulders perfume and think of Doreen Burke; this miserable substitute paid little attention to personal grooming, wore the same clothes for days running, and rarely brushed her hair. Completing the loss of discretion and decorum, this woman who went by the name of Doreen, but looked and behaved nothing like her, began to live from one drink and one man to the next.

Judging by appearances, she was bent on destroying by rejection everything that had meant anything to her before, including her children. There had been two before the twins—a boy and a girl, Rollie and Glenda—and now she all but handed the responsibilities of motherhood over to Glenda. But as soon as she was old enough to go out on her own, Glenda left, leaving it up to Rollie, who was in the seventh grade at the time, to function as the parent, getting the twins ready for school in the morning, cleaning house, doing the laundry, cooking the meals, basically taking care of two boys and a mother.

During this time friends who had a hard time believing Doreen could fall so low so fast did what they could to slow her descent. Even the family doctor, who was treating her for various alcohol-related ailments and who felt she was a better woman than this, spoke up and appealed for her to drink less, if only for her health. But she was impervious to admonitions and advice, and by 1972, 2301 Ridgecrest Drive, the Burke address, was a bleeding sore in a neighborhood that had become staunchly middle class. The house not only needed painting and the yard watering, those who had ventured inside were appalled at the clutter and filth. Clothes were strewn around the floor and furniture; the sink was piled high with dirty dishes, which accounted for the candy wrappers and fast-food containers spilling from the overfilled garbage cans. When the doors and windows were open the place reeked like an open container.

Rumors of drunkenness and promiscuity had been making the rounds of the neighborhood for some time when Doreen scandalized the gossip-mongers by letting a stranger move in. They said her judgment was as pickled as her system when she decided to bring Dave home. The guy was ten years younger and a half-foot shorter than Doreen and looked like an unwashed hippie. The last job he'd had was in a traveling carnival and since then he'd been drifting. The only thing they had in common was a preference for Schlitz and they could waste whole days guzzling a case of it. It was painfully obvious to others that this guy was a sleazy hustler, a worthless freeloader taking advantage of a pitiful, lonely widow who was crashing, but she would hear none of it. The closest she would ever come even to explaining would be a letter to an old friend living out of state, in which she admitted, "There's no fool like an old fool. But what a lover!"

That same friend remembers when, not long after receiving that letter, she returned to Farmington: "Doreen called and said she was coming over. We hadn't seen her since our return and she staggered in with a six-pack in her hand, already drunk. And she insisted we have one with her—this is in the morning, mind you. Well, she rattled off about this guy, who gave me the creeps when I saw him, but she insisted he made her happy. And, I don't know, it just seemed like she was trying too hard to convince us she was doing great when it was apparent her life was going down the drain. Then I stopped listening and started worrying about her driving home by herself."

Just when people began to wonder how much longer she could go on living like this, on a July afternoon in 1973, Doreen collapsed as if she'd been hit on the head with a hammer. A brain aneurysm, the doctors said. According to friends, "Her body just said, Enough, I can't take it anymore."

Dead at the age of forty-five, it was a pathetic conclusion to an immeasurably sad life. And a tragic epilogue was added when, not one year later, her son Peter was picked up for the cold-blooded murder of three alcoholics.

Even though they were fraternal twins, you hardly knew they were brothers. Early on they had to deal with the reaction of strangers who made a fuss over how alike they looked, how you couldn't tell them apart. But their mother's taste in boys' shirts had a lot to do with that—signal flags and checks, bought by the pair—and Paul, the secondborn, knew there was a distinct difference between them "from day one. He was always a lot bigger than I was. And I guess you'd have to say he was more mischievous to begin with too."

Neighbors with children were also quick to single out Peter as the problem child when he was still a toddler. Tom Hynes, before he became assistant district attorney, lived several houses down from the Burkes, and remembers that whenever Peter Burke was around his kids, someone usually ended up crying. Invariably, the instigator was Peter. "If I knew he was around, I kept an eye on what was going on. I always felt uneasy about him. He would barge in and grab something from one of the kids, then push them to the ground. He was that kind of kid."

In school, as early as the second grade he was recommended for a special-education class. "Adjustment problems" and "Lack of achievement" were given as reasons. He stands out in the memory of his third-grade teacher because "He did not have a normal facial expression. It was very, very cold. No emotions showed on his face whatsoever. And very, very calculating. You never knew what he was thinking." She was used to kids that age expressing themselves with joyous spontaneity, and remembers Peter Burke sitting at his desk watching her with a dour expression, a solitary black rock rising out of a sea of jubilant faces.

Even at home he was trouble. His older brother's and sister's rooms were off-limits, but if he felt like it he would go in anyway, rummage through their stuff, and if he found something to his liking, claim it as his by right of want. And that wasn't the only time he behaved as if everything around him was there for the taking. If he felt like going for a bike ride he would walk around the neighborhood and when he spotted a two-wheeler not in use, simply take it without asking. This willful and heedless attitude found its most extreme form when he started stealing money from his mother's purse. With sixty, eighty, a hundred dollars in his pocket he would head downtown, buy himself lunch, mosey over to a department store, and purchase a bunch of new toys . . . treating any of the neighborhood kids who wanted to come along.

Naturally his mother, who lived from check to check, was put out with him when he pulled a stunt like this. But curiously, Doreen was lenient when it came to disciplining Pete, and reacted defensively whenever he was criticized to her face. Mothers in the neighborhood, when they came to her with a complaint or tried to talk to her about her son, found she refused to listen. Trying to make sense of the bond she seemed to feel with Peter, one neighbor attributed it to the fact that when he was just two months old he contracted whooping cough and almost died; and because Doreen came so close to losing him then, she was overprotective of him ever after. Whatever the reason, Doreen was closer to Pete than any of her other kids, and it was the impression of those who were aware of this that he took advantage of it, and could have gotten away with murder.

The relationship between the twins was not as harmonious, by any means. Blood ties in no way meant kindred spirits, and the difference in their personalities led them to be referred to as the "Light Twin" and the "Dark Twin." Paul was outgoing, well liked, easy to get along with. In the summer he was always on the go, playing outside, participating in a pickup football or basketball game with the neighborhood kids. Pete, on the other hand, was an extreme introvert who gave you the feeling he didn't like people and didn't trust them—an attitude, it hardly need be said, that did not win him many friends. He didn't seem to have the least interest in sports, and if he wasn't hanging out at home with his mom, he would often just stand on the street corner, smoking cigarettes and watching cars go by. To passersby it seemed he was giving them the evil eye, reviewing various options, and about to do the devil's work.

According to Paul they both knew right from wrong, but Pete "was always going to do what he goddamn pleased." Although the reasons for many of his actions were totally obscure to his twin brother—like when he took a hammer and went out in the yard and beat holes in the fence, or when he got the pruning shears from the garage and went around the house pruning the shrubs down to nothing—what was all too clear was his total lack of conscience. "Sorry" was not a word in Pete's vocabulary. He would never apologize for his misdeeds, or give the impression he had any misgivings about anything he did. He could walk away from a wrong as if it wasn't his bother because it was past, without thinking about the consequences or seeming to care much if they caught up with him.

Pete was always doing what he shouldn't. "All I heard about was Pete did this, Pete did that. He was always out of line, it seemed," his brother remembers. And because Paul managed to avoid trouble, people would say to Pete, "Why can't you be more like your brother?" Paul was constantly held up as an example of goodness that contrasted to his badness. This was true to such an extent that it fostered a resentment in Pete, and rather than try and compete with his better half on terms not of his own choosing, he would punish him, take it out on his smaller brother in a variety of ways, ranging from petty to nasty. It might be a pinch, a shove, or a punch, and it might be the destruction of something personal. Paul loved airplanes and would painstakingly glue and paint model planes, only to have Pete bust them up in reaction to a reprimand that included a reference to Saint Paul.

Their respective performances in school were another difference. Throughout elementary school Paul received good grades and praise from teachers on his report cards, while Pete was absolutely unproductive and a constant behavior problem. By the time he was in junior high his Student Discipline Report read this way: "Disrespectful to Mrs. Alvis. Attended open house bugging teachers. Skipped 6th period. Didn't come to school. Suspended from school. Cigarettes in his pocket. [His brand was Kool.] Goofing off in study hall. Lighting firecrackers." And finally, "Ten swats."

Corporal punishment with a wood paddle was still in use in the Farmington schools, and stoically Pete Burke had absorbed the record number of swats ever administered to a student in a single session. But the punishment left him unfazed, and school authorities miffed. Recalls a vice-principal: "There was only so much you could do with someone like him. The code he lived by was such that the reasonable deterrents didn't seem to make any difference to him."

At one point both boys were tested by a guidance counselor, and even though Pete was hard to test—"He was quiet and surly, difficult to work with," according to the examiner—both were found to be possessed of an equal share of smarts. They were found to have IQs in the range where, if properly motivated, they could be considered college material.

Taking it as a challenge to find out what was holding Peter back, what was wrong with him that he did not feel what other kids that age seemed to feel, the counselor arranged for a conference with Doreen Burke, who showed up for the meeting late, intoxicated, and uninterested.

By this time most of his teachers were aware he came from a household where domestic tranquillity was unknown, but there existed a disagreement between faculty and administration on just how to handle him. His English teacher, Barbara Alvis, remembers feeling caught in the middle.

I got Peter Burke when he was in the ninth grade and he stands out in my mind as a constant problem. He was disobedient and disruptive; he was hostile, impudent, and unmanageable. He wouldn't do his work, he would sit in the back of the room and . . . periodically I would check the students' desks and there was a lot of writing on his. Four-letter words, shocking language, scrawled into the lamination. I wasn't particularly afraid of him, but I kept a close eye on him and never felt I could turn my back on him. I didn't trust him. He was just one of those kids you have to keep your finger on all the time. At times I was worried about losing control of the class with him in there.

On several occasions I went down to the principal's office and spoke to Mr. Crowley about him. But Mr. Crowley was very, very sympathetic towards Peter Burke because of the home situation. I assumed he'd had dealings with the mother before because he said there was no point in trying to talk with her, she would not respond. And he himself did not seem to want to do much as far as punishment because of that, which

*put me in a difficult position. It was clear to me that he was a
boy who had been let go. There was no control at home. And
people like Mr. Crowley, they didn't want to do anything because they felt that, you know, somebody had to express some
love and compassion for a child like that.*

*I didn't feel that way. I felt that he was getting away with far
too much and if somebody didn't draw the line . . . well, I had
a friend who taught next to me, and we both commented how
he was the type who was going to end up in the New Mexico
Boys School someday.*

He didn't like school, sports were a bore, he didn't have any
close friends—the only thing he did express an interest in was
cars. He was always checking out cars. When he was just ten
years old he was leaving the house and going downtown to the
auto dealerships to admire the new cars in the showroom windows. An avid reader of *Car and Driver* and *Motor Trend*,
often he was more conversant about the new models than the
salesmen. "The only thing I ever heard him say he wanted to
do with his life," Paul remembers, "was test cars for the motor
magazines."

By this time it was just the twins and their mother at home,
but Doreen's need for companionship meant there was a steady
stream of men coming around the house. When she decided to
let one move in with her it introduced a whole new dynamic of
discord, particularly with Pete. Used to being his mother's
favorite, he was particularly resentful at this expansion of the
household by someone who dominated his mother's attention.
Chronically unreceptive to instruction or authority, he refused
to recognize this substitute-father's right to tell him anything.

Neighbors report looking out their windows at night and
seeing Pete sitting by himself on the curb in front of his house,
while his mother partied inside. It did not surprise them in the
least when they heard he had run away.

*Pete wasn't my best friend or anything. He lived in the
neighborhood and I felt real sorry for him, which was the main
reason I hung around with him. I knew his mother was an
alcoholic and the guy she was living with was a big drinker
himself, 'cause I walked by the house on my way to school and
I'd stop and pick him up and they'd be there with drinks in their
hands. Either started early or were still going. I knew Pete for
two or three years and never saw her sober once.*

One day we were walking to school and Pete said he wanted

to get away from his family. I had no problems with my family,
I was just adventurous. I'd always wanted to go someplace
where I hadn't been before, so I was ready to go wherever the
wind blows. He wanted to go to Dallas, where his sister lived.
So instead of going to school we were off and running for
Dallas.

We had less than two dollars between us. We just stuck out
our thumbs and caught a ride to Albuquerque and kept going
from there. We didn't do much eating or sleeping. Where we
did sleep finally was in Amarillo. We were hanging out in the
lobby of a Ramada Inn and this bellhop let us stay in a room
that a couple had checked out of early. So we stayed there
about four hours, took a shower, then left. An hour later we
were picked up by the highway patrol for hitchhiking and they
called our parents. End of trip.

Pete was a pretty moody guy who didn't seem to give a shit
about anything. Always seemed like he was angry at life. There
was absolutely no parental control at home. He could come
and go when he wanted, stay out to all hours, and nobody
cared because they were drunk. Or if his mother did say some-
thing he paid no attention for the same reason.

Some of the things he did, I don't think he thought about
what would happen, because he'd never had to answer to
anybody. I don't remember him being especially aggressive.
Oh, he was kind of mean to animals. He didn't like cats or
dogs. He'd boot a cat if it walked up to him. As far as people,
I don't know that he liked a whole lot of people either. I mean,
he was pretty much afraid of people I think. He wouldn't stand
up and fight anybody. Even if he was in the right he wouldn't
stand up for himself, so a lot of people used to pick on him. If
he did hurt someone, I don't think it would have made a lot of
difference to him because I think he thought when he was hurt
nobody gave a shit about him.

Not long after he was returned, Pete asked his older brother
if he could move in with him and his wife. He said he couldn't
take being around home anymore. He was told he would be
welcome as long as he lived by the rules of their household.
He'd always had trouble with authority; nothing turned him
cold like being told what to do. But anything was preferable to
living another day at home, he said, and moved in with Rollie
and Mitzi.

Several months later his mother died. Although Pete showed
it least, it was the opinion of his siblings that he probably felt

it most. Now the oldest brother became the legal guardian of the twins, and after selling the house, feeling the need of a change of scene and responding to an offer of employment elsewhere, Rollie moved to Forks, Washington. Less than a year later the company he was employed by went out of business, so they returned to Farmington. This was in March 1974.

Throughout this time Rollie's wife had grown increasingly concerned about Pete. Citing his rebelliousness, his inability to communicate, and his cruelty toward his twin brother, she arranged for him to see a family-oriented therapist. Surprisingly, he didn't object; but when she thought about it she decided his willingness to go into therapy had less to do with an admission he had a problem than with the fact it would get him out of school.

Enrolled in Farmington High School as a sophomore, he remained an introverted person of limited friendships with one exception. He took up with another student that no one else seemed to like either, a kid by the name of Vernon Crawford.

Dr. Rada did not read the results of the psychological report on Oren Thacker until after he had conducted his own interviews with the youth, but his conclusions closely paralleled those of Dr. Quenk. He found Thacker lucid in his description of events on the Saturday night in question, willing to admit he was not without sin, but a long way from confessing to murder. He said that he, along with the two other youths he implicated, had assaulted an Indian male, and that it was something he'd done on a number of different occasions, but he insisted that he in no way expected the situation to end in death, and swore that when they left the Indian was definitely alive because as he walked away he heard him groaning.

Though he admitted that he had smoked a joint of marijuana on the drive out, Thacker denied it had any serious effect, or that his use constituted a history of drug abuse.

The youth was polite almost to the point of being obsequious with Dr. Rada, and struck him as a basically passive youth with a poor self-concept. There was reason to wonder about the character of this passivity—someone with a better image of himself would have asked himself, What am I doing here? Or he might have blown the whistle on the others. Or at the least extracted himself from the situation. But when he followed a standard course of questioning, branching out on the basis of what was said, nothing Rada heard made him feel the boy was so disabled with mental illness he did not know the nature of his acts or that they had come out of a sick mind. Thacker seemed to him to be little worse than your classic follower.

Likewise, Dr. Quenk encountered a boy who was courteous and cooperative, whose performance on the Weschler Adult Intelligence Scale indicated "he has a superior grasp of social mores and values, as well as superior abstracting and organizational abilities," but was someone who "has not yet developed his internal resources that would provide the necessary attention to details and motivation to achieve [his] aspirations. Coupled with this is his need for approval and recognition from others so that in the presence of persons with status he would behave in a courteous and somewhat dependent manner."

In itself this trait was not necessarily a deficiency, unless it suggested something deeper, which it did to Dr. Quenk: "Signs were also evident that Mr. Thacker has difficulty in delaying gratification of his needs. . . . His judgment in some instances would be impaired, resulting in behavior which would be impractical and at times deleterious to himself."

Taking it one step further, "It is very likely he would do things on a dare in order to obtain recognition and approval from his peers."

Boyd Thacker knew the oil-field business inside out. A ruddy, rugged fellow who talked like a backwoods hillbilly, he was partners in a firm that trucked water out to drill rigs for making mud (a standard procedure used to wash out the fragmentation generated by the bit). He was at home in the oil patch, but of late was spending less time in the field than he was functioning as a "customer man." He'd hear on the news that AMOCO was going to drill fifty new wells, so he'd find out whom to talk to, call him up, and say, Hey, why don't we play a little golf tomorrow afternoon? Yeah, okay. So they'd meet at the San Juan Country Club and play a round or two, and he'd pick up the tab. And when they went in the clubhouse afterward, maybe they'd play a few hands of "customer gin," where he let the old boy win a hundred bucks. Then he'd buy dinner and drinks . . . and when the time came for AMOCO to start operations, when they needed water delivered, Boyd got the call.

His wife, Joyce, was a different story. She was a tiny woman with a bouffant hairdo, sharp features, and refined tastes, who kept an immaculate house decorated in the French provincial style. She doted on her puffy wire-haired terrier, was active in the Lutheran church and assorted women's organizations, and every other week hosted a two-table bridge group. There was absolutely nothing about Joyce Thacker that would place her with a hard-working, hard-drinking roughneck, and two big-footed boys who were the spitting image of their father.

Boyd Jr. was the oldest by twenty months and he would always be two steps ahead of his younger brother, Oren. More mature, more popular, better-looking, the superior athlete. Oren, it almost seemed, dropped out of the sibling rivalry race at the starting line, as though he knew he could never measure up no matter how hard he tried, so why bother. But then it could have been his temperament too, because he was always a happy-go-lucky, supremely easygoing type who never took life that seriously; who, by his own admission, "was content to go find a shade tree and watch it all go by."

In school, though he was never perceived as a real discipline problem, he was quickly identified as a poor student, a boy with low ability and no motivation. When asked what he wanted to be when he grew up, he would answer "A lumber-jack," and giggle. He was a D and F student who thought it was funny when he flunked a class. Those who believe a per-son's penmanship reflects the mind at work will find it signif-icant that when he entered the eighth grade, his English teacher was appalled to discover "He could barely write. I don't re-member if he was left-handed, but there was such an odd, cramped slant to his tiny letters, it seemed that way. And there would be so many misspelled words it was hard to read what he wrote and make sense of it."

Other teachers would recall him as a boy who seemed to constantly be auditioning for the role of class clown. He had to make a flip and funny comment about everything; he would deliberately misunderstand their questions in order to get a laugh; if someone got in trouble, he would snicker. His junior high science teacher remembers, "By the things he would say you would think he was ten years old. One time we were talking about the clouds around the planet Venus, and how, if they were out of the way, we might be able to see the surface. Oren piped up, 'Why don't we take a big fan up there and blow them away.'"

Most of the time his bad puns and witless remarks left his classmates groaning, when the effect was comically intended. For this reason he is not talked about in high regard. "Having fun was Oren's thing," remembers a classmate. "Whatever was fun, whether it was picking up on someone else's practical joke, or doing something stupid, like throwing spitballs across the classroom, he was one of those type people. And he had a little bit of a reputation for being gross. I can remember him in the junior high locker room, spitting a lugee on the ceiling and watching it drip to see who it fell on.''

Moving in a world of lowered expectations, where he appeared to take a certain pride in getting by with the least amount of effort, Oren dressed the part. He would come to school with his hair greasy and disheveled, as though he hadn't bothered to brush it after waking up that morning. His shirttail would be hanging out in back, the buttons on the front misaligned; his shoelaces would be untied and his fly open. These may have been the days when anti-fashion statements among teenagers were in vogue, but Oren Thacker's ensemble did not strike his classmates as having been cultivated with any thought, as in the case of the nerd who wore loud plaid pants and two different kinds of shoes. It was more like, well, you have to have clothes on or they'll throw you out of school. This was in contrast to his older brother's preppy neatness.

It was almost inevitable that a kid like this would be given a nickname inspired in that devastating way kids have of zeroing in on a playmate's peculiar trait, and by their attention, turning it into a flaw that sometimes seems to shape character and direct the course of a life. In Oren's case, his peers had dubbed him the "Missing Link" because everything about him seemed to suggest that he had not quite completed the evolutionary cycle.

Physically the nickname was apt: His thick lips, big ears, and deep-set eyes under a heavy brow gave him a distinctly simian countenance, to which was added an odd birthmark—a bald spot the size of a half-dollar on the top back of his head. It fit with respect to behavior, too, according to the nickname's author. "He knew just enough to stay out of serious trouble, just enough to get by in the world, but not quite enough to be considered a full member of the human race.''

Once perceived in this light, everything Oren did and said seemed to fall in line with what you'd expect of someone who had not quite finished the transition from ape to man. Or so it appeared to those he ran around with:

"I remember sitting in his room, he had a telephone in there, and he would call strangers on the phone and record the conversations with a little attachment you stuck on the receiver.

But before he dialed he'd stuff his mouth full of crackers, so when someone answered he could hardly be understood. He'd pretend like he was trying his best to talk, and would be so convincing the guy on the other end would get concerned. 'Son, are you okay?' he'd ask. 'You want me to call a doctor?' Stuff like that. And afterwards Oren would play it back and laugh like hell . . . the Missing Link.

"Once we were out hunting in this box canyon north of town, and Oren was running all over creation so I lost track of him. Anyway, I'm walking along and all of a sudden a rabbit jumps up and runs off. So I aimed, and just as I pulled the trigger, Oren's grinning face pops up in the sights between me and the rabbit. When he heard the bullet zing by—it must have missed his head by inches, if that—he went straight up in the air and landed flat . . . the Missing Link."

Over time, you would think that to have every slip and blunder turned into anecdotal evidence for those who got their kicks needling you would wear thin. But it was no big deal to Oren, who never stuck up for himself. He not only endured kidding about his shortcomings, he would laugh along, even when he was the butt of a joke, as though it were happening to someone else.

"One day Boyd and Oren were at my house, it was a Sunday afternoon late in the day, and we were watching a football game. Oren had fallen asleep in a chair in the den, and my dad happened to come along. When he saw Oren like that, he snuck out and came back with a can of shaving cream that he squirted on Oren's hand. Then he tickled Oren's nose with a feather until he slapped at it, thinking it was a fly. Out of a dead sleep Oren jumped up. And he stood there for a moment, wiping shaving cream out of his eyes, looking like he didn't know whether to get mad or cry, before he got this goofy grin on his face and he said, 'Golly, you guys, you really got me. Way to go.' "

Though basically a good-natured kid, there was a side to his equanimity that concerned his more astute observers, and that was his susceptibility to forceful personalities, which in adolescence usually turned out to be the troublemakers. Oren was impressed by them, drawn to them; and he wasn't above getting into a little bit of trouble himself to win their approval. Unfortunately, he was often unable to recognize when they were laughing at him instead of with him, and it became a minor amusement for some of the tougher ones to purposely egg Oren on, encouraging him to show off and make mischief, just to see him get into trouble. Being the kind of kid who was capable of thinking to himself, Okay, you're my friend, you're daring me, so I'll do it, who would try just about anything if he thought it would be cool or neat or new, the Missing Link obliged them.

Trouble, it sometimes seemed, followed Oren Thacker even when he wasn't looking for it. "Dusty" Downs, a classmate in junior high school, is the right person to talk about this quality:

"Whenever I think of Oren Thacker I think of . . . I had him in an English class in the eighth grade, and this one day the teacher stepped out of the room momentarily, and as soon as she was gone these two kids got in a fight. They were rolling around on the floor and whatnot, and got close to Oren's desk. Now Oren—he used to wear these wingtip shoes that might have been his dad's because they didn't fit him, were real loose, and he never tied the shoelaces. And when these guys rolled into Oren's desk, somehow one of his shoes came off his feet and got under them. So he tried to get it back, but ended up getting tangled in with them, and was in the middle of things when the teacher walked back in the room. All three were sent down the hall and got swats. And Oren had had nothing to do with the fight whatsoever, he was just trying to get his shoe back."

Looking back on it, looking for the reason all of what followed came down on Oren, that scene would prophesize for Dusty Downs the way Oren Thacker's luck ran: It always seemed he was dealt the bad hand.

By the time Oren was in high school, relations with his parents had become so strained that, to those who came to the house, Oren "had to sneak around to do anything." They didn't see his mother that much, but they would hear her screaming at Oren when they stood outside. Oren Thacker turn that stereo down. Oren Thacker what are you doing now? Oren Thacker look at the mess you've made.

At times, Mrs. Thacker's obsession with cleanliness made it seem that her kids were boarders in the house. Things always had to be just so. Friends who entered Oren and Boyd's room, noting the beds were made with military neatness, all clothes were hung up, and the general lack of clutter, would sometimes remark, "Gee, guys, what's wrong here?"

Mr. Thacker wasn't home a lot, and when he was he often

had a whiskey or beer in his hand, both of which seemed to make him cranky. You never knew from one day to the next what kind of temper he would be in. Some days he acted like he remembered exactly what it was like to be young, and if one of his sons wanted to borrow the truck he'd say, "Sure, go ahead, enjoy yourself." Other days he would be grouchy, unpredictable, and capable of crushing plans with a "No" that would be explained with a "Because I said so." End of conversation.

Boyd Jr. and his father seemed to get along slightly better than Oren and his dad, which could be attributed to Boyd's success in athletics. He was a starting end on the Farmington Scorpions football team—while the donkey's tail was always being pinned on Oren.

Keillor Haynie, a high school chemistry teacher who lived next door to the Thackers, had his doubts about the boy ever since he began to find empty billfolds under a piñon tree in the backyard where his lot cornered with theirs. Although he couldn't prove Oren was the culprit, he didn't think it was Doc Coates, who lived behind him, or Jack Morgan, his neighbor on the other side who was a state representative at the time. And when Haynie turned the wallets over to R. T. Tolliver, a principal at the junior high school Oren attended, who lived across the street, *he* checked the IDs and it turned out the wallets were being stolen out of a phys-ed class Oren was in.

What lightened life for Oren was the way his older brother included him in his own circle of friends. If Boyd went downtown for a Coke, Oren came along. If he went rabbit hunting in Chokecherry Canyon, Oren was welcome. If Boyd and his friends got into a pickup game of basketball in the driveway, Oren would be there. They got along well, which was unusual for brothers so close in age.

Nevertheless, even though Oren was included he was generally perceived as a tag-along, and was known to be somewhat overhearty in his effort to establish his right to be there. Not that he would initiate anything—the only time he went first was on a dare—but you could always count on him to join in any activity enthusiastically.

Significantly, when he was asked to list his four best friends on a questionnaire distributed to students his junior year in high school, all the names were of seniors, and all had been his brother's friends first.

In his own class, because of his propensity for getting into trouble and his slovenly appearance, Oren was not considered exactly socially acceptable. The few friends he did have his own age tended to be the independent types who, like him, lived by a day-to-day, moment-to-moment, from-one-good-time-to-the-next philosophy; kids who, on weekends, in shared paroxysms of mindless youthful energy, were into taking risks.

For a while, bashing trash cans was their sport. Armed with machetes and baseball bats, they would cruise down an alley, jump out, and whack at the trash cans. Oren developed a reputation as the clean-up hitter because when he started swinging, sometimes he would get carried away. On his way back to the car, after doing a trash can, he was likely to take out the headlight on a parked car. It wasn't that he was such a violent person or got off on vandalism, more that he was excitable.

According to his friends, they began rolling Indians as a lark. "We'd go down to the Copper Penny, hold a couple dollars out, and them Indians would come up and they'd stick their head in the window, 'cause we'd talk real low, and we'd grab their hat, spin out, and throw dirt all over them. It was just a kid prank."

Three incidents, it seems, turned it into something more.

The first was the Kevin Arnold accident. Several days after it happened, Oren and a friend walked over to the yard where the wrecked Corvette had been towed. "That really hit us. You could tell they'd been to the Pizza Hut before it happened, because there was pizza and blood all over the inside of the car. It was bad."

Tommy Kitchens was along on the second: "This one night me and Oren decided we were going to go roll Indians. And just by chance, as we were going down this alley, we came across an Indian stretched out on the pavement that somebody else had already wasted. He was hurt pretty bad, bleeding from the side of his head where it looked like he'd been hit with a brick. So we went and called the police. They told us, You see that again, don't bother calling."

The whole business of drunk Indians getting away with murder, and the impression that the cops had given up on the problem, appeared to disgust Oren. And it provided him and his companions with a rationalization for their nocturnal adventures. When they felt the need to justify hurting these people, they talked about it as a way of sending a message to the Indians to clean up their act.

The third, and perhaps most significant, development was that around this time he took up with Vernon Crawford.

They were never best friends. There was a lot of guys closer to Oren than Vernon. Oren first got to know him when they had a morning class together. Since they were always in the same spot at the same time, they would often go to the 7-Eleven for something to eat before class started, or they would eat lunch in Vernon's car, the only place on campus besides the designated areas where they could smoke cigarettes and not get in trouble.

Nor was it a friendship in which they drew one another out, or talked about things. Explaining the camaraderie he felt, Oren once said, "I always thought he was sort of a lonely guy, off-the-wall and kinda weird. Maybe that's why I liked him. Because nobody else would be his friend. I'm sorta that way."

When they started rolling Indians together they did not do any serious beating at first, they just harassed Indians. Usually there were other kids along, but as Vernon's kicks became uncomfortably rougher the ranks thinned until it was just Peter Burke and himself.

Originally the hearing was scheduled for Friday, May 24, but Dr. Winslow and his team had not completed their evaluations by that time so they were given an additional two weeks. The new date designated by the court was Friday, June 7, the day before the annual Sheriff's Posse Parade.

8

THE CAVALRY GHOSTS
OF CENTURIES PAST

While Coalition leaders dismissed as a flanking maneuver the charge that their organization was a front for professional agitators and seasoned political subversives trying to exploit the crisis, they could not deny that a certain amount of support *had* come their way from the American Indian Movement. AIM's involvement was not as much as Mayor Webb or the citizens of Farmington believed, but it was enough to be a source of disagreement between Wilbert Tsosie and John Redhouse.

From the start, Tsosie had welcomed AIM's interest, wanting the support of as many Indian people as possible. He had not personally dealt with AIM before this, but felt their presence would swell the Coalition's clout. White Farmington would sit up and take notice when the names of its notorious leaders, Russell Means and Dennis Banks, were invoked. No smart city official was going to ignore the Coalition if he thought much about what had happened at Wounded Knee, and put AIM and the CNL together.

Redhouse, having had the benefit of observing AIM in action in Gallup, was wary of the group and skeptical about their benefits. He didn't have a problem with those Navajos who claimed a membership in AIM, of which there were only a handful, most of them recent converts. What he objected to was the kind of thing that had happened at the second march: a cameo appearance by John Trudell, national chairman of AIM, who flew in to shake hands with the marchers—*We're with you, brothers. Keep it up!*—and make a few idle threats before catching a plane back to Minnesota.

Prominent in his memory was a scene in Gallup that, to his way of thinking, captured and caricatured AIM. During the time when Navajos were protesting the Intertribal Ceremonial a group of Sioux affiliated with AIM pulled into town costumed up like nineteenth-century warriors and asking for a traditional blessing ceremony. At some trouble, not to mention expense, it was arranged. But when the medicine man showed up wearing Bermuda shorts and a ball cap, the AIMers acted as if some trick were being played on them, and succeeded in creating serious bad feelings, never mind a canceled ceremony.

While Tsosie and Redhouse may have seen AIM as playing different roles in their struggle, both recognized that association with a group widely recognized as the militant defender of Indian rights on a national scale had the effect of elevating the issues raised in Farmington into the grand struggle being waged by native people across the country. And both knew very well the strategic importance of continuing to connect what was happening in Farmington to a larger Indian history.

In this regard, it would be closer to the truth to say that *they* were using AIM. The national press snapped to attention at the mere mention, and Coalition leaders were savvy enough to know that national exposure through the media could only help. For this reason they had cultivated contacts with the press, and staged events with a strong sense of theater and cameras and deadlines in mind.

One measure of their success had been their ability to turn Farmington into a national dateline. Read alone, the headlines on the stories filed from Farmington made it sound like they were winning the good fight: "Murders Move Navajo Tribe from Passive Life to Protest," *Rocky Mountain News*. "Triple Murder Brings an Echo of '60s Strife," *National Observer*. "Navajo Activism Forcing Clashes between Cultures," *Washington Post*. "Farmington, N.M., Is Beginning to Harvest Fruits of 100 Years of Indian Bitterness and Frustration," *New York Times*.

If the Coalition got its way, that would be just the start—not only of national attention but of outside intervention; for just as the mayor had decided not to talk directly with the Coalition but rather to deal with the tribe, the Coalition had decided that *their* efforts would be better spent if they went over the heads of city officials to the United States government.

"What we wanted was a seat at the negotiating table," John Redhouse remembers. "The city refused to recognize us, to address the things we were raising. Instead they ignored and badmouthed us. So we wanted federal people involved. If the feds came into Farmington and listened to our complaints, it would give us respect. It would keep our position of strength intact. And it would force the city to respond meaningfully to our charges—which was exactly what they did not want to have to do."

As a result of the slayings, the protest activities, and the community unrest, the U.S. Commission on Civil Rights in Washington, D.C., had received letters, petitions, and other appeals, including concerned inquiries from several congressmen, requesting an inquiry into the potential violation of the civil rights of American Indians in the Southwest. By mid-May the Commission had decided a closer look at the charges was warranted and dispatched staff member John Foster Dulles II, and Gerald Wilkinson, director of the National Indian Youth Council and a member of the State Advisory Committee, to Farmington to collect information, gather testimony, and assess the validity of the accusations.

Wanting to hear the Indian side of the story directly from the complainants themselves, Dulles and Wilkinson met with more than a hundred area Indians at the San Juan Episcopal Mission and listened to more than six hours of testimony. Members of the families of the slain Navajo men, seated in the front row of the church hall, stood and expressed their grief, suffering, and concern that justice would not prevail. There followed a series of Navajo speakers who told of unscrupulous business practices, including overcharging and inflated interest rates for Indians, and personal and property crimes against Indian people that went unaddressed by local law-enforcement officials, including beatings, rape, robbery, and other serious felonies. There were also several reports of Navajos who had lost their lives because the local hospital refused to treat Indians.

What the representatives heard was disturbing, but what moved them as much as the universal examples of racial prejudice—consumer fraud, economic exploitation, discrimination, and injustice —were the petty harassments and humiliations that made up an Indian's reality. They could only imagine what it must be like to live with a steady barrage of slights and aggravations, day after day, each incident like a tiny splinter that worked its way beneath the skin and gradually festered. They could only guess what living under those conditions over the years did to the spirit.

The next day they met with Mayor Webb, other county and city officials, law-enforcement personnel, and knowledgeable individuals, and their overall impression was that there was a tremendous lack of understanding on the part of officials as to the extent and nature of the problem they faced.

An exchange with the mayor typified the problem. As it was written up afterward, "The mayor . . . blamed all of the recent unrest on outside troublemakers and affirmed his belief that the Navajos in Farmington are not dissatisfied and do not support the actions or tactics of the militant groups which have intervened to exploit the recent Navajo killings. . . . The main problem with the Navajos, according to the mayor, is that they have not yet become a part of our civilization."

Before leaving town staff members were quizzed by local reporters about the results of their investigation, but they refused to answer any questions other than to say that, as soon as it was written, a report containing their findings would be forwarded to the national office for action.

What they kept to themselves were the determinations they had already reached, and the recommendations they had decided they would make. In their analysis, Farmington was permeated with deep, divisive racial attitudes that went largely unacknowledged by the authorities. The report they would submit would contain this summary: "There is a clear atmosphere of hostility, racial tension, and polarization which threaten[s] to provoke a serious, and possibly violent, confrontation between angry Navajos and apparently unresponsive and complacent white community leaders."

Having concluded that the agency could, and should, play a major role in this urgent and critical situation, they intended to call for Justice Department intervention to assure that the criminal justice process was fully and fairly executed with regard to the deaths of the three Navajo men, and for a more intensive investigation into the status of civil rights of Native Americans in northwest New Mexico, to be followed by full public hearings.

Journalists sent to Farmington to report on the unfolding events had a lot of fun profiling the community's personality, variously describing it as a place "where burly men with knotty forearms rise and stand before their chain store television sets when the first pre-football strains of the National Anthem sound," and where people live "a life of fried chicken and potato salad, with sweet pickles, uncomplicated by crises of the soul beyond the lonewolf lyrics of a country-western tune." But not one writer made any reference to what made it such a dangerous place for minorities. For that they needed to talk with the local FBI agent, from whom they would have heard that the Bureau had identified the Farmington-Aztec area as a center of rabid conservatism, and a major mail drop for federal fugitives moving around the country robbing banks to raise money for white-supremacy groups. And they would have had to have known that Chief of Police Roy Kerr was receiving phone calls telling him all he had to do was give the word and at the next march enough oil-field hands and power-plant people would show up to put a bloody end to all this demonstrating.

Local tempers were turning mean. People in Farmington were resentful of the way the entire town was being slandered for the crimes of a few, and they were tired of demonstrations they thought were uncalled for since the ones who had done the murdering were in custody.

The coffee shops around town provided a forum where one could hear local sentiments, and some of what was said was alarming. Where we went wrong, according to Carroll Fisk, a realtor in Farmington for more than twenty years who made no secret of his dislike for Indians, was in not getting rid of all of them when the West was won. "The way I feel, if you're gonna invade a country with a mind to resettling it, you don't leave any who was here before. Kill 'em all and be done with it. To the conqueror goes the spoils. That's been the history the world over. And where they've done it that way, there are no Indian problems."

Which led to the second mistake, the one that most rankled not only Fisk but a lot of others: "The way the government, after knocking the Indians down, decided to pick them back up, at a cost to all of us."

Many felt that if anybody had a right to gripe about equal rights, whites did, and arguments making this point scored heavily in the letters column of the *Farmington Daily Times*. Wrote Donald George of Farmington:

Will [the Indians] please delineate just what "privileges" the whites enjoy that Indians are denied? They eat in the same restaurants, shop in the same stores, attend the same shows, enjoy the same parks and recreational facilities, and the same protection under the law.

Where can the average white man go for free medical and dental care? Free legal advice? Will I ever be exempt from paying state income and sales tax? Will institutions of higher learning lower their entrance requirements for me and then accept substandard work as passing? The answer to all of the above is no. The only so-called "privilege" accorded the white man is one of paying taxes to keep a large segment of the American public on some kind of dole.

As for the accusation that Indians were being exploited by liquor establishments: "[It] is so asinine I have to bite my tongue to keep my composure when I hear it," opined another Angry Citizen. "I can remember a time in the early '50s when the Navajos went to the Supreme Court and challenged New Mexico state law prohibiting the sale of liquor to Indians. The law was found unconstitutional as it should have been. Now that the Indians can legally purchase liquor, they claim it is a tool of the white man to exploit them. The initial decision to take a drink is a FREE ACT of the individual will. I reject the theory by BLEEDING-HEART type sociologists that the conditions imposed by society are responsible for a person's drunkenness. If this were true we would all be alcoholics because the exigencies of life are imposed on us all and no one is exempt. Individuals are responsible for their drunkenness, not society."

All this bottled-up indignation hardened attitudes among the average citizens of Farmington, and their feelings were mixed and shaken by continually infuriating behavior on the part of the Coalition. People resented it when verbal insults were hurled at duly elected officials, when their mayor was burned in effigy, when the symbols and institutions which they regarded respectfully were belittled. At one march a veteran had to be restrained by friends. "Twice in my life I've been ready to go to war," he said later. "When the Japs bombed Pearl Harbor, and when I saw all them *Ya-tah-hey*s marching down Main Street, and one of them had an American flag draped over his butt."

A series of incidents heightened the tension. The local newspaper reported that police were investigating an incident in which a white Farmington woman was allegedly attacked by three Navajo men. According to the report, she had been trying to locate a residence in Hogback, on the edge of the reservation, and when she had asked directions of three Indians in a pickup they charged at her. She told police she repelled one man by kicking him and the other two by firing a .22-caliber pistol into the air.

Then city councilman Jimmy Drake received a death threat: a letter from Minneapolis, written on Holiday Inn stationery, warning him that his days were numbered. It had been unsigned, but AIM's headquarters were located in Minneapolis, and Drake had no doubts who had sent it.

Then word got out about what happened up at the Haynie place.

For some reason he could never quite figure out, about 90 percent of the people who came to Keillor Haynie's front door were looking for Boyd Thacker, who lived next door. His oilfield hands, even people who knew him, they were always getting the wrong house and Haynie would have to tell them, "Next door."

When Haynie read in the newspaper that Oren Thacker had been charged with murder, and saw that the identifying information listed his home address, he groaned. If their own friends couldn't get it straight which house was Thacker's, and if someone took a notion to get even with the killers' families, there was a good chance his own could find itself in the line of fire.

"Guys I knew said, 'Hey, Keillor, don't you worry about it, it won't happen.' And I said, 'Easy for you to say. Those men who were killed, they were fathers. They had families. I can see how their side would be upset.' "

As a fire chief he'd been on well over a thousand runs, and he'd seen people shot, knifed, run over, burned up: killed every way imaginable. Not only did he know anything was possible, he knew the value of anticipating the worst and taking preventive measures. The first thing he did was make a trip to the hardware store where he picked up three sets of stick-on numbers. One he put on his mailbox, another above the garage door, the third on the back gate. A person would have to be blind not to see that his house was 3601 Sunset when Haynie was through hanging up all those numbers.

Next he scattered fire extinguishers throughout the house, down the halls, so if someone threw a Molotov cocktail or something of that type there would be an extinguisher close by.

Same way with the guns: "We scattered them too. You take three or four steps and you could find yourself a rifle or shotgun."

Finally he had his wife, Jocile, and sixteen-year-old son, Ronnie, memorize the telephone numbers of the fire and police departments and practice dialing them in the dark, so if something happened they would not have to turn on any lights.

They lived in this domestic state of alert for several weeks, and during that period of time, other than having to listen to carloads of Indians drive by hollering names at them, nothing eventful occurred. And probably nothing short of an all-out assault—howling Indians storming the fort walls—would have justified the preparations of the Haynie household. In that regard, what finally did happen on May 4, the night of the high school prom, was anticlimactic, though at the time it was frightening enough.

"My wife left the prom early, and after picking up my son at my brother's, she came home. No sooner had she closed the door and turned on the lights and here comes this Indian trying to break in the front door. Just like the drills we'd practiced, Jocile started dialing, while Ronnie dropped two double-ought buck in the shotgun and closed it. When Jo told the police what was happening, they said to her, Well, we'll have a unit up there in a little while. Then she told them, Listen, we live next door to the Thackers, and the dispatcher said, We've got a unit on the way. The guy had taken off by the time they got there, but all night long, every five minutes, a police car passed my house."

It's said that after that the gun peddlers in town did a booming business. Untrue. Some even pulled their handguns, rifles, and shotguns off display, locking them in back rooms so if a bunch of Indians broke in and overpowered a clerk they couldn't walk out the door with enough guns and ammunition to stock a small army. Besides, most of Farmington already owned firearms. The difference now was they started carrying them. Some wives never went out without a pistol in their pocketbook. One man started openly carrying an M-1 carbine in the gunrack of his pickup—with a bayonet affixed to the barrel.

By the end of May the animosity in Farmington was palpable. Whites and Indians passing in the street looked into each other's eyes prepared to interpret anything other than a smile as an indication of hostile intent. From passing vehicles racial slurs were shouted, and thinly veiled threats against the lives of Indians and whites alike. One liquor store owner warned, "I'm not gonna lock my store up and leave. I'm by damn gonna stay here and one of those suckers so much as rattles my door I'm gonna blow him away."

While a war of nerves was being waged between the Coalition and city officials, armed citizens began to patrol the streets in pickups, tuned to the police band. They considered themselves an unofficial civilian militia ready to back up law enforcement and help keep the peace. But to hear them talk among themselves, they sounded like they were itching for a showdown.

Everyone was afraid that under stress, or accidentally, someone would do something drastic, spooking the other into a reaction that would precipitate an outbreak of violence. That was how most wars started, with a minor incident that escalated into guns away.

An editorial in the local paper—"Time for Cool Heads"— preached caution: "There are hot-heads on both sides of this dangerous situation and all right-thinking people should be aware that the situation can get out of control by an incident which can be the spark for mob action." But no one believed that would make any difference.

"It's like sitting on a powder keg," police chief Roy Kerr stated to the press. "What we have here is a highly explosive situation that is just waiting for someone irresponsible to touch it off."

By June 1974, Farmington was a ticking bomb. It seemed like just a matter of time before gunfire would shatter the tense truce that had been maintained since the last war between settlers and Indians.

To be sure, nothing can concentrate the mind of a community like a loud and foul-mouthed minority launching rallies to protest redneck prejudices, with signs, banners, bullhorns, and a local television crew recording it all for the evening news. But in the forum provided by the letters column in the *Daily Times* one heard the voice of moderation pleading for Anglo and Indian to "get it together," "live in harmony," "join in common prayer." There was even a place for humorous satire, as a local wit came up with the idea of a contest in which Rule Number One was: "Coalition leaders are permitted to mention established facts only 22 percent of the time. The rest of the time they must spew a smokescreen of vulgarities in order to conceal the specific problems of Native Americans in the city." Rule Number Two was: "City administration members are allowed to speak as many platitudes as they desire. They must not however, under any circumstances, say anything that would lead the populace to the conclusion that they have any constructive ideas for alleviating the problem."

The editors chimed in with an editorial that sounded like a sermon: "In this difficult time of deep emotion there is a danger that a closing of hearts could force a blind stumble that could topple red and white into a dark place of unbridled emotion. Qualities of humanity must prevail over pettiness in Farmington. City officials must show a renewed willingness to walk an extra mile with their Indian brethren. . . . And the Coalition for Navajo Liberation must not allow the zeal of idealism to become the passion of hate. . . . Violence can be avoided. In the name of humanity, it must. Blood on the streets of Farmington would be a tragic indictment of all men in that city—Indian and non-Indian."

But this was not the feedback the Custer of Farmington was getting. Via phone calls at home and in the office, and conversations on the street, people were encouraging him to stand up to this anarchic element and put the Indians in their place. "They were telling me not to give an inch. There was actually resentment that I had ever been willing to meet and talk with the Indians." Especially vocal were the downtown merchants angered at a substantial decline in weekend trade.

There were times when Marlo Webb felt like taking the hard line. He was fed up with heated, threat-laced confrontations at the city council meetings. For the town to be subjected to false, fictitious, and unwarranted charges, and to have been unable to get any cooperation from the troublemakers and accusers, enraged him. And he knew only too well how the downtown merchants felt: Every weekend his place of business was being picketed and boycotted by Indians, and before this he had done most of his business on weekends, two-thirds of it Navajo. So he, perhaps more than anyone else in town, was suffering economically.

But his internal anger and frustration went unexpressed—other than an occasional shouting match in the city council chambers—as he also felt that in his position as mayor of Farmington it was his responsibility to prevent violence, to keep the peace and people from getting hurt.

Just how precarious the "peace" was became evident at one of the marches. As it happened, Mayor Webb was out of town that Saturday and councilman Bob Culpepper was in charge. As was the custom, he, along with the chief of police and other ranking city officials, was present at a temporary command headquarters that had been set up several blocks off Main Street, adjacent to the lot where the state police, dressed in battle gear, were positioned. He was kept informed by walkie-talkie of the progress of the parade, and at one point was alerted to the fact that the marchers had halted near one of the Indian bars where the leaders were making inflammatory speeches. This was in violation of the conditions of the parade permit, in which it had been stipulated that the marchers could not stop at any point along the parade route for a rally. The thinking had been if they were allowed to stop the leaders could get the crowd stirred up and that could lead to stone-throwings and fire-settings.

Culpepper communicated to the officers along the route that the crowd must not be allowed to remain in place. When there was no movement, Culpepper found himself in the position of either enforcing the conditions of the parade permit or backing down.

Well, you can only run a bluff so long, he thought to himself, and ordered the troops to move in. "Whether they got wind of it, or everybody was playing a game, who knows," Culpepper remembers. "At any rate, the troops had no sooner left the marshaling grounds than the parade continued. So they came back, and it was just a close call."

In their relentless quest to make the summer of '74 a significant turning point in Navajo history by creating and dramatizing issues through protest marches, the leading spirits of the Coalition for Navajo Liberation, as well as antagonizing most of white Farmington, were inadvertently alienating themselves from significant sectors of Navajo society. Many Indian people had difficulty reconciling the Coalition's methods with its objectives. Maybe the intention was to make lasting improvements in race relations, but so far the demands and demonstrations seemed to be having just the opposite effect. A rise in the number of drive-by shootings at hogans and sheep on the reservation was just one indication things had gotten worse.

Even the *Navajo Times* took the Coalition to task in an editorial: "In their public burning of an American flag, members of the Coalition for Navajo Liberation demonstrated a disappointing willingness to outrage their fellow citizens. This deliberate engaging in the politics of insult deeply offended many Indian and non-Indian citizens for whom the flag has a deeply rooted emotional significance."

A case in point was provided by the post commander of the Veterans of Foreign Wars in Shiprock, who wrote Fred Johnson the following letter, and sent a copy to the *Farmington Daily Times*:

> We express to you our deep sadness over the manner in which you and your Coalition are demonstrating in Farmington. Certainly, we are not telling you not to demonstrate. That is your decision. However, the manner in which you conduct your demonstrations is of concern to all Navajos.
>
> Our concern is directed primarily towards burning, tearing, and defacing our American flag and wearing the flag upside down. Many Navajos died fighting wars for that flag. To burn or tear the flag or dishonor it in any way is the same as dishonoring those many Navajos who died fighting for that same flag.
>
> We do not condone unfair or unjust treatment of any person. . . . But, there is a right way and a wrong way to protest injustice and unfairness. Burning our flag causes all people to turn against us. Instead of being able to resolve the problem, it creates more.

Individual Navajos were not the only ones to publicly question and condemn the Coalition for using tactics that were raking up resentment in the white community. Speaking for the chairman and members of the tribal council, Andrew Benallie, appointed to head the Navajo Commission on Civil Rights, damned the Coalition in public statements for their "displays of arrogance, self-righteousness, and a total contempt for decency and their own tribal leaders. On the one hand, we are calling on the Anglo people for understanding, respect, and compassion. Yet these self-righteous individuals have demonstrated before the public the very image we are trying to erase from the history books and the movies, the image of Indians as savages and uncivilized." He went as far as to urge fellow Navajos "to reject the Coalition, their goals and their philosophies that poison the minds of our people."

Even Rena Benally had withdrawn her active support. Since the first bereavement march she had grown uncomfortable with the Coalition's combativeness and now she no longer participated in the weekly protest marches.

Despite a lack of tribal solidarity, the Coalition remained convinced of the justice of their cause and maintained that they still had the backing of a decisive majority of those 20,000 Navajo who lived in the San Juan River Valley. They reasoned that much of the uncertainty among their tribesmen could be attributed to an unfamiliarity with the traditions and techniques of public protest. They maintained that theirs was a vanguard movement still in its formative stages, and that the "liberation" of an oppressed race that historically has been subjugated and humiliated was always going to encounter resistance from within. Some of their fellow Navajo, they cynically suspected, had probably been influenced by Mayor Webb, whom they didn't put above sweetening a deal on a new pickup at his dealership for their vocal support.

Redhouse's assertion that "there's a sell-out group in every oppressed people, oppressed nation, who see their security, if not their salvation, in serving the interests of those who dominate them," although a harsh claim that served *his* interests to think so, was not an entirely unfounded opinion. Navajo identity had begun to erode in the thirties and forties, and the fifties and sixties were confusing times for many Indian people who had been educated in off-reservation boarding schools where they had been indoctrinated to align themselves with progress, which translated into assimilating themselves into white society. If a person did not have a strong sense of place in the world or pride in his cultural heritage, an activist orientation did not come naturally.

In response to the criticism they had received for their desecration of the American flag, while admitting there were two schools of thought on this issue among Navajo, the Coalition perceived the Stars and Stripes as a symbol of oppression. Thousands of Navajo people had died at Fort Sumner under that flag. That flag flew over the offices of the Bureau of Indian Affairs, which to them represented a force opposed to self-determination. In their eyes the United States government was the main source of the problems the tribe faced today. And while it may have been true that some of their people were veterans of American wars and proud of their service, many of those who served under the American flag had come home to a life of poverty and discrimination and felt betrayed.

"So that's where we were coming from," explained Redhouse. "There had to be some forcing of the situation. Our school of thinking had to be laid out and dealt with, whether it was understood or rejected or whatever. People had to know that our patriotism was to our people. To the Navajo Nation, which had its own flag. That's what we wanted to project: a new way of thinking about country."

The Coalition leaders were well aware that militancy charged its price, but felt there was no alternative. They knew Indian people in this country had always had to resort to militancy to protect their interests. It was one of history's lessons: Sometimes people have to fight for their rights, and if you were Indian, make that every time.

Besides, they genuinely believed that almost every Navajo would agree with their basic premise: Race relations between Navajos and Anglos in Farmington needed improvement. The disagreement lay in what it took to bring about change. The Coalition did not think significant social and political change could be achieved in an orderly manner. Its leaders felt that the normal channels had been tried and had not worked. They felt Farmington needed to be shown they meant business, and the most productive course of action at this point lay in forcing the powers-that-be to confront the issues, and making demands and insisting they be acted upon. They felt that by taking a stand now, a big stand, ten years from now, twenty years down the road, their people would be less likely to be facing physical and cultural genocide. They wanted this to be a time in history when the line was drawn and ever after Navajo people were accorded equal respect as fellow human beings.

It was probably unavoidable that a politics based on dramatizing racial grievances would produce some counterproductive excesses. Nor did the improvisational character of the movement lend itself to the formulation of sustainable programs, and the discomfort that inevitably accompanies the conflict between established ways and new directions was always going to scare off the multitudes. But the Coalition justified all these risks and drawbacks by placing them in the context of its higher objectives—and all things considered, its leaders had not done badly. Their activities had awakened a new spirit of activism among many Navajos which was resulting in a reexamination of existing relationships between the Indian and non-Indian community. The city of Farmington had been unable to suppress their protests, they had succeeded in garnering an impressive amount of favorable press coverage, and there were indications the legitimacy of their efforts was going to be backed up by the findings of the U.S. Commission on Civil Rights. But whether the "Indian problem" in Farmington would be resolved by any of these developments remained to be seen, and they had yet to actually secure specific concessions from the city.

Indeed they had been far more successful in collecting death threats. Although Redhouse's home phone number was supposed to be unlisted, on a half-dozen occasions the phone had rung late at night and when he answered he could hear a jukebox and loud voices in the background, then a gruff voice warning him if he kept it up he would be the next Indian found dead in the hills outside Farmington.

History suggested such threats should not be taken lightly, but the leaders of the Coalition were not in a frame of mind to be intimidated. If anything, they felt almost invincible. They were buoyed by a quixotic certainty that history was on their side. A feeling of rightness about their mission gave them added confidence. And strongest of all, they felt they were protected by the Holy People.

It had been after one of the marches that Tsosie had been approached by a Navajo veteran who told him his grandfather was a medicine man who had incredible powers, derived from the knowledge of uncommon ceremonies that had been used extensively before contact with the white man. He said his grandfather had performed a ceremony to shield him from danger before he went to fight in Vietnam, and having survived battle scenes where those on either side of him were shot and killed, he was convinced it had worked. He had offered the blessings of the same ceremony to the leaders of the Coalition, and a sing had been held one night on the bluffs overlooking Farmington.

Many of the ritualistic details had been new to Wilbert, so he listened closely to the medicine man intone the story of a contest for the world in which a mythological Navajo warrior warded off the attack of a monster. In the end it became a prayer that was supposed to clothe them in a suit of supernatural armor which would give them strength and protect them from their enemies.

And then help came from an unexpected direction.

In response to the social disruption of the 1960s the Department of Justice had set up the Community Relations Service (CRS), an agency whose sole purpose was to assist cities and towns experiencing civil disturbances and racial conflicts. The agency worked under a very low profile, so low that some likened it to the Mission Impossible team. Gus Gaynett was a forty-year-old Hispanic with the CRS in 1974, assigned to crisis response. He was dispatched strictly when conflicts had reached the overt state of street activity, demonstrations, and violence. He was working out of the Dallas, Texas, office when a report came in that the situation in Farmington had gotten out of hand, and because he had experience with the Red Power movement, he was given the Farmington assignment.

By this time in my career I had been all over the U.S. and was involved in almost every major confrontation, so I had a good idea what could happen when these "liberation" movements brought internal civil unrest to a community. Very few police departments were prepared to deal with them. That had not been part of their training, so their responses often were not very . . . sophisticated. And our experience had taught us that the people in these movements were no longer afraid of the police. Just because you had a machine gun, that wasn't going to stop them. You were going to have to use it. Those dynamics, at a point in time when the climate in the country was that minorities were going to take steps to make changes whenever they thought change was necessary, made for a dangerous situation.

As a mediator you do not become involved in the investigatory aspects of a situation. In fact you go to lengths to avoid involvement with intelligence agencies. You are there as a third-party neutral. You have to appreciate the fact that in any adversary situation both sides believe their position is the correct one. You don't try to legitimize either side, but rather try to find, within the context of a lot of work, some medium ground that both sides can agree on without necessarily giving up their specific positions.

From my perspective, both sides had legitimate concerns. Farmington was like many other small communities caught in the middle of something like this. The status quo had been dominant for a number of years. They were not aware that Indians perceived themselves as being discriminated against. And the bottom line is, in cases like this there is always some merit, however minor, in some of the allegations. I don't think any system is 100 percent foolproof against inequities. Often there are problems relating to structure that sometimes transcend ethnic or racial issues, because in almost every system the people governed aren't always going to be pleased with the people governing. The Native American community was taking the opportunity to raise questions of great concern to them. And they were making demands which, seen in that context, certainly had some validity.

The town, well, at first the mayor felt threatened and was adamant about the fact that he wasn't going to cave in to these folks. He felt the whole thing was being run by outside agitators. That the leaders wanted violence and were simply seeking publicity. I pointed out that he certainly did not have to tolerate violations of the law. On the other hand, he did have an obligation to try to address the issues that had been raised that were in fact relevant. To ignore the issues simply because a specific group is raising them whom you consider anarchists or militants should not be the motivating force that determines whether or not you are going to address the issues. In other words, you don't ignore the issue because you don't like the people raising it. I tried to impress upon him that it was not his right to restrain people from voicing an opinion, however distasteful it might sound.

This effort involved going back and forth, rather than getting the opposing parties together. Our role was to keep the lines of communication open between protesting Native Americans and the authorities because there was very little communication, and no trust level.

I was trying to provide a vehicle for a frustrated minority group who has all but given up on the existing political structures to work through the system—by using our process. I did not say to them their position was correct, or that it was incorrect. There were times when I did debate with them the merits of the issue as I saw them from my perspective, and said I did not think, based on my experience, they had much chance of getting this particular concession, or that, and here's the reason why. And I would point out, when it was apparent to me, there's something here I think the city is in a position to concede to you, providing you are willing to negotiate, and this is an opportunity to prove you can do that. And then, of course, if that doesn't work you still have other options available to you which are more drastic if you should so choose.

One of the things they needed to recognize was that nothing in life is free and people have to be willing to pay a price for whatever it is they are seeking. That meant if they wanted to benefit from the system they had to be willing to participate in it.

The common ground here was I don't think either side truly wanted violence or confrontation. All wanted stability and harmony in the community, and this was the basis for discussion.

The challenge was finding out what had to be done to accomplish that.

You never know for sure what will happen afterwards, but when I left my assessment was the tension level and potential for violence had been significantly reduced.

From the mayor's point of view, it had. Having the situation analyzed historically had been a major development for him. To hear someone put what Farmington was going through into the context of a trend among minorities that was occurring domino-like across the country gave everything a larger clarity. When you found yourself in the middle of a grand tableau of events, sometimes it was impossible to give full and serious consideration to all the undercurrents, so it helped having it called to his attention that this was a time in history when those who felt they had a reason to advocate change or challenge the status quo were tilting wildly at the white establishment, that what the militants were seeking was what they perceived as their rights but they did not know how to go about getting it done working within the system so they adopted the techniques refined by minority and youthful anti-war protestors; and that's what this was all about.

Communication between the Coalition and the city administration continued to be tenuous, but the mayor felt more confident about providing responsible leadership now that the Justice Department had prepared him for what to expect. "They drew a blueprint out for us. This happened today, this will happen tomorrow, and a month from now you can count on this happening. It was almost as if a book had been written they had read and were following line for line. We knew every weekend what was coming before it happened. That's the reason we were able to resist. To face and confront what was happening to us without violence. Justice didn't miss a lick."

Adopting a conciliatory pragmatism and conducting himself in a low-key, statesmanlike manner, the mayor, while continuing to maintain that the community itself was not prejudiced, conceded in an interview in the *Navajo Times* that the rapid growth of Farmington in the past twenty-five years very well may have left a gap in cultural understanding.

"Many of our new residents have come from other areas of the country where they had no knowledge of Indian culture or history and where they had never met an Indian. They come here and have little contact with our Indian residents, and when they see Navajos lying drunk on the streets, they make the generalization that all Navajos are drunks. Longtime residents of Farmington know that this is a false stereotype and we must do what we can to educate our fellow citizens to the dignity of the vast majority of the Navajo people.''

Reversing his previous position of refusing to meet and talk with Coalition leaders, he now said he would gladly meet with them to keep them abreast of developments, and extended an invitation to them ''to demonstrate their good faith and sincere desire to better the conditions of the Navajo people and to work together to better the relationship of all members of the community by supporting the efforts of the Navajo Relations Committee.'' When they rejected his offer on the grounds the Committee was political in its inception and designed simply to appease Navajos, and insulted his initial appointments as ''Uncle Tomahawks'' and ''Redneck John Birchers,'' he did not debate with them, he let their ill-tempered remarks speak for themselves, which he believed proved to any thinking person that the Coalition was not seriously interested in problem-solving and was unable to rise above its own rhetoric.

Holding to a moderate line, his handling of the Saturday marches shifted focus so that rather than preparing for trouble, the objective was to prevent it. ''We always let them take the first step, we never initiated anything. They would have loved for us to storm their parade so they could yell 'Police brutality.' That was one of the things Justice cautioned us about. Not to react strongly, not to take the initiative on anything. The only affirmative thing we did was move the parades off Main to the back streets so all the merchants would be impacted the same.''

The payoff for pursuing a strategy of ''putting oil on the water'' came soon enough. Mayor Webb felt jubilantly vindicated as, with each passing week, he began to notice that the size of the crowds the Coalition was able to turn out on a regular basis seemed to be dwindling. Sometimes it couldn't even be called a parade, just a bunch of people packing the streets listening to a few of the leaders make speeches. If this kept up it would soon get to the point where it would not even be necessary to block off streets along the route on Saturday, they could just put a police escort in front and back, and it would be business as usual.

Thinking back, it was hard for Mayor Webb to believe that all this craziness had been going on for less than two months. Looking ahead, he allowed himself to feel that unless some-

thing unforeseen happened, his town had escaped civil warfare.

On Thursday, June 6, all three of the examining psychiatrists
flew to Farmington where they were met at the airport by
sheriff's deputies. Maybe it was their awareness that Farmington was a town under siege, but it could also have been the
presence of riot guns and armed men in uniform, or the way
they were handled with the care and caution of government
witnesses in a high-stakes trial—at any rate, it was their distinct impression that as much as serving as functionaries of the
court, the deputies were present to provide police protection.

They were driven directly to a motel in Aztec, and once they
were checked into their rooms they stayed in. Dinner was
delivered to their door, and they were not allowed to leave until
called for by the deputies first thing the following morning. At
the district court they were hustled through a back door, then
led to a large courtroom where they were to wait until called to
testify. The last deputy to leave locked the door behind him and
assumed a guard's position in the hallway.

The reason for all these precautions could be seen en masse
outside the courtroom windows, where a crowd composed pre-
dominantly of Indians milled around. They weren't unruly;
there was no sense they were preparing to assault the courthouse; but there was definitely something ominous and vaguely
threatening about them. When, every so often, one would stroll
over to the courthouse windows, cup his eyes, and peer in, the
conversations inside would come to an abrupt and uneasy halt.

All three physicians sat in that big empty courtroom all day,
leaving only when the deputies came and escorted them to the
San Juan Country Club for lunch and again when they were
taken, one at a time, to a smaller courtroom where the hearing
was taking place. All except Dr. Cummins, that is, who was
informed that his testimony was essentially irrelevant since the
boy he evaluated was fifteen and by law could not be treated as
an adult, no matter what. (And at a slow point in the afternoon,
Dr. Cummins slipped out the back door and managed to remain
inconspicuous as he went shopping for an Indian rug to take
home with him so the trip wouldn't be a total waste of his
time.)

When Dr. Winslow entered the hearing chambers, the only
people present were Judge Frank Zinn, Vernon Crawford and
his parents, his defense attorney Felix Briones, and the assis-

tant district attorneys. Taking the stand, Winslow glanced at the parents. This was the first time he'd seen them since they had come to his house, and there had been no subsequent conversations. They seemed extremely nervous and looked at the floor a lot. So did the boy.

As the man who presided over the evaluation team, Dr. Winslow was asked for his general thoughts on what was going on with these youths. He replied that in his judgment three distinct psychological forces were at work in these crimes. First of all, he felt that the youths were to some extent reflecting local attitudes toward Indians. He stopped short of calling them racially motivated crimes because none of the youths had expressed an obsessive hate for Indians. Race may have been a subtext, but it was not the main issue. What he said was that the negative feelings the community harbored toward Indians set a tone that ultimately trickled down to these youths, creating an ethos that made this kind of behavior possible. Because assaulting drunk Navajos was even seen as acceptable behavior by a segment of the population, it was probably easy for these youths to rationalize "rolling Navajos" by thinking, He's a bum, he deserves it.

"If you're going to attack somebody it might as well be somebody you don't like, and the community disapproves of," Dr. Winslow summarized.

This environment of entitlement, he went on to say, provided these three individuals with a screen on which they had projected private individual conflicts. To a certain extent internal turmoil came with the territory for fifteen- and sixteen-year-olds. A lot of changes were taking place and often they were not prepared for the emotions generated by the development of their reproductive systems. They tended to do more "acting out" of early life problems, to behave impulsively. At younger ages the urges weren't there; by eighteen they had more control. At this age, there were always conflicts around sexual issues. The difference here was that with these youths those conflicts were associated with the process of victimization, raising the question: Had these youths been sexually traumatized themselves, and were their crimes an act of striking back?

As Dr. Winslow explained, "Someone who has not been abused himself may have strong feelings, confusion, and conflicts around sexual issues, but he can usually express them verbally, symbolically, through sublimation in socially accepted ways. Those who have actually suffered personal trauma tend to be disorganized and are more likely to express the functioning of their bodies in a disorganized way."

Relating this back to the crime, if these youths had been injured by past experiences in ways that left them with unresolved aggressive feelings, and were living in a social environment that tolerated abusive behavior toward a particular group of people, this, then, could account in a general way for their involvement in these acts.

Finally, he said the examiners felt that at some point the "group process" had taken over. They did not feel that any of the youths would have behaved with the same murderous intent on his own because individually none of them registered as an assertive, secure type. And consciously, each of them knew that while rolling Indians may have been winked at, killing them was wrong. But an evil synergy seemed to take place when they came together under these circumstances. Each, seeing the other excited, had found his own level of excitement augmented, and their passions had built to a fever pitch until a single killing personality was created.

A report containing the specific findings of the psychiatric evaluations had already been submitted to the court, so both prosecuting and defense attorneys knew how Winslow was going to testify. Nonetheless, he was asked for the record whether, in his opinion, Vernon Crawford understood the nature of the charges brought against him, the purpose of these proceedings, and whether he was capable of cooperating with counsel and competent to stand trial? To which Dr. Winslow answered in the affirmative. As to Crawford's sanity at the time of the commission of the offenses he was charged with, Winslow said there was no doubt in his mind that this boy was not legally insane. And he went on to describe a "character disorder."

Then, to Dr. Winslow's surprise, the questioning shifted to whether or not he thought Crawford's illness was treatable. It wasn't that this question was not germane to his testimony; in fact, the very purpose of the hearing was to determine whether the sixteen-year-olds should be bound over into adult court, a decision which hinged on whether or not they were deemed amenable to treatment. It was just that Winslow had expected he would have to make a more vigorous defense of his findings.

Afterward he would comment, "Obviously, at least to me,

they had decided to get this settled as quickly and coolly as possible. They wanted a disposition, and I don't think they wanted a big adult trial. Nobody came out and said that. It's my speculation. But I had testified at trials before this, and a lot more since, and I have never been treated so gently by either side as I was with that group.''

Reflecting years later on his response when the ADA asked him if Vernon Crawford would be amenable to treatment, Winslow would begin by saying, ''When you're dealing with adolescents you don't have a history to be able to say he or she is always going to be this way, because this is the way they've behaved in the past. So there's a strong tendency for most of us, including lawyers, to think that this or that kid might make it yet; that even though he's done something as serious as this, he's still in his formative stages and maybe he'll learn from this experience. Since you don't have any basis for saying he's not going to get well, you like to think rehabilitation is possible and you don't like to throw the book at him. Even now, unless I had good evidence that everything had been tried with a kid, I'd be abhorrent not to give him every opportunity to be rehabilitated.''

And so he testified he did not feel that Vernon Crawford was suffering from difficulties that were necessarily going to lead him into a long career of violence and antisocial behavior, and that he had every reason to believe the boy could be rehabilitated into an ordinary citizen with the proper kind of guidance and treatment and training. At least he had found nothing to tell him this would not happen.

Dr. Winslow was pressed a little on this point. On one weekend this boy participated in the murder of one man, and the very next weekend he was involved in killing two more men. What, from that, suggested he was capable of learning from his behavior?

That was enough to make him wonder what was going on in the boy's head that would prevent him from responding to the guilt he must have felt, Dr. Winslow admitted. But he did not feel that two weeks was enough time to say the kid was incorrigible. If it had been going on for two years, that would certainly have decreased the prognosis.

There followed a discussion about whether or not there was a facility within the state of New Mexico that was equipped to treat these juvenile offenders. Anticipating this question, Dr. Winslow had made some phone calls to the New Mexico Boys

School at Springer to update his information about its staffing, counselors, and treatment programs. It was his feeling that while it may not have been the best treatment facility in the country, it was safe and would give these boys a probable chance at rehabilitation.

Following Dr. Winslow into the hearing chambers was Dr. Rada, who was asked similar questions about Oren Thacker. After paraphrasing what he had written in his report, Dr. Rada was asked about Thacker's capacity for rehabilitation. He said he felt the boy was genuinely remorseful, that he recognized what he'd done was wrong, that he regretted his involvement, and was determined to change his ways. Summarizing his report, Rada stated, "[Thacker] understands the nature and quality of his acts and their wrongfulness. In my opinion he is not in need of psychiatric hospitalization, nor longtime confinement in a penal institution, but would most likely benefit from an extended period of probation with strict requirements to ensure he does not involve himself in antisocial conduct or behavior."

As he left the courthouse that day, Dr. Winslow reflected on the decision facing the judge. In a case like this the discretionary powers of the bench were absolute. Even if the psychiatrists and lawyers agreed that a kid had a horribly distorted personality, had committed a heinous crime, and was a wretched candidate for rehabilitation, the judge had the latitude to say, I'm keeping him in the juvenile justice system. Likewise, in a case where all the examiners voted for rehabilitation, the judge also had the discretionary right to bind a youth over for adult trial.

Although it had been the consensus of the evaluation team that Crawford and Thacker deserved an attempt at rehabilitation, Dr. Winslow felt that the case against a bind-over was not overwhelming and he, for one, was not convinced he knew what the outcome would be. What he did know was that either way the judge decided to go, there would be shock waves.

By early June the Coalition sensed a loss of momentum. Their rallies were no longer generating the same numbers or passion, and they attributed it directly to the intransigence of city officials and their stalling tactics. Something needed to be done to regain the initiative, and a meeting was convened at the Skyliner, a restaurant attached to the terminal of the Farmington Airport, to discuss ways of reenergizing the movement.

One suggestion was to highlight each march with a theme: Demonstrate one week against the liquor dealers, the next for more cultural education in the schools, and then in protest of the energy corporations headquartered in Farmington. While that idea sounded good in the long run, everyone felt that more drastic action needed to be taken soon, along the lines of provoking a confrontation.

Until now, even though the threat of violence had been both explicit and implicit in many of their statements and actions, the Coalition's activities had remained nonviolent. Now serious discussion was given to raising the stakes. Talked about was a plan to exact revenge on the town teenagers—sneaking out to one of their party areas, ambushing one who strayed too far from the others, leaving him to be found the way the Navajo victims had been found as a message that violence against Indians would be answered in kind.

Also considered was the staging of a sensational clash between the forces of racism and its victims that would, of course, be witnessed by the media, who would, naturally, play a dual role: assuring them of a wide audience, and serving as a buffer against excessively brutal consequences.

It was decided that all these plans for escalating the tempo of their protest activities should be put on hold pending the outcome of the court hearing for the three suspects in the slayings. After all, that was what had started this whole business. And the circumstances of the crimes were the supreme manifestation of ingrained problems, from alcohol abuse to violent racism. How these individuals were handled would reveal how serious the justice system took their acts.

The hearing was scheduled for Friday, June 7, and an incident occurred two days prior that added tension to the buildup. When the Coalition applied for a parade permit for the upcoming Saturday, for the first time since they had started marching it was denied. The reason, they were informed, was that a parade permit had already been issued for Saturday, June 8. It was the occasion of the annual Sheriff's Posse Parade.

The Coalition was disgruntled. They claimed that the parade had been intentionally scheduled in order to give the city a legal excuse to deny them the right to march. That wasn't true and they knew it, but that fact was conveniently overlooked because by now it had become almost a sport with them to continue to be troublesome, to keep the pressure on and not let the city relax until issues were resolved.

That Friday, John Redhouse was in Wilbert Tsosie's office at the Equal Employment Opportunity Commission headquarters and they were discussing ways of raining on the Sheriff's Posse Parade when a call came from Rena Benally. "I'm in Aztec along with the family members of the other victims," she said, "and they won't let us attend the court hearing. Will you please come over?"

Perhaps a hundred people were milling around on the lawn outside the San Juan County Courthouse, and when Tsosie and Redhouse arrived they were swarmed. Everyone was talking at once so it took them several minutes to figure out what was going on. Apparently the proceedings were closed to the public, which made everyone on the outside suspicious that some kind of a deal was being cut on the inside.

The Coalition leaders approached the courthouse door, where they were denied admittance. Hostile words were exchanged with the uniformed officers standing guard, but no explanation or concessions were given. Not until a break in the proceedings, when assistant district attorney, Byron Caton, stepped outside to talk to them, did they receive any indication as to what was happening inside.

Caton explained that the judge had invoked a statute that barred the public from being present at a hearing involving the disposition of juveniles. "Not even newsmen are allowed in," he said.

When Redhouse voiced his objection, citing the right of at least the victims' families to know the basis for the legal determinations in a case as personal to them as this, Caton shook his head. "I know, but there's nothing I can do about it."

Redhouse aimed a glare at the courthouse.

Caton shrugged helplessly. "I'm trying like hell to get these guys bound over to adult court. Please, have faith in the system."

When Redhouse said nothing, Caton turned to leave. But before walking away he softly noted, "John, that one kid's crazy. He didn't call them Indians or men. He called them 'things.' "

They remained at the courthouse all afternoon but received no word of the decision. They had to wait for the evening news to learn the results:

"A hearing was conducted today before District Judge Frank Zinn at the county seat in Aztec to determine what action should be brought against the three white youths accused of the

Navajo triple slaying. Because of the recently enacted State Juvenile Code the proceedings were not open to the public and Judge Zinn would not permit relatives of the Indian victims, their counsel, or representatives of the news media into the courtroom. The results of the hearing were released this evening, and the district attorney's motion to bind over two of the three juveniles for adult prosecution has been denied. The youths were sentenced to attend the New Mexico Boys School at Springer for an indefinite period, not to exceed their twenty-first birthdays.''

When John Redhouse heard the sentence he was livid. ''I remember thinking, Damn! They let them off. But I wasn't really surprised. In fact I expected it. It was vindication for what we'd been saying all along: The white man's damn criminal justice system discriminates against Navajos and favors whites. And I felt they shouldn't be allowed to get away with it, that *now* was the time to initiate a physical confrontation.''

The way things turned out, it was almost as if this was the way it was supposed to happen.

A CNL meeting was held at the Indian Center the very next morning to discuss the court hearing, and the outcry of suspicion, indignation, and disgust within the Navajo community at the sentences was unanimous. It was felt that a license for malice had been extended to murder. Not only would the three killers be freed in a couple of years so they could slaughter more Indian people, the leniency of the punishment would incite further crimes. Clearly, to those present, the decision had unzipped and exposed the dirty double standard of justice in Farmington, for no one doubted that if the races had been reversed and three Indian teenagers had tortured and murdered three of the town's white citizens, they would not have gotten off with a legal spanking.

Tempers were flaring, anger building, when someone hurried breathlessly into the hall to report that he had just come from the Sheriff's Posse Parade and seen a unit of U.S. Cavalry soldiers dressed in nineteenth-century-style uniforms and riding horses.

The news was potent. The "Long Knives" were the Navajo's Nazis. The U.S. Cavalry had commandeered the brutal subjugation of the Navajos in 1864. For a contingent of them to parade through Farmington was like having Nazi storm troopers march through downtown Tel Aviv.

As one, those who had gathered at the Indian Center that

Saturday poured out the doors and headed toward Main Street to witness this outrage for themselves.

The parade was led by a group representing the Veterans of Foreign Wars and carrying American flags. There was a band present, as well as fifteen queens from past rodeos, candidates for political office perched waving from the backseats of convertibles, and a tank deployed by the National Guard. A distinct law-and-order character differentiated this parade from the protest demonstrations that had filled the streets the previous weekends, and in the applause from the Anglo onlookers for the uniformed men who passed in review one could sense a statement of support that was meant to be heard by Coalition members, who stood on the sidewalks observing the proceedings with arms folded, scowling behind their sunglasses.

Sure enough, a cavalry contingent composed of six mounted men, one carrying the Stars and Stripes, all dressed as frontier troops, was part of the festivities; and at each stage along Main Street, as they passed the ovation became more pronounced.

As the Coalition leaders watched, they hastily conferred on the meaning of the cavalry unit, and it was a consensus that it could only mean the city of Farmington was going on the offensive. The day after a court hearing which sent a clear message that Anglos could get away with murder if the victims were Indian, the authorities were trying to make a show of force by inviting a cavalry unit to participate—a cavalry unit that brought back memories of how the Navajo had been massacred, most notably at Canyon de Chelly, Arizona, and of their long exile to Fort Sumner.

"I interpreted it as a warning to us—You didn't win in the past, and you can't win today," Wilbert Tsosie said with deadly evenness.

John Redhouse grunted his agreement. "The parade committee was deliberately baiting us."

How long such a moment had been in the making was a matter of perspective: over a hundred years to some, mere months to others. What all would agree upon was the Coalition was about to get what it had been asking for: a chance to test the limits of its power against the forces opposing it. And while whites in the crowd jeered and imitated Indian war whoops, Tsosie and Redhouse stepped into the street to block the passage of the cavalry ghosts of centuries past.

Witnesses, white and Indian alike, disagree on who is responsible for igniting the melee that followed. According to some Indians, when the city police failed in their attempt to disperse the blockade, one of them shouted "Charge," and the cavalry unit spurred its mounts forward, the flag-bearer lowering his standard like a lance and thrusting it at one of the Indians, and that's how it started. The police version, on the other hand, is that the fault lay with the Indians who, on top of disobeying the order to clear the street, threw firecrackers at the horses, which sounded like gunshots. What is indisputable is that the undercurrent of racial tension which had gripped Farmington for the previous seven weeks broke the surface with the first pop of a tear-gas gun, and all hell broke loose.

As someone who observed the fracas, the spectacle of officers in blue helmets chasing long-haired youths down streets and thrashing them with nightsticks before hauling them off to idling paddy wagons on charges of disorderly conduct and disturbing the peace recalled the way the authorities dealt with Vietnam War protestors in the sixties. To many of the almost fifty Indians arrested that day the replay went further back than that: to the 1860s. Only this time instead of being rounded up and incarcerated at Fort Sumner, they were herded into a cell and confined behind steel bars in the Farmington jail.

3

RED POWERS
OF DARKNESS

9

WHITE MAN'S JUSTICE

The decision not to try the three youths as adults for their crimes angered more than the Indian community: The leniency of the sentence caused an uproar in white Farmington as well. A sheriff's deputy summed up public reaction best: "I don't go along, and the next old boy don't go along, with a fifteen-, sixteen-year-old kid who knows right from wrong and does something like this getting off with two years at Springer. I mean, it's just not right. I don't care whether the people they killed were white, Navajo, black, whatever. On a deal like this a kid that age ought to be held responsible for his actions. They're big enough to kill somebody, they're big enough to pay the penalty."

Whatever else they might have felt about militant Indians marching down Main Street, few were prepared to defend the decision. Left to wonder what kind of justice had been done, many were hard-pressed to come up with a better explanation than the one advanced by the militants: White man's justice allowed horrible things done to Indian people to go unpunished.

In the days after the ruling the public search for someone to blame for what was being called "a travesty of justice" focused on the man who presided over the case, Judge Frank Zinn. His decision to bar newsmen from the hearing, as it was reported in the *Farmington Daily Times*, had initially raised questions about the fairness of the proceedings. ("As the reporter asked the judge to scan a copy of the Children's Code which has been interpreted as allowing news media at closed juvenile hearings, the judge walked quickly past the reporter into the courtroom, commenting that he knew what was in the Children's Code and adding, 'I decline to acknowledge its requirements in this case.' '') This was followed by an editorial entitled ''Judicial Secrecy'' which criticized Judge Zinn for being ''insensitive to the public interest.'' It read, in part:

> While we think the judicial process should take every precaution to protect the right of a defendant—adult or juvenile—to a fair disposition of a charge or allegation, it is difficult to see how the barring of reporters from Friday's proceeding could contribute to that protection.
>
> Rather, the judge's decision leaves too much room for doubt in the minds of many who feel the public is entitled to know the legal determinations in a case which has attracted as much attention as the one in question has.
>
> The judge's action in barring newsmen from the hearings fuels the suspicions of those who already have decided that the suspects will not receive just punishment for the crimes.

The editorial in the Aztec daily spoke more to the public response:

> It is safe to say that the reaction following news reports of the hearing was loosely along the line that Judge Zinn should be hung, drawn and quartered, or inflicted with some such punishment for having been so soft on the three boys.

This was not the first time a decision of Judge Zinn's had drawn the ire of the community. Several years earlier, a few days before Christmas, when passing sentence on a college student who had been caught unloading 800 pounds of marijuana from a plane into a van at nearby Navajo Lake, Zinn had given him a deferred sentence, remarking, ''This is a present from Santa Claus.'' Townspeople were ready to string him up then too.

Nor were those who pled cases before him always sure of the conventions he adhered to. ''Zinn was notorious for telling the public to kiss his ass by his actions,'' Assistant District Attorney Tom Hynes would recall. ''The greater the outcry and outrage from the newspaper and the public in a case, the more likely he was to do the opposite of what was expected.''

But just because Judge Frank Zinn refused to explain or justify a controversial decision to the press or public, that didn't mean he didn't have his reasons, or believe that what he was doing was right in the light of the law. As he would say to me some fourteen years later, in the first interview he would give on the case, he was simply following the advice given him by his father, a former state supreme court justice.

"He said never be concerned about what he called the Four P's—Politicians, the Press, Preachers, and Pedagogues—and what they have to say to you. Because they don't really care about the answers to their questions. Most of the time they've got something else in mind and are addressing their constituents, not you. So don't even bother to reply."

It was a Caribbean cruise that designated Frank Zinn the judge in this case. At the time he lived in Gallup, where, as district court judge, he heard all the criminal cases in McKinley County. But there weren't enough cases in that sparsely settled county to keep him occupied full time, so he spent ten days each month in San Juan County, where he handled half the civil cases and all the disqualifieds with Judge James Musgrove of Farmington. Normally Musgrove would have handled this case, but he happened to be on vacation at the time. "I guess I was just lucky," Zinn would wryly suggest later, the irony lying in the fact that of all the cases he would be involved with as a jurist in a long and distinguished career, this one would put more of his conscience and personal feelings at odds with the law than any other.

Zinn was a New Mexico native, born in Tucumcari but raised in Gallup, where his father went to work in 1922 as the assistant district attorney. He remembers Gallup when it was a shoestring town, a mile and a half long, a half-mile wide, population of 5,000, which owed its existence to the railroad. Kids had the run of the town in those days, or so it seemed to him as one of them, and the most exciting thing to do was pursue autographs from the big shots who came through town on the Chief. Sometimes they wouldn't bother to leave the train, but stood on the observation decks smoking and gazing at the scenery; sometimes they would dine at the magnificent Harvey House; and sometimes they stayed over to take an Indian Detour out onto the reservation. Signed 8×10 glossies of cowboy star Tom Mix and silent screen siren Clara Bow topped Frank Zinn's collection.

Watching all those interesting and important people come and go on the train, the yearning to someday be a railroad engineer would stir his imagination. But this was only once in a while, because he knew ever since he started thinking about such things that he was destined to become a trial lawyer, just like his father. It was knowledge born in the county courtroom, where he spent much of his free time watching his father prosecute cases with an eloquent mix of folksiness and flamboyance. The drama of a trial was as exciting to him as a movie, his father had a starring role, and the performance kept his son spellbound. "I thought it was the best show in town, and never wanted to do anything else but what *he* was doing."

One other aspect of his boyhood deserves mention: Although there were only a few Navajo students in school with him, none he was close friends with because they were shy and tended to keep to themselves, he grew up with a deep affection for them. And for their parents, whom he'd see come in off the reservation on their way to and from town jobs. He believed the Navajo were gentle folk, and the fondness he felt toward them included a protectiveness that would remain with him as an adult.

Frank was twelve when the Zinn family moved to Santa Fe in 1932, but he would return to Gallup, moving back in 1959. Both he and the town had changed a lot during those years. Social programs created during the New Deal years and after had improved the economic lot of the town as well as the tribe. "You've seen the old cartoon that's captioned, 'There's money in poverty.' Well you bet there is. You put money in the hands of poor people, they spend it. You put money in the hands of rich people, they invest it. There's a big difference. You figure the Navajo people, or any people living on a reservation, they live free—pay no rent, pay no real estate or sales tax, seldom buy insurance—so everything goes in their bellies or on their backs. And where do they take their money to get what goes in their bellies or on their backs? To civilization. And that doesn't mean the nearest trading post, where they'll be extended a credit line that will gouge the hell out of them. They come to town. And when they return, their pickups are loaded."

As well, drinking had emerged as a major social problem for the Navajo, now that it was legal for them to buy liquor. He recognized there were peculiarities to Indian alcoholism, the most significant being that they drank what they bought before they went home for fear of being arrested for possession by the Navajo Tribal Police. But he also believed "the idea of people drinking to excess isn't any different among Indian people, as far as I can see, than it is among any other people depressed and living in poverty. Go to any big city and you can find all the drunks you want. Gallup was no different.''

In the meantime Frank Zinn was graduated from the New Mexico Military Institute with a commission as a second lieutenant in the cavalry, enrolled in law school at American University in Washington, D.C., and no sooner completed his third semester when he was called to do his part in fighting World War II. He served as a platoon leader in a tank unit in France, and when the war was won he finished law school, returning to Santa Fe and criminal defense work in a practice already established by his father and older brother. Several years later, following in the footsteps of his father who had been active in state politics, he was appointed to the post of assistant attorney general. As prestigious as that sounded, he found himself doing most of the work for the attorney general, which prompted his decision to run for the office himself in the next election. He lost, but ran again to get the bitter taste of defeat out of his system, and won that time around.

Six months later he would resign. His public reasons were given in the form of sardonic quips: The joy was in winning, an attorney general was basically a ceremonial position, he didn't want to have to run for reelection every two years. The truth behind his decision was the governor of New Mexico at the time, John Burroughs, had come to him with a problem: A new judicial district was being formed which took in McKinley County, the people in the Gallup area would resent an outsider being forced on them, and since Zinn grew up in Gallup would he accept the post as judge? He would, he did.

He was thirty-eight at the time, and he had some difficulty making the transition from a practicing attorney who had "defended a lot of rotten guys, some of who were acquitted, some who went to the pen, but my batting average was enough to keep me in business," and a judge who must divorce himself from advocacy, "put your personal feelings on the shelf, keep both cheeks on the bench, and deal with issues as objectively as possible." But he liked trials, enjoyed the theatrical aspects of criminal cases, believed that "adversarial tension" was a requirement of the judicial process much in the way "aesthetic tension" was of value in art and literature. Only when both sides were represented with vigor and intelligence would justice be served. It just wouldn't do to have a district attorney blazing away while a defense attorney shuffled papers and sharpened pencils. On occasion Zinn would sustain an objection no one had made when he thought an attorney was not paying proper attention.

While he would earn high marks as a no-nonsense, decisive judge ("Someone's got to call balls and strikes," would become his motto) whose sentencing was often unconventional (he would put some people on probation who everyone thought deserved stricter treatment, and send others to the penitentiary people thought ought to have been set free), his popularity in Gallup was such that he would have opposition during the first primary election but after that nobody bothered to run against him. His reputation as a fair and intelligent judge, always one step ahead of the lawyers trying a case before him, was augmented by his "progressive" attitude toward crime and punishment, particularly as applied to Indian people.

According to Zinn, "The determination of what to do after a person is found guilty should concern itself with things like what's best to prevent this person from being a danger to society in the future, and what might change his ways. Sometimes you just lock him up for twenty years. That'll change his ways sure enough. But when trying to figure what's best for society, to me that means what will cost the least in terms of future crime or in caring for these people. Just because the law attaches a penalty to the crime, to me that doesn't mean it should be applied to everybody regardless of his circumstances. The idea of making the penalty fit the crime is madness. I think the penalty should fit the person."

From the standpoint of the criminal prosecution of Indian people, given what he knew of the Navajo and their ways, he believed the law ought to accord them special considerations. Their culture and upbringing prepared them for a different world; and so, when their behavior came into conflict with the rules of white society, he treated them accordingly. "Whites don't have a corner on crime or criminality. If an Indian did something ugly, I didn't have any compunctions about sending him away. But I have to admit, if the crime was not violent I dealt with them like children. I'd do things like put them on an honor system."

An example would be, "An Indian steals a car to get transportation home. Not to claim it as his, not thinking he's getting away with something, just uses it for a ride home. So he gets in someone's car, takes it out onto the reservation, parks where the road ends, and walks the rest of the way. What do you do? It's a crime and it's a problem and it needs to be dealt with. But in those days you could get five years in the penitentiary for doing that, and to take some of these guys who are half-crocked when they 'borrow' a car to get home and give them five years—that just doesn't make sense, particularly if the car wasn't damaged, or if it was the insurance took care of it, or the owners weren't adamant about prosecution. So what I would sometimes do, in conjunction with the sheriff, who also recognized the special needs of young Navajo men, was let him set up his own system of parole and probation. Though it would have been considered highly improper and a risk by many, I would release the prisoners to his custody, and he would tell them their lives were in pawn to him. They had to report to the sheriff's office periodically, just like going by the trader with whom they had pawned something, to pay the interest to avoid a forfeiture and to extend the redemption period. And if they didn't report in or if they committed some other offense, then they forfeited their freedom.''

In part, it was his compassion for and understanding of the Navajo that created such strong personal feelings about the case against Crawford, Burke, and Thacker. In a twist on the incipient legal question of whether the offenders should be treated as juveniles or adults, he saw the victims—drunk and defenseless Navajos—as children. And in previous cases where people had offended against children he usually gave them the top of the penalty section. The maximum sentence allowable.

The more he learned about what had happened in Chokecherry Canyon, the more intense his feelings became, until, by the time the transfer hearing was held, he had come to the conclusion, ''I'd handled a good many homicides, but never one as abjectly evil as this case.''

The fact that this was a case that had generated a lot of community heat and, from the standpoint of publicity, was in danger of becoming a media circus didn't complicate things personally for Judge Zinn. Nor did it impact the way he conducted the proceedings. By this time in his career he was adept at handling the press, to a large extent because he had a realistic understanding of their imperatives. He knew they were always in a hurry to make that day's deadline. He believed that most reporters did try to respect the bounds of objectivity and truth, but that entertainment values had softened hard news standards, putting a premium on the most sensational aspects of a story. Which was understandable. He wouldn't presume to

tell them how they should do their job—just as he didn't expect
them to try and tell him how he should do his.

This business of a reporter waving the Children's Code statutes in his face, claiming press entitlement to attend the hearing, had been staged to create news itself, he suspected, which
was why he had brusquely dismissed the request. It was true,
the statutes did permit accredited representatives of the news
media to be present at closed hearings, but it was a discretionary permission, and in his mind and his court the right to
confidentiality in a juvenile hearing took precedence over any
kind of public interest that might have been served by allowing
the press to sit in. It was a summary ruling on his part that
would result in indignation, suspicion, and editorial complaints, but he didn't give it a second thought.

In the state of New Mexico a bind-over procedure had to
prove that the offense was serious enough, that the child was
not legally insane, and that he was not amenable to treatment
within the existing facilities of the juvenile justice system.
Based on his previous experience with the assistant district
attorneys, Tom Hynes and Byron Caton, Zinn felt they probably had a strong case going for them. They were not the type
to charge what they didn't feel they could prove, and as a
general rule nobody pushed for a juvenile transfer to adult court
unless he had a hot case, from both the public standpoint as
well as the evidential.

The first order of business in a transfer hearing involved
testimony on the crime itself—evidence that substantiated a
crime had been committed, which could take the form of statements or confessions, and in this case took the form of Peter
Burke relating his account of the whole pitiful tale as if he was
describing going to a football game on a Saturday afternoon.
He laid it out in a monotone: We stuck a firecracker up his nose
and he kind of batted at it and we all laughed about it. . . .

As he listened to Peter Burke's cold-hearted chronicle of
torture, Judge Zinn found himself struggling to control his own
emotions. He might have been able to understand it if these
kids had taken one Indian out into the hills and, while knocking
him around, got carried away, one doing something, the other
saying *Gee, this is fun. Let's do this*. . . . Or maybe daring the
other—*Come on, you afraid?*—and both of them getting carried away. But after doing one they had had a week to think
about it, to reflect on their actions, to wonder how it could have
happened, to regret it, and that was not what had happened.

The very next weekend Burke and Crawford had gone back out for seconds and thirds, taking two this time and doing them in the same night. He had no doubt that if they had not been caught they would still be doing it, the numbers mounting as long as they got away with their crimes.

Zinn felt that such total and casual disregard of other human beings' right to life left little hope for redemption, particularly when not one iota of remorse seemed to be present. He'd said it many times, even though he knew it was an improper sentiment for a judge to admit to, that there were people in this world who deserved killing, and often the defendant in a murder trial should be given a medal for what the law wouldn't permit or civilization condone. But in this instance, as he listened to Burke testify to how he and Vernon Crawford burned and battered their victims, he found himself feeling that Crawford was the one who should be done away with.

These were interior musings, of course, never given voice, not allowed to influence any of his rulings, and not technically relevant to the question confronting the court. The guilt of these individuals was not being contested. Nor was the nature of their crime at issue. The matter to be resolved was how they should be treated, as juveniles or adults, which was wholly dependent on the testimony of the psychiatrists.

As the prosecution qualified the men who had evaluated the youths, establishing their right to express their opinions as experts, Zinn's thoughts drifted ahead. In his mind he ran through the scenario of what would happen if he did bind the sixteen-year-olds over for trial as adults. Recent Supreme Court rulings had put the New Mexico death penalty law in limbo, so the worst the two kids could get if they were convicted of murder was a life sentence in the penitentiary. A judge who presided at the transfer hearing was automatically disqualified from hearing the trial in criminal court, so he wouldn't be doing the sentencing; but based on his experience, he guessed Thacker would probably be put on probation and Crawford sent to the pen. For how long, he wasn't sure. More than likely the kid's attorney would plead, make a deal for manslaughter, and get him out in seven or eight years. *If* he lived through it, and there were no guarantees a sixteen-year-old in that den of snakes would make it out alive.

But all these thoughts were a form of mental chess that was checkmated when the psychiatrists testified that neither of the kids met the legal criteria for insanity or incompetence, and nothing in their examinations, or the records, indicated that they were incapable of rehabilitation.

On a yellow pad Judge Zinn kept a checklist on which he tallied the basic elements that needed to be established for a bind-over. If any questions went unasked he would speak up. His obligation as trial judge was to amass all the information available and develop a full record. It was at this point in the hearing that he knew the outcome.

"A trial judge always knows the elements you have to have, in this case, for a transfer. There are just certain things that have to be there. And you wait, and you listen. And if the evidence doesn't come through, bingo, she's a goner. You haven't got a case. That's what happened here. It was the burden of the state to prove beyond a reasonable doubt that these were real bad guys with propensities to commit crimes who would be criminals forever, there's no use wasting time trying to salvage them as human beings. But the only state witnesses testified both *were* amenable to treatment. They were the experts, this was their opinion. They left me no choice. I couldn't willfully go contrary to the expert testimony. They left the court with no hinge, no fulcrum, no nothing. You've got to have *somebody* saying that at least one of these kids is a hard-core sociopath before you can bind him over. If I'd have gone against them because I felt differently, it would have been an appealable ruling and would have been overturned."

Although there was little need for deliberation on his part, Zinn called a recess anyway, during which, on a visit to the men's room, he speculated on what had happened. It appeared to him that the prosecutors were let down by the medical testimony, that the diagnosis was not what they had anticipated. And he felt much of the same disappointment he imagined they did because he would have liked to have bound these kids over. In particular he had a strong reaction to Vernon Crawford, whom he understood to be the ringleader. He felt no sympathy for that one. Maybe the kid had problems, but he knew what he was doing, and just didn't care. Some people were just no damn good, the judge thought. Had no feelings for anybody—other human beings or themselves. They were the kind of people you wouldn't mind killing yourself.

Because he would have liked to have sentenced that kid as severely as the law allowed, and at the same time knew that those ignorant of the process would probably interpret his judgment as an act of favoritism confirming judicial discrimination against Indian people, he felt doubly bad. For almost twenty years, ever since he donned his robes, he had personally worked to reverse discriminatory practices in law enforcement that were rampant in the bordertowns. Indians got it both coming and going. Crimes against whites were prosecuted vigorously, while there was a laxity and failure to prosecute crimes committed by Anglos against Indians, as well as by Indians against Indians. It was an unavoidable shame that this case, which was probably the worst you could imagine, would be interpreted as fresh proof that justice depended on the victims' race.

When court was resumed he announced his decision, denying the motion for a transfer. He took note of the audible relief expressed by the Crawford family, as though their son had been acquitted, and moved swiftly through the list of statements required for the record. Because both the defense and prosecuting attorneys were entitled, at this stage, to disqualify him from sitting on the juvenile case, he asked them if that was their preference. They stipulated and agreed it was all right for him to proceed, and the youths were then arraigned all over again.

The rest of the day was spent attending to formalities. He heard from the director of the Boys School at Springer about the capacity for existing facilities to treat kids of this disposition, and what kinds of programs were offered. He'd heard it many times before, and knew that Springer did not truly offer a real therapeutic option, just a structured environment. That was all they'd had for years. But the reality of the situation—the fact that there was no correctional institution in the state that really was equipped to rehabilitate anybody—was not supposed to matter. What did matter, by law, was that the youths were deemed amenable to any kind of treatment, anywhere in the world, period, because the true purpose behind the statute, which indeed was the philosophy behind the whole juvenile justice system, was simply to give kids a second chance.

When it was all over, the judgment rendered, and all three youths sentenced to the New Mexico Boys School at Springer until they were eighteen, after which they could be detained on a year-by-year basis until they were twenty-one, at the discretion of Springer authorities, there was the public fallout to deal with. But even though he felt personally frustrated, and divided in heart and soul, Judge Zinn never let on to the press or the public the nature of his own emotions. He read the editorials criticizing the way he handled the case, and he was aware that public opinion felt his judgment sent the wrong signal, suggesting that the law only winked at crimes against Indians, even encouraging the continued robbing and rolling of Navajos if the worst you could get for killing them was Springer. And he disagreed, totally. If he had been inclined to speak out he would have argued, "You don't make examples out of people in a case for public reasons. You just can't do that. I can't do that. It's not right. A case has to live within its own context, and the identity and circumstances of the victim are not part of it really. Furthermore, people who behave this way are not conscious of the punishments. They don't weigh their acts and say, 'Let's see, if I kill a cop I'll go to the gas chamber.' Most criminals don't care what the consequences are and don't consider them. That's particularly true of violent criminals. A case like this is a one-shot deal. It lasts for two days and it's over, forgotten. How long does the tone of a bell keep ringing unless somebody's whacking the clapper? It just doesn't happen. Oh, the media people and schoolteachers, people at that level, they'll talk about how dispositions encourage crime. They say this is dreadful, a bad example for youth, and so on. But the people down in the sewer don't pay any attention. I don't feel this case made one nickel's worth of difference to those who roll Indians."

The travesty, to his way of thinking, would have been if he had allowed public fervor to get ahead of justice, as it had, in his opinion, in the 1920s in the Sacco-Vanzetti case.

Judge Zinn did not take murder lightly. This was a man who, while fighting the Germans in Europe, once put a gun to the head of a man under his command who was about to execute two captured German soldiers, the same man who had saved his life in action days before, because he made a distinction between murder and killing in wartime. If he could have, he would have dealt as severely with Vernon Crawford as the law allowed. But he believed the decision he'd made was right in the light of the law.

As bad as he felt, there was another way of thinking about it. He wasn't so sure the best place for kids like this *wasn't* back on the street. Few of these kinds of people lived out normal lives. Bad things had a way of happening to bad people. Somebody or something got them for you.

*   *   *

Within an hour after Judge Zinn announced his decision in closed court, the proper papers were signed and the three youths were hustled through his chambers to a county car parked behind the courthouse. Deputy Bruce Brimhall drove and Deputy Chuck McGee rode shotgun. This was not their first trip to the New Mexico Boys School in Springer to deliver juveniles, but never before had they been concerned about an ambush by a lynch mob bent on stringing up their prisoners. They remained tense until they had motored past the uniformed officers positioned like sentries at the end of the alley, driven down the shady back streets of Aztec, and turned finally onto the Bloomfield Highway. Only then were they confident the ruse had worked, that the boys had been successfully ferreted out of town before the Indians were aware of the decision and did something drastic like surround the courthouse.

Handcuffed and squeezed together in the backseat, Crawford, Burke, and Thacker seemed oblivious to the threat. To the amazement of the deputies, Crawford and Thacker even managed to find their predicament amusing, talking and snickering like it was all a big joke. Brimhall, who had been the first officer to arrive on the scene when the first body had been found, and McGee, who had responded to the call on the third body, exchanged wry glances. Neither man was happy with the court decision. Maybe the law had been complied with, but considering the brutality of the crimes and the sadistic manner in which these three had gone about them, they did not think Springer was enough of a sentence.

At one point during the drive, when he heard the conversation in back turn particularly nasty—"I heard one of 'em say, 'Them squaws were more fun 'cause they fought harder and we could screw 'em in between' ''—Brimhall found himself so disgusted he had to suppress the urge to detour up a remote dirt road, take them out one by one, and deal each a hard hand of personal justice.

Around Santa Fe, however, the lapses in the backseat banter lengthened. As they passed through Las Vegas the boys grew even more subdued. It was almost midnight when they exited the interstate at Springer, a depressed little farmtown pocketed in the rolling shortgrass plains of northeast New Mexico, and for miles not a word had been spoken. Wondering if his passengers were so cold-bloodedly blasé they had fallen asleep, Deputy Brimhall searched the rearview mirror. Three sets of eyes blinked back at him, like barn owls. The deputy smirked in satisfaction. Reality was sinking in. No more fun and games.

Once the paperwork was completed and the responsibility for and rights of the three kids were officially turned over to the Boys School officials, the deputies left without a parting word, or an ounce of sympathy. They were waking up the manager of the Oasis Motel in downtown Springer at just about the same time Crawford, Burke, and Thacker were being shown their accommodations: cinder-block cells higher than they were wide, furnished with a thin mattress, a seatless porcelain toilet, and a stainless-steel sink. "Lockup," the maximum-security wing at Springer, was designed to humble the tough guys and troublemakers, and let newcomers know that this was no boys' camp, it was a juvenile prison.

At 6:15 the next morning someone banged on their doors and ordered them up and moving. They were told not to lie down again until lights out at 8:30 that evening. If they were tired of standing or pacing and wanted to sit on their beds, that was okay, but their feet had to be firmly placed on the floor at all times. They were also told not to look out of the sliver of a window in the steel door, or to try and signal to other boys in the next room or across the hallway, or to talk (even to themselves), sing, hum, or whistle. If they wanted anything they were instructed to place a sheet of paper underneath the door with the written request and wait for the staff to answer.

Their doors were opened four times that day: once at each mealtime, when a guard slid a tray of food across the concrete floor like chow in a kennel, and again when they were led to a shower area. "Wash them bugs off," a surly corrections officer barked.

Then it was back to their cells and more time to think about the past that had led them there and the future that was going to be the same for an indefinite number of days, and to ponder the meaning of the cryptic and haunting bloodstains that painted the walls of their cells like cave art.

For the remainder of the day following the tumultuous, tear-gas–throwing melee on Main Street, Farmington braced for an aftershock. Aided by a contingent of specially trained members of the State Police Tactical Force, Farmington police, many garbed in combat suits and helmets and carrying rifles, patrolled city streets. It was reported that riot-control teams were being rushed in from Albuquerque, Santa Fe, Espanola, and Gallup. As if that were not firepower enough to restore calm to the city, Mayor Marlo Webb announced that after conferring with Governor Bruce King and advising him of the situation, the National Guard had been placed on alert and would be called up if further assistance was needed.

Although the outbreak of violence had been a grim enactment of a scene local police officers had anticipated for five previous Saturdays, all things considered, the disturbance had been quelled and order restored with remarkable efficiency. The only injury requiring hospitalization was a brain concussion suffered by a Farmington police officer struck by a car driven by Wilbert Tsosie's sister; the major damage to downtown was a smashed plate-glass window at the Indian Room, a Navajo arts-and-crafts business.

Appearing at police headquarters shortly after the downtown area had been cleared and secured, city officials, wearing attire more appropriate to the golf course and backyard gardening chores, were briefed by the authorities. After a tour of the downtown streets in a police cruiser, the mayor showed up and promptly issued a statement praising the conduct of all law-enforcement personnel for their professionalism and restraint. Calling the violence "regrettable," he said the confrontation proved once and for all that "the Coalition for Navajo Liberation has been more interested in creating issues than in solving problems."

In spite of the efforts by the mayor to give the impression that everything was under control, the racial climate remained dangerously volatile. Anglos were irate because Navajos who had been allowed to march peacefully had not accorded the same right to the Sheriff's Posse. There was talk that white vigilantes, organizing out of the Veterans of Foreign Wars hall, were preparing to launch an offensive (and it was taken seriously enough that a special undercover intelligence unit of the state police was immediately dispatched to investigate). Meanwhile, on the reservation side of the San Juan River, Indians from all over the area were amassing in a show of support for the Coalition. Angry speechmakers attacked the justice system in Farmington, claiming events had proved that the Coalition had been right all along. Some CNL hotheads even advocated taking up arms and storming the city jail to free their leaders.

The storm did have an eye, however, which began to take shape the morning after, when several hundred concerned Indians assembled at the San Juan Episcopal Mission to decide what action should be taken. Opinion was divided almost evenly between those who wanted to continue along the path of confrontation with city officials and those who did not believe the demonstrations and marches had achieved any progress, and felt the time had come to court compromises.

Spearheading the latter group were three prominent Navajo figures, including a former state representative and a tribal councilman. Predictably, in the heat of the aftermath, their moderate proposals were defeated by a voice vote of boos, but when they left the meeting in disgust, as they were climbing into their pickups they found themselves thronged by people who agreed with them. Encouraged, they decided to move swiftly to solidify the consensus and drove to the closest pay telephone where they called Mayor Webb and asked if they could meet with him. Dismayed but not surprised by the parade incident, the mayor sensed in the conversation an opportunity for a breakthrough in relations with "responsible representatives" of the Navajo people, and he went them one better. He told them he would arrange for a meeting to be attended by other city officials and law-enforcement representatives that very evening at Farmington City Hall.

The news media, naturally, were tipped to the meeting and the *Daily Times*'s front-page coverage struck a celebratory tone. "COALITION SPLINTER GROUP CALLS FOR END TO MARCHES" ran the headline, followed by a two-column story whose tone was set by a lead—"The first step toward healing the break in Farmington's Anglo-Indian relations was taken Sunday night in a conciliatory meeting between city officials and Indian representatives"—that was maintained through to the last sentence: "The meeting ended on a note of goodwill as both city officials and the Indians . . . clasped hands and smiled, all promising to meet again."

But there would be no dancing in the streets yet. In fact, once the Coalition leaders were released from jail, they would immediately begin beating their war drums and denouncing the defectors as Benedict Arnolds.

While charges had not been stacked against the thirty-four Indians arrested in the fracas, enabling most to post bond the next day on misdemeanor charges of disorderly conduct and disturbing the peace, Wilbert Tsosie remained behind bars. Grabbed from behind (a picture of a Farmington policeman bear-hugging him would fill a half-page in the next issue of *Time* magazine), Tsosie had broken free and was running down the sidewalk when he was tackled by two white youths who held him down until officers caught up. After he was handcuffed he'd been jerked to his feet and brought face-to-face with a classic moment in the lives of civil-rights activists: The terms of the struggle have changed; a line has been stepped over; it's open combat now, and suddenly you find yourself looking into the ferocious eyes of a skull-basher.

Raising his nightstick, a Farmington policeman sneered, "You've been asking for this."

It wasn't Wilbert's weak bleat, "Police brutality," that halted the blow; it was a second officer with a cooler head who stepped between them, whispering to his partner, "Not now. Not here."

With the nightstick jammed against his throat as if he had already tried to break away and had to be restrained, he was marched to an idling police car and shoved headfirst into the backseat. Cussing, his nemesis joined him, the second cop jumped in the front seat, and a third put the car in gear.

"Make a move. Come on. Give me an excuse," the one beside him taunted.

Pressed against the door, Wilbert held himself rigid.

"What do you say?" The cooler head was addressing the driver. "Shall we take him for a ride?"

For a single terrified moment all Wilbert Tsosie's self-assurance vanished. He knew very well what could happen and he was powerless to change anything. They could say he tried to escape and in the process of subduing him an accident took place. They could say he pulled a knife and their reaction was in self-defense. And it would be his word against three of theirs—if he was around to plead his case, that is. His eyes danced desperately, but he did not change his position.

To his tremendous relief, the driver would have none of it. Not even the talk. "Cut that crap out," he snapped. "And don't mention it again."

When they arrived at police headquarters he was lifted out by his hair and given the bum's rush inside. The next time he would see daylight would be Monday morning, when he was led out the front door like a risk-flight convict: with cuffs on his hands and hobbles on his feet that forced him to take short shuffling steps. Heavily armed guards delivered him to his arraignment at municipal court where he was charged with battery on a police officer and unlawfully disturbing a lawful assembly, both second-class felonies. Bail was set at $30,000,

and it was posted by his father. By late Monday the leader of
the Coalition was back on the streets.

In the days that followed, while other Coalition members
palavered about what strategy should be used to take advantage
of the "berserk overreaction by Farmington Nazis," as they
were characterizing the parade disturbance, Wilbert Tsosie was
distracted by his legal dilemma. Not that there wasn't an over-
lap. In fact, an intriguing offer had come his way that very
much connected the two interests, but in a way that presented
complications for him.

At the arraignment he had been represented by an attorney
who worked with him at the EEOC, but afterward he'd been
informed that his friend's position did not permit him to represent Wilbert in a criminal proceeding. He recommended another attorney, whom Wilbert called for an appointment. After
listening to Wilbert's version of the events, this man stroked
his chin and said he would take the case, but with all the
publicity it was going to be a difficult case, time-consuming,
costly, and he would need a thousand dollars up front.

Wilbert blinked. "Huh? I don't have that kind of money."

The lawyer shrugged, leaving the impression he wasn't sorry
about that.

Back at his office, Wilbert was sitting at his desk staring into
the middle distance, where the seriousness of his situation was
dawning, when the phone rang. The good news was it was a
lawyer calling to donate his services. The bad news was that
what he expected in return amounted to a devil's pact.

The guy was calling from South Dakota, where he listed
among his many clients the American Indian Movement. And
at first he said all the right things. He made Wilbert feel like an
honorable warrior returned from battle. He said he had been
involved in cases like this before, and no sweat, when he was
through, Wilbert would be a national hero. There was only one
thing he said Wilbert would have to be willing to do.

"What's that?"

"Go to jail."

It was not even a consideration. "No. Uh-uh," Wilbert said.
"I just got out of jail and I don't like the place."

"Don't worry, I'll coach you," he heard the voice on the
other end of the line say, as if he hadn't heard. "Think of it as
a performance. Act outrageous. Make them gag you. Make
them drag you kicking out of the courtroom. The cameras will

record every minute of it and I guarantee, the national spotlight will shine on you and your cause.''

"But do you guarantee I beat these charges?'' Wilbert asked. The man sighed. "That's not the name of the game.''

"Well, I've got some felony counts against me,'' Wilbert reminded him. "That could mean the state penitentiary.''

"A small price to pay for the cause of racial justice,'' the man replied.

Wilbert shook his head as if the man were sitting across from him, not in an office somewhere in the Midwest. "No. I ain't going to no penitentiary.''

Again, the man on the other end seemed not to be listening. "Just give me the word, brother. My plane is waiting. I'll fly out today if you give me the word.''

"No. No thanks,'' Wilbert said, and hung up feeling the adrenaline rush that follows a close call.

The next conversation with an attorney was more to his liking. Once again a liberal attorney was volunteering his services, but unlike the one from South Dakota, James Toulouse of Albuquerque did not talk like he might sell tickets to the trial. The two lawyers shared a reputation as men with radical sympathies for minority causes who entered courtrooms armed with First Amendment defenses, but Toulouse had a more long-term view than his ideological comrade, and less faith in the power of publicity. Realizing that most of his clients in these cases were young and idealistic, and that once they matured they very well could develop into fine leaders, he did not want to see career potential ruined by a criminal record. And leadership, not martyrs, was what he felt the Navajo people needed.

If there were some who thought and hoped that once the sting of the tear gas was washed from the eyes of the Coalition, and after the city had seen itself characterized on national network television as a synonym for cities across the Deep South where major civil-rights battles had been fought (a report on the riot was beamed across America on the evening news), each side would take a step back, realize how close they were to igniting a racial war, and discover the means to a neighborly reconciliation of their differences, it was a short-lived dream. If anything, the situation deteriorated.

First, the city and the Coalition got into a rock-throwing contest over the presence of the horsemen in Old West cavalry uniforms. Tsosie called it evidence "the city was willing to promote racial scorn.'' He said that by blocking their path, ''the Coalition for Navajo Liberation has successfully shown we are not to be mocked by a public display of our oppressors.''

The charge that the city had deliberately been baiting the Coalition was denied, of course. A Mrs. Schofield, co-chairman of the parade committee, incensed by the suggestion that the selection of parade participants had been politicized, proved to be a feisty point person in the ensuing debate. The cavalry unit had been planned as a special attraction before the Coalition was even in existence, she stated. It had been arranged through the local army recruiter as a way of promoting his recruitment program. ''Nobody travels a thousand miles to get into the kind of trouble that happened Saturday,'' the lady pointed out. As for regrets about insensitivity, she said that instead of the six-man contingent they had this year, ''It is hoped that we can have the entire twenty-five-member drill team for next year's parade.''

On a more informal level, a number of people chuckled over the fact that the cavalry soldier who had been holding the American flag, and who had jousted with one of the militant Indians, was a black man, pitting one minority member against another. ''That's no big deal,'' John Redhouse would say when the ''joke'' making the rounds reached him. ''Buffalo soldiers killed a lot of our people, too, under that flag. And there were Indian scouts.''

Then, the special Navajo Relations Committee which had been appointed by the mayor with great fanfare collapsed on the night of its very first meeting, when an Anglo committee member objected to the use of profanity by a member of the Coalition, sparking a verbal confrontation, on-the-spot resignations, and the eventual dissolution of the group.

This was followed by a series of legal maneuverings by both the city and the Coalition. Attorneys for the city of Farmington went first, filing motions to deny the granting of additional parade permits to the Coalition. As explained by Mayor Webb, ''There have been five marches in Farmington since the first weekend in May. Each one has forced us to draw law-enforcement personnel from other areas where they are needed. And by blocking traffic, the marches hinder the business of city merchants. These factors, together with the persistent threat of an eruption of violence during a march, make further marches a clear and present danger to the welfare of the community.''

The city succeeded in obtaining a state court injunction against the parades, but when Toulouse, on behalf of the Coalition, took the issue before a federal district judge, the constitutional right of Navajo Indians to come to Farmington and air their grievances in a peaceful manner was upheld. The city again sought to enjoin further Indian demonstrations in state court, and the outcome was an agreement between Coalition and city attorneys which permitted continued parades as long as the Coalition abided by stipulated guidelines on routes and procedures.

Retaining the right to march was only the first of a series of moves taken by the Coalition to strengthen its position in the aftermath of the Main Street "riot." In an effort to keep unity in the ranks and the support of conservative Navajos, Tsosie and Redhouse decided it would be smart to diversify their activities, to rely less on demonstrations as the main method for addressing issues and more on the courts.

Drawing on his legal background, Fred Johnson took the lead. Basing legal action on public nuisance statutes, he filed a petition in district court to close six "Indian bars," alleging that they were the cause of daily violations of municipal, county, and state laws such as drinking in public, littering, reckless driving, and disorderly conduct.

And then, finally, the U.S. government entered the picture. In a letter dated June 10, two days after the parade disturbance, J. Richard Avena, regional director of the United States Commission on Civil Rights, filed a report to the commissioners in Washington in which he stated "the racial tension in Farmington has intensified dramatically in the past few weeks." In addition to the confrontation on Main Street, he cited continued instances of harassment (a Navajo man walking alongside the road was attacked by a group of knife-wielding Anglo youths) and murder (on Sunday, June 9, the bodies of three more Indians were discovered in the Gallup area—stabbed repeatedly). His report was so alarming that it prompted John A. Buggs, staff director, in Washington to fire off a letter to William Saxbe, attorney general of the United States. "The situation in Farmington . . . has moved significantly beyond the specific incidents (killing of three Native Americans). . . . The Commission is aware from its series of investigations and public hearings on and near the Navajo Reservation that incidents frequently occur in bordertowns that violate fundamental constitutional rights of Native Americans. The history of bordertown areas is replete with issues ranging from economic oppression to the effects of the brutal psychology that apparently is operative in the community—that Indian life is somehow less valuable than that of other Americans. We believe the situation to be intolerable. We believe that the Federal Government must utilize all of its authority to enforce the equal protection of the laws guaranteed by the Constitution to all Americans. . . . Intervention [is] necessary to break the violent, brutal cycle that is a reflection of systemic bordertown problems."

A series of interagency memos resulted in the decision to follow the recommendations of the New Mexico Advisory Committee and pursue a deeper, more extensive investigation, coupled with public hearings.

All along, the Coalition had wanted a full-scale public hearing. So they kept in close contact with members of the State Advisory Committee, hoping for an information leak. It came the last day of July, when they were informed that the representatives of the U.S. Civil Rights Commission would be coming to Farmington at the end of August for three days of open hearings.

Their orchestration of the announcement into a public relations coup was masterful. The Coalition's leaders went to Albuquerque on August 1 and called a press conference at which they demanded the hearings be held immediately. In the absence of hearings, they said, they would "issue a national call for continuous demonstrations in Farmington each day of the month" and would march until hearings were scheduled.

The very next day, the U.S. Commission on Civil Rights formally announced its plans to hear testimony concerning civil-rights issues affecting Native Americans in the Farmington area in late August. To all the world it appeared that the Commission had caved in to the Coalition's demand.

In the aftermath of the "race riot" Marlo Webb daily found himself on the receiving end of press inquiries. The wire services, state newspapers, national magazines; reporters, stringers, free-lancers—all came to town to follow up on Farmington's Indian problems, and all, in his opinion, came with a liberal bias.

He would be cooperative. He would be courteous. He would assume they were in pursuit of truth and tried to be factual in his replies to their questions. But even as he spoke he could sense they already knew what kind of story they were going to write. Before they ever arrived in Farmington they knew it was the Home of the Provincial Bigot. Without researching the situation they knew the lineup: it was Farmington vs. the Indians, like some traditional school rivalry, and there was no doubt which team they were rooting for. They came to expose racial prejudice in a backwater western community as if it were a private assignment that was only coincidentally linked to their job as journalists.

He tried to tell them different. He would say, "You're looking for something like what happened in the South, but you won't find burning crosses or lynchings by the Klan here." He would get a flat look back, and knew if he protested any louder they would suspect him of being part of a cover-up or conspiracy.

Thanks to deadlines, most of the press was in and out. But some hung around as if hoping to be on hand for the next violent outbreak. For a scene like the one promised by the manager at Sambo's: "Hey," he was supposed to have said. "Ain't none of them sonsabitches gonna pull a sit-down again in here. They try to and I'm gonna get on the CB, tell all the truckers in the area there's free coffee at Sambo's, come on down. I'm gonna fill the seats with my kind of people, and we'll see what happens."

It was an impossible situation for the mayor, and when he learned that the U.S. Commission on Civil Rights was planning to hold public hearings in late August, he was afraid it was only going to worsen things.

Mayor Webb did not see the need. He thought it would be a waste of taxpayers' money. He was concerned that "outside intervention" could only aggravate matters. And after polling community leaders, who agreed with him unanimously, he notified the Commission that he was not requesting nor did he endorse the hearings.

But even as he registered his objection he knew it was a lost cause, and when he was informed they would proceed as scheduled, with or without his blessing, not to be completely shut out he made it known that he wished to participate as a witness.

The hearings were held in an auditorium at McGee Park under irritating conditions. The weather was hot and humid so the doors were kept open for ventilation, admitting hordes of flies and periodic gusts of dust. Numerous times the testimony was drowned out by nearby road equipment sprucing up the grounds for the San Juan County Fair and proceedings had to be temporarily halted. The audience was restless, constantly shifting in their seats, sitting for an hour or two and then leaving for fresh air or refreshments at a hastily opened stand across the grounds. One of the few attendees who remained for the entirety of every session was Mayor Marlo Webb, who not only sat through hours and hours of continuous testimony in a hard, straight-backed chair, he took notes the whole time. And after three days of exhaustive testimony, his suspicions were confirmed. A pre-hearing briefing had assured him that these would be impartial hearings, not adversarial proceedings, but the contrary was the case. It was apparent to him that a major propaganda event was being staged, a mock trial in which Farmington was the defendant, the Coalition for Navajo Liberation the prosecutor, Commission representatives the judge and jury, and the outcome predetermined. The entire blame was going to be laid on the community.

A parade of witnesses alleged that Navajo people were not treated equitably in schools, businesses, courts, jails, and hospitals, and were the victims of consumer fraud, economic exploitation, and employment discrimination, which perpetuated poverty and helplessness and the despair that led to drunkenness. Altogether they painted a dire picture and predicted more violence if the situation were not turned around soon.

The mayor had heard it all before and thought most of the criticism had a rote quality. But the Committee was obviously impressed and appeared to him to be deeply moved. And so, when at last the mayor strode to the witness table for his turn, feeling he had nothing to lose, he prefaced his remarks with a frontal attack on the credibility of the Committee, likening these hearings to agitprop.

Mr. Chairman, members of the committee, ladies and gentlemen. For the past two days we have heard a great deal of testimony concerning the relationship of the Anglo community with its Navajo neighbors. . . . The record has been filled with emotional statements, broad charges of discrimination, [and] many statements of untruths. . . . Up to this time I have found my preassessment of these hearings confirmed and my worst fears realized.

(PAUSE)

Mr. Chairman, I have documented evidence that the majority of this committee are members of the Communist Party and this hearing is being held for the sole purpose of contributing to the overthrow of this government.

(PAUSE)

Before some newsmen dash out of the room to phone in a headline, let me explain—I have made this malicious, unfounded, and untrue statement only to make a point. The statement, if left unexplained; as most of the testimony up to now has been, would stand in the record as fact with no proof necessary or required. Such has been the case in these hearings. Accusations have been made without documentation, broad charges made without specifics being asked for or cited.

I believe that this failure to cross-examine, to insist on proof, or to even question most charges is indicative of the attitude of this committee . . . [and] the committee's preconceived judgments and personal prejudices.

George Washington once said, "Truth will ultimately prevail if enough pains are taken to bring it to light." As a believer that there is no compromise for truth, I intend to see that truth does prevail.

He proceeded to contradict the statements of the majority of the preceding witnesses, and paint an entirely different, far more benign picture of the Indian situation in Farmington. But even as he spoke he sensed the futility of his endeavor, and believed that rather than educating the Committee he was speaking for the record.

10

WHISPERS OF
WITCHCRAFT

Immediately after the court hearing Rena Benally went to the Sheriff's Department in Aztec to pick up what remained of her husband's personal effects.

I explained to the officer on the desk that I was told I could come back and pick up his things after everything was over. He looked at me and said, "Is everything over?" I said, "No, I don't think it will ever be over." He stood there thinking about what I'd said, then he said, "Okay," and went to a back room. I could see him looking for Benji's things, and from time to time he would stop what he was doing and look back at me. He was coming back when the phone rang. He could just have given me what he had, but he didn't. He answered it and made me wait. And he kept looking at me while he talked.

I got his silver ring back. There was a tag on it that said it had been taken off Peter Burke. And I got his shoes back. You could see the scratch marks underneath where he had tried to push himself back from the ledge. There was sand and blood mixed together along the soles. They gave me his shoes and one sock.

I asked where his jacket was. "May I have it, please?" I said. "Even if it's burned, I want to take it home." I didn't want anything of Benji's left in that place. The man said it was too far gone—"unsalvageable," he said—and they had thrown it away.

He kept staring at me, listening to every word I said, watching how I acted. He really wanted to know how I felt about everything, but I wouldn't let him. He asked me if I wanted to stay and have a cup of coffee and talk. I said, "No, thank you." I just wanted his things. That's all I said and walked out.

He followed me out. I looked back once and he was standing in the door watching me. But I just kept walking.

Once she had retrieved the last of the "evidence," Rena went through a Blackening Ceremony, a rite designed to remove the contamination of contact with the dead. Her body was rubbed with greasy mutton tallow, then wiped with the ashes of weeds burned on a flat rock. According to custom, this made her invisible to the malevolent ghost of her husband's spirit. Then her husband's things were prayed over, the medicine man sang, and she was blessed. She did not wash for four days, and when finally she did bathe, according to traditional belief she was now safe from the illness and misfortune that were believed to haunt those not protected by the ceremony.

As for her feelings about the outcome of the court hearing, Rena had come to a place of uneasy resignation. Although her Christian upbringing had oriented her toward forgiveness, to think in those terms went against the grain of her emotions. For this reason she had steeped herself in prayer and there, it seemed, she had found the grace to put her feelings aside and let the Lord's will be done.

Her response had not been typical among those related to the victims, however. Others, left with a more active residue of resentment, were not content to let the court's verdict be the final one. They also would turn to deities, but not for solace. Rather, they sought satisfaction through clandestine Navajo spiritual practices.

At least this was the theory that I wanted to investigate, and the reason I approached Rena and asked her to arrange an interview with a medicine man. I knew the *haatali*, as medicine men were called, as well as doctoring and performing priestly functions, were ceremonial leaders. When confronted with problems they could not answer with natural knowledge, it was said they consulted with spirits to find solutions. And for money and gifts and sometimes as a favor, they would even invoke supernatural assistance on behalf of The People.

I was aware that helping me with research had made Rena's life less comfortable. I'd heard that the same people who had blamed her for her husband's death resented the fact that she was cooperating with me. And yet I got the distinct feeling that Rena also enjoyed her involvement with my investigations. I liked to believe that it was because she had faith that a worth to this story would eventually be acknowledged by those currently condemning her.

Her response to this request was the closest she had come to just saying no, and when I asked her what bothered her about it she expressed a serious concern for my welfare if I pushed too hard for information on the witchcraft angle.

"Why? Do you think someone is going to put a hex on me?" I asked with a pinch of sarcasm.

The look she gave me said, You never know, which had the exact opposite of its intended effect. I don't think she realized the extent to which the notion there were people in this world who could attract and manipulate unseen forces animated this story in my mind.

For this reason, the next time I asked her if she would locate a medicine man for me to talk to, I tried to assure her that this was not so unusual a request. White anthropologists had been conducting this kind of inquiry for years. I also told her I had no intention of making specific references to the nature of our relationship, the purpose of my inquiry, or the acts that sparked my interest. I said I even preferred that he *not* have any background to work with, because his responses would be cleaner that way. Finally, I said I was willing to pay.

I was startled when she simply said, "When do you want to go?"

I looked closely at her. "Right now."

She hesitated. "I can't say for sure he'll talk to you. . . ."

"Of course not," I hastened to acknowledge. "That's for him to say."

It took us the better part of an hour to get there from Farmington. We followed a two-lane blacktop west toward the stacks of the coal-fired Four Corners Power Plant that were puffing sulfurous plumes of pale smoke skyward like a gas geyser, turning an otherwise clear day hazy and leaving a film of dust on the postcard views of Shiprock Peak. Then, at a side road without a sign to mark it, she directed me to turn left down a rough and rutted lane that led across and along an irrigation ditch, which brought us to a fenced compound of packed dirt. On the far side a rectangular cinder-block house built in the shade of a cottonwood was surrounded by the usual debris that collects around homes in Navajo country: broken-down vehicles, a doghouse and an outhouse, leaning stacks of cedar firewood, all of which composed a playground for loose-running chickens. But the obvious center of the compound was a newly constructed hogan. You see them all over this country: circular or six-sided dwellings, many constructed of earth and stone and covered with sod, their doorways always facing east. But this one was as close to a suburban doctor's office as you're going to find on the reservation. It was apparent the medicine man I was about to meet ran a thriving practice.

There was a pickup parked in front, and as we pulled up an elderly couple hobbled out of the hogan. There are traditionalists on the reservation who feel that the power once held by medicine men to work magic through special ceremonies belongs to another age. They point to the radio towers bristling on the bluffs above Farmington where religious ceremonies used to be conducted, and recall the caves along the San Juan River that were flooded when Navajo Dam was built, and say that the sacred sites have been desecrated. They refer to the Squaw Dances that are advertised in the newspaper, the sandpaintings for sale in the trading posts, the sacred songs played on the radio, and say that all these were given to the Navajo by the Holy People and were not to be shared with others. They believe that for magic to work it must be covertly practiced, in ritually prescribed ways kept within the tribal family. The soul and strength of the Navajo, these doomsayers contend, have been bled by exposure and commercialism. Nonetheless, religious ceremonies continue to be held and are widely believed to be effective. A family is not going to pay $1,000 for a Yeibichai sing or $2,000 for a Fire Dance (the going rates) if they doubt the value of traditional rituals.

Watching the couple depart, I thought about how these people had come here believing this man still owned the knowledge and power to cure the sick in mind and body through ceremonies, songs, prayers, and herbs, and I wondered if they were going away better than they came. I also wondered how I would assess the outcome of my visit. Since it was information I was seeking, not treatment, would I come away wiser? Just as I knew that a Navajo family could call on a medicine man to heal human suffering, was I about to find out about rituals that could be performed to direct harm to people?

I let the couple leave before I parked, and for a moment Rena and I sat there, saying nothing. I have no idea what she was thinking, but I was asking myself if I had already made a misstep and we should have called ahead of time. And what—scheduled an appointment with his secretary?

Rena broke the silence. "I'll go in first and talk to him."

I watched her go, noting her tentativeness and appreciating her position as my cultural ambassador. Rena had said she did not personally know this medicine man, only that he had a good reputation and was one of the few who spoke English. When she disappeared inside, I immediately went about organizing my thoughts into an order that prepared me for what I imagined was going to be my strangest interview to date.

The situation was far from clear. Through a network of hearsay and gossip I had been led to believe that family and friends of the slain Indians, feeling disharmony and anger at the outcome of the white man's judicial system, and a need for action and retaliation, had gone to a medicine man who, acting as a witch doctor, had cast a curse on the three youths. Of course most white folks I talked to scoffed at the idea. When I mentioned the witching rumor to Lieutenant Miller, a dubious expression dimpled his face. So I asked him, "Wouldn't it strike you as just a little bit strange if, in fact, all three youths are dead?" His eyes bored into mine. "Not half as strange as the way they done those Indians," he answered, as if nothing more needed saying.

A number of other Farmington people had just as much trouble taking Navajo witchcraft seriously. I heard comments like, "What kind of story is that? A ghost story, that's what." "People are free to think as they please, but in my book belief in the supernatural is pure superstition. It's just another one of those Indian bugaboos." And, "There's no such animal," a reference to the fact that Navajo witches were also called "skinwalkers" because it was believed they could turn into wolves, coyotes, or bears.

There were some, however, whose experience inclined them to keep an open mind about these things, particularly when they had been personally involved in incidents that defied rational explanation. A retired criminal investigator for the Bureau of Indian Affairs told me about a case he had been called in on that still made him scratch his head. "This was over near Tuba City, and someone was placing bird feathers on graves in a cemetery. That had people upset since it was supposed to mean a hex was being put on the surviving family members. The Navajo police looked into it, and found animal tracks that appeared to be dog or wolf leading away from the graves for about a mile, and then vanishing. So they called me. All right, white man. We want an explanation. Well, I went out there and I picked up the trail leading out from the cemetery, and they were right, it was dog or wolf tracks, and I followed them to their end and then there was nothing. Nothing but a hogan but it was a good fifty feet away. A person would have had to have been an Olympic vaulter and then some to cover that distance and not leave any sign. But there were none. And the ground had not been brushed or disturbed in any way. I thought, Hey Joe, slow down. Maybe there's something to this.''

In the time I'd spent in Farmington I'd spoken with two Anglos who said they had heard from Navajos themselves about the curse. One was a woman who had trained as a ''healing therapist'' under a Navajo medicine woman. Assured that she was not some pseudo–New Age mystic but someone highly regarded in the community, I contacted her and we spoke at length. She admitted that her teacher had mentioned something about this and it was her understanding that a group of medicine people had gathered and decided it was not right for these three youths not to have to face up to what they had done in this lifetime. So they had concentrated on collecting the negative energy (her words) the boys had directed toward their Indian victims and reversing it. Turning the evil around so it worked against the evildoer, in other words. I asked her if she would arrange for me to meet with the medicine woman. She did not think the chances of that happening were good, but agreed at least to bring up the subject the next time they got together. A month had passed by the time I called her back. Yes, she had spoken with her teacher. No, she would not discuss this matter with me. And the way the therapist characterized the refusal it sounded like she'd been made to feel foolish for asking.

My second source on the subject was a reporter on the local newspaper who was interviewing *me* for a change, I suspect to see whether he had missed out on a story with larger implications than he'd previously thought. When I mentioned the whispers of witchcraft he said, ''It's no rumor. I knew the guy who threw the curse.'' I looked at him casually. ''Oh? Tell me about him.'' He related a story about a party he'd gone to some years back that was also attended by a well-known medicine man who had bragged that he was the miracle worker who had cast the spell that sentenced the boy-killers to death.

I had my reservations. From what I'd read, shamans and sorcerers were not braggarts. Indeed, it was my understanding that once their power to direct evil was known, they lost it. That was one of the reasons the subject was shrouded in secrecy. By some accounts it was also written that when a source of witchery is revealed, he is marked for death.

Thinking to myself, So there are charlatans in that profession too, I nonetheless asked the reporter how I could get in touch with this individual.

"That would be hard. He died in a car wreck not long after that."

My gaze shifted to Rena who was standing in front of the hogan, gesturing for me to come; and grabbing a leather satchel in which I kept a tape recorder and notepad, I jumped out of the car and hurried down a path of bootprints toward her. When I reached the doorway I stopped and peered inside—and winced at the betrayal of all my expectations. I'm not sure what I imagined the interior of a medicine lodge to look like, but I know I didn't think that it would be indistinguishable from a Route 66 roadside attraction, which was my first impression. Taking in the cheap veneer paneling on the interior walls, crayon-colored Indian blankets for drapes on the windows, and a series of Taiwan tapestries I'd seen displayed for sale out of the back of panel vans in Albuquerque (several contained American flag imagery and one was a tribute to the United States Marine Corps), I made a swift internal readjustment.

I went in. A man was standing with his back to me, stoking the fire in a sheepherder's stove set in the center of the hogan, its pipe chimney rising through a smoke hole in the roof. Not until he was finished with his chore did he turn to meet me.

He was a robust man in his fifties whose crew cut and black-framed glasses gave him a stern look. He wore cowboy boots, jeans, a white T-shirt under a blue nylon windbreaker, and could have passed for a construction worker were it not for the jewelry. Rings on every finger but his thumbs. A watch on one wrist and a turquoise-encrusted bracelet on the other. A fancy belt buckle and several necklaces. Earrings studded each lobe. When he shook my hand it was not the light finger-brush customary among Navajo, but a firm grip that subtly seemed to test the strength of my own handshake. He gestured toward two folding chairs and as I took one, Rena sat in the other, and he sat across from us. Resting his hands on his knees, he gave me a perfunctory nod that I took to mean, Go ahead.

I returned his gaze, wondering what Rena had told him and how he had sized me up. Did he think I was a latter-day hippie looking for a Native American guru? An unenlightened seeker of higher consciousness? I hoped not, but just the thought sat me up straight. In spite of my lowered expectations, I wanted to present a demeanor that said I was here to be edified by him, without appearing suspicious or gullible.

In a soft hoarse voice he asked me, "What do you want to know?"

I decided I might as well go straight to the heart of things.

"Have you ever applied your knowledge, your powers, to a criminal case in a white man's court?"

He answered as though he were on the witness stand and this was sworn testimony. "Yes."

"Would you give me an example?"

His English, when he spoke in sentences, was rougher than I had wished. In fact it was so broken and slurred he might have had a speech impediment. But I got most of what he said. Using a method of divination that employed crystals and water, he had been able to see a missing person or guilty party, and describe them in sufficient detail that those who came to him were able to identify them by name. At times he had also been able to tell in what direction they lived or where they could be found, and in that way he had been of help in court cases.

"Have you ever performed any ceremonies designed to influence the outcome of a court case, where Navajos are involved?"

He did not respond, so I gave him a hypothetical.

"Let's say an Anglo commits a crime against a Navajo, and his family is afraid justice will not be done. Can a medicine man be of help?"

"Yes," he replied.

"How?"

From his coat pocket he removed an eagle-bone whistle and blew several shrill notes. "I use this," he said. "I go outside. I blow the whistle in the Four Directions. I pray. I sing. The answer comes."

"What ceremony is that?"

He shrugged. I thought maybe he misunderstood the question so I asked, "Is that part of the Blessing Way? The Enemy Way?"

For the first time he smiled. He said he did not know the ceremonies by name so he couldn't say this was part of that. A situation was presented to him, he knew what had to be done, and he went about doing it. That was how it worked.

He did not elaborate, even though I tried to prompt him with a half-dozen more questions, trying to get a fix on the particular ceremonies. I wanted to hear more about the incantations and rituals. I wanted to hear him talk about the magical medium of ceremonials in which certain Holy People could be invoked to assist the Navajo through special supernatural powers. In other words, I wanted him to make the spirit world more palpable to me.

"You said that you are able to see people in crystals and water. Would you show me how this is done?"

That request presented no problem, and he reached for a red Sears toolbox, flipped it open, and removed a beaded leather pouch. Loosening the drawstring, he took out a clear glass which he set on a table. Underneath was a jug of water. After the glass was about one- third full, he swirled the water around and held the glass out in front of him, tipping it at an angle. He said all he had to do was look into the water and pictures appeared.

I nodded. "I've heard about this power. And I'm told some medicine men can look at a photograph of a person through crystals and water, and see things no one else can. Is that so?"

He nodded.

"Would you be willing to look at some pictures and tell me what you see?"

Beside me I heard a rustle that was Rena either changing her position or squirming in her seat.

When the medicine man nodded again, I reached down into my satchel and withdrew a page I had Xeroxed out of the 1974 Farmington High School Yearbook. It was a junior class photo page. The faces of thirty students looked out, and among them were Vernon Crawford and Oren Thacker.

"Do any of the faces stand out, or strike you as unusual in any way?" I asked, handing him the page.

He scanned the page from top to bottom, stopping several times for a closer inspection, before looking up at me. "I see a lot of things," he said.

I realized that was probably true, and that perhaps the way I had set this up was unclear. I had thought maybe a certain face would jump off the page at him, but that was just the way I construed the test. Apparently he needed to have a better idea what I was looking for.

Leaning over, I pointed to Vernon Crawford's picture. "Can you tell me anything about this boy?"

He held the glass over the photo, appearing to use it like a magnifying glass, moving closer, to the side, as though searching for a proper focus. At last he found it and said emphatically, "I see a bear."

"A bear. What does that mean?"

"He is big and strong. Pushes his weight around and uses his strength against people. He's uncontrollable, has a short temper. This boy's a brute."

"Anything else?"

Again he held his glass over the photo of Vernon Crawford. "He smokes."

I recalled the comment of one of Crawford's teachers who said how strongly he smelled of cigarette smoke when he came to class.

"A lot of stuff," the medicine man added.

"Meaning?"

He just looked at me.

"You mean pot?"

He nodded.

I remembered classmates telling me how Crawford was frequently stoned. And the marijuana and paraphernalia police found in his car after it was impounded.

"How can you tell that?" I asked.

"Green spots. On the side of his head," he replied, and extended both the page and glass to me, as though they could be seen by anyone who looked. But although Crawford's face swam in and out of focus, I saw no green spots.

Leaning back, I reappraised the man sitting across from me. I did not believe he knew why I had come, and even if he did, that did not explain the character and accuracy of his observations.

"What about this boy?" I asked, pointing to Oren Thacker's impish face.

Seconds later he informed me he was seeing "A deer."

"And what's the difference between a bear and a deer?"

"You know how a deer is. It's not like sheep. It doesn't stay in a flock. It wanders the hills. This boy is wild like that. Acts crazy. He's unstable. Don't know what he'll do."

That was the way Oren Thacker's mind worked all right, I thought.

"Anything else?"

After studying Oren Thacker's photo for a moment longer, he returned to Vernon Crawford's picture. This time when he looked he saw something but he did not speak right away. He seemed to look closer, a second time, for confirmation.

"What?" I asked.

"There is witchcraft associated with this boy," he announced.

I pretended to be surprised. "Witchcraft?"

Putting the water glass down and handing me back the page, he didn't answer.

"Can you tell me more about that?" I requested.

"I've been doing this for eighteen years and I haven't been able to find much out about witchcraft," he said.

"Do you know who does it? How it's done?"

He shook his head. "No. I know it goes on though, because I've undone it for people."

He went on to say he had no expertise in this area, it was outside his jurisdiction. I wondered if he knew more than he was saying and just wasn't telling me, but I did not think it would be appropriate to probe any harder. I could tell he wasn't comfortable with the subject, and the motions he was going through returning the water glass to its pouch were as much as telling me the session was over.

Reaching for my wallet, I placed a twenty-dollar bill on the table beside the red metal toolbox and rose to leave. At the doorway, I paused, hoping for some final exchange, but his back was turned to me again and he was stoking the coals in the sheepherder's stove.

The New Mexico Boys School was established in 1909 when the citizens of Springer donated their stately, three-story brick courthouse to the Territory of New Mexico. Since the town had lost its status as the county seat ten years earlier to the coal-mining town of Raton, forty miles to the north, the grand old edifice had stood empty.

The town would remain the site of the state's juvenile reformatory, but in time the stolid redbrick courthouse would retire and become a museum, and an expanded facility would be erected on 2,500 acres west of town. Designed to hold approximately 200 kids, it is a cottage-type residential treatment center that features seven lodges, a gymnasium complete with a swimming pool, an academic and vocational building, and a cafeteria with an up-to-date bakery. As with juvenile reformatories elsewhere, the Boys School at Springer tries to prepare a delinquent youth for a positive reentry into society by providing him with a variety of educational opportunities, plus some job training, along with individual counseling.

A considerable amount of publicity preceded the arrival of the three youths from Farmington. Not only had they made headlines on the outside, their offenses were far more severe than any of those committed by the population at large on the inside. Crimes against property was the big category: burglary, auto theft, petty larceny. Now and then, in the past, there had been a kid committed for killing someone, but the circumstances were usually mitigating. A stabbing in a gang fight. The shooting of an abusive father. In 1974, Crawford, Burke, and Thacker were the only boys admitted for murder.

And yet none of the three struck the staff members who evaluated them during their "orientation" period as incorrigible delinquents. In spite of the violent nature of their crimes, none of them came with a long history of law-breaking habits, whereas many of the others had previously spent time in a correctional facility.

Once they were given physicals, interviewed by the consulting psychiatrist, and assessed by a central classification committee, they were assigned to different lodges. It was automatic that so-called brothers in crime were separated. There was too big a chance that if they were placed in the same quarters they would reinforce each other for the wrong reasons.

When the "new" facility was built in the fifties the lodges had been named for letters in the alphabet. Since then they had been renamed after trees, to give the grounds the ambience of a summer camp. Oren Thacker was assigned to Cedar Lodge, Burke went to Redwood, and Crawford to Elm.

The layout of all the lodges was basically the same: a sleeping area furnished with bunk beds; a day area appointed with chairs, tables, couches, and a pool table; a TV area; a locker area; and a shower area with half-doors on the toilet stalls. In the center of the open setting was a security station where seasoned juvenile correction officers (JCOs) maintained around-the-clock surveillance. With the help of rounded mirrors the size of hubcaps mounted at strategic places around the inside of the lodge, from where they sat they could view every wall and every corner of the building.

Although an Individualized Treatment Plan was alleged to be developed for each inmate—particularized programs directed to each boy's needs, supported by the intensive psychological sessions—the fact of the matter was that the Boys School did not offer uniquely tailored treatment regimens, nor was therapy in the professional sense a major part of the

Springer experience. Indeed, at the time, psychiatrists and psychologists generally were not held in the highest esteem at Springer. In the opinion of one former staff member, "Ninety percent of the psychiatrists I've met have no business passing themselves off as authorities. They went to college, had a problem, didn't want to discuss it, so they took psychology classes to find the answer to their own problems. Got so many hours in and ended up majoring in the field. My feeling is that a lot of them do more harm than good." While not a point of view that received official endorsement, the sentiment that you didn't need to have a licensed psychologist involved before therapeutic results were achieved was shared by a lot of people at Springer.

According to Steve Hill, director of programs at the time, "What we find is that the kids have an easier time relating to the staff they spend time with, be it the JCOs who supervise their daily activities, the teachers they come into contact with, the maintenance crews working around the campus, than they do to a stranger, no matter how many academic stamps of approval he has, who pulls the kid out of his living situation, takes him into a room, and tries to root out the cause of his problems. There are several reasons for this: That's who they are living with; that's where problems are coming up; and that's where they're going to get immediate feedback, which is important. So what we try to do is promote the idea of the para-professional. To give all the staff some in-service training so when a situation comes up they can counsel the kids. We think that if you take a person who is able to empathize with others, is a good listener, and shows sincerity, that with proper instruction he can do as good as or an even better job than a psychiatrist."

The treatment philosophy at Springer relied on Glasser's "Reality Therapy," an approach that did not look at a kid's record, see a string of priors, and automatically assume the kid was a hopeless case. But neither did it allow him to lay responsibility for his behavior on his past. Just because his father was an alcoholic or his mother ignored him, that did not justify his breaking the law. It said, in essence, that here he could start out from scratch. It stressed the idea that everyone had the option of changing his ways. And following this, it tried to motivate the kid in a positive direction.

Realistically speaking, no one at Springer expected the kids there to walk out with all their problems solved. What they hoped to do was get the kid looking into his strengths, cultivate his ability to deal with and overcome difficult situations, and give him some trade skills so when he left the facility he was enthusiastic about the future.

Predictably, some you would feel good about, some you wouldn't know what to think, and others you would expect to see back in the custody of the Department of Corrections. More or less, that was the breakdown of what the staff would come to think about the prospects of the three youths from Farmington.

By almost every conventional measure, Vernon Crawford turned his life around during the two years he spent at Springer. He would represent his lodge on the student council at the Boys School, working for the betterment of school programs, which earned him the right to represent the Boys School at the state convention of student councils to exchange ideas with students from public schools across New Mexico. His superior academic work and positive attitude would gain him a place on the honor roll, and after he had completed the G.E.D. program and received his high school diploma, he took a college-level correspondence course in philosophy through the University of New Mexico. Perhaps most impressive, he would help found *RAP*, the student newspaper, and taking a particular liking to journalism, he would rise from reporter to assistant editor to executive editor all in a matter of six months. So profound was his apparent change and growth, so distinguished was the record he left behind, that he would be remembered as a model student, cited for years as an example of successful rehabilitation.

According to those who were in a position to observe this remarkable transformation closely, Crawford, through no fault of his own, did not have an easy time of it at first. Although he was obedient and polite around staff, and appeared to have little difficulty adapting to the rigorously structured routines of reformatory life, the nature of his offenses caused him problems. The "Shots," as they were called, the tough kids who liked to swing their weight, felt they had to put the newcomer with the "name" to the test. He was constantly reminded that he was an "Indian killer," and was challenged verbally and physically to prove he was as bad as his reputation.

But he was not inclined to play king-of-the-mountain and he refused to be goaded into a reaction. Indeed, it struck the JCOs working in Elm Lodge that, if anything, the kid was a walking case of guilt and remorse. He refused to talk to fellow students about the acts that had gotten him into trouble and would walk away when asked. To disassociate himself from the person everyone seemed to think he was, he went so far as to answer to a different name, taking on his first name, Cody, and dropping Vernon. It was only in his art class, in his drawings and paintings, that one could find evidence that malevolent urges still coursed through his system. The same fascination with grotesque and morbid imagery that had shocked his public-school teachers became even more extreme at Springer, startling seasoned instructors who thought they'd seen everything.

Not long after Crawford began serving his sentence, Dr. Winslow had an occasion to visit Springer. While he was there he was taken aside by Damon Wicker, the school's art instructor, who "seemed very, very concerned. We went into the room where they did arts and crafts and he showed me the artwork that Crawford had done. They were huge pictures of daggers and decapitations and dripping blood. Just a gory mess. When I saw them I remember thinking to myself, This kid has a more serious psychopathology than I originally thought. The poor teacher, he didn't know what to do. It was my impression he had a lot of experience with boys but was not a well-trained art therapist. Seeing the tremendous alarm on his face, I told him I would talk with the consulting psychiatrist and ask him to keep an eye on the kid. I suggested perhaps these expressions could be of use in helping the kid work through what was disturbing him. But to be perfectly honest, *I* wasn't sure if maybe it would just be best to leave some of that stuff buried."

Damon Wicker taught graphic arts at Springer at this time, and he was probably the most popular instructor on staff. A former cowboy on the rodeo circuit, ex-marine who had seen action in Korea, he was real with students and willing to try innovative approaches to meet their individual needs. He had little faith in psychology—his gripe was that it dwelt on the past and didn't provide people with a way of starting fresh—and he could see that Cody was not finding any answers from his sessions with the psychiatrist. Frequently he came back from them in worse shape than he went in, and when Wicker would ask how things went, Crawford would brush the question aside but Wicker could tell emotions had been stirred that left him unsettled.

So he encouraged the boy to express himself through drawings, and when what Cody produced was what you expect to see from someone who felt trapped in a box with no way out, or lost in a tunnel that had no end, Wicker decided to recommend something that he'd seen work wonders on others. He referred Cody to a scriptural passage about a man who had done horrible things but turned his life around through repentance and obeying the gospel. The next thing he knew the boy was asking for more—and to make a familiar story brief, before the year was out Cody Crawford walked down the steps of a baptistery in Raton, New Mexico, confessed that he was lost and needed to be in fellowship with Jesus Christ, and after he was taken under the water he came up a new creature in the Kingdom of the Lord.

The staff at Springer were familiar with so-called jailhouse conversions, and usually it meant a superficial change at best, something done to impress the authorities or get a kid out of a jam. A lot of these converts would draw pictures of Christ on the walls that, hollow-eyed and with a crown of thorns, were almost indistinguishable from drawings of the Satanists. Rarely did their religious beliefs have an effect on their behavior.

So they were not naive, not without experience. And when word got around that Cody Crawford had repented his sins, accepted Christ as his Savior, and the Almighty had forgiven him, there were those who scoffed, questioned the sincerity of the change, and doubted the therapeutic value of these kinds of conversions. There was more to rehabilitation than saying the right things, going through the motions of a ceremony, they pointed out. It must show itself in a completely different attitude, the development of positive thought patterns, as expressed in the actions of daily life.

Damon Wicker had counseled Crawford, warning that this was just the beginning, he would be faced with skepticism, and that the way to deal with it was to simply commit himself to the Lord's work. In other words, continue to study and actively serve the church. By following up on his commitment, taking it to people around him and trying to enlighten them to the grace of God, Wicker told him "you can replace, erase, everything that was worldly and evil in your background." And in addition to the blessings God would bestow, the disbelievers would eventually come around to accept him as a "new creature."

For Cody Crawford, the question of how to put the past behind him had been answered. He continued to meet periodically with the psychiatrist, but because his attitude was so entirely different—he was more interested in praising the Lord than in self-analysis—it got to where their conversations were brief and superficial. He was on fire, and along with his new outlook had come a sense of purpose that he was convinced would lead him to a brighter future.

With evangelical ardor he plunged into the Lord's work. Inspired by those apostles who had been beaten and imprisoned, and who ended up converting their jailers, he began to preach and teach fellow students at the Boys School. He established a regimen of Bible study and volunteered for projects helping other people. And the rewards were immediate, as holiday invitations to visit and stay in the homes of Church of Christ members in Raton poured in. Almost as important as the Lord's forgiveness, to him, was the brethren's acceptance.

It was at the home of "Doc" Skow, a longtime Raton veterinarian and an elder in the church, that Cody met Leesa, a nice, pretty, high school senior, who adopted him like a sister. Charmed by what she saw as a touching innocence—she knew he must have done wrong to be committed to Springer, but what affected her the most were his shyness and insecurity, his fumbling attempts toward human contact and fear of rejection—she took great delight in guiding his reentry into society: going for Cokes and dragging Main, introducing him to her friends, and having long heart-to-heart talks.

For a long time she did not know the specifics about his past. They had known each other for almost a year before he told her about it in a letter he wrote from Springer. On his previous visit to Raton she had told him about her boyfriend problems, and now he was following suit with a painful disclosure of his own. "It warmed my Christian soul for you to confide in me all your troubles. I know you trust me and I am going to trust you too. . . . I don't think you know why I'm here. It's because me and two other guys got in a fight with three other men and we killed them. I'm what is termed a murderer. But that was when I drank, smoked pot, popped pills, and other super dumb things. Also before I had Christ. But I'm a new person. I don't believe I'm the same Cody Crawford who did that. . . . I told you this because you're a friend and I know you'll understand and care and not condemn and judge. . . . All I ask is a second chance at life. Jesus is giving me this. But it's hard and I need friends to lean on.''

She was unaware that his version of his crime contained peculiar manipulations of fact. In a subsequent conversation he would distance himself even further from his acts, claiming not only was it an event that took place on a single night, but that his memory of what transpired was obliterated by prodigious amounts of drugs and alcohol. But even if she had known the truth it wouldn't have mattered because, being a young Christian herself, and seeing how important her reaction was to him, she felt a higher calling to accept him for the person he was hoping to become.

Custody of Cody Vernon Crawford had been originally remanded to the New Mexico Department of Corrections for a period of one year, after which he could be released or, if it was felt that his rehabilitation had been slight or extended efforts were necessary to encourage attitudinal and behavioral changes, legal custody could be extended for an additional period of one year. Although his individual progress by the end of that first year indicated changes that, under normal circumstances, would have warranted his release consideration—he was on Step 4 of a Five Step Program, which usually meant, with continued good behavior, he would be out in a month or two—because of the severity of his crime and the feeling of the administration at Springer that there would be a public outcry if he was let go after serving only one year, a petition was filed requesting further institutionalization.

The fact of the matter was that any other student, having established a similar record, would likely have been released. Crawford was functioning well, he seemed to be motivated, and he had succeeded in impressing a range of people to such an extent that they were willing to make special efforts on his behalf. Those efforts were spearheaded by Damon Wicker who, through his contacts at the Sunset Church of Christ, a training center for Church of Christ preachers in Lubbock, Texas, now set the wheels in motion to try and place Cody, upon his release from Springer, in Lubbock Christian College, a small private college populated by about 1,200 students whose parents sent them there in hopes that a continuing Christian influence would guide their sons and daughters through the perils of the college years.

At that time, the dean of students at LCC was Dick Laird.

He had never before accepted a student who was presented under these circumstances, but he was intrigued—not only because he had confidence in those people who were speaking up for the youth, but from what they had to say this was someone whose involvement in Christianity had put him back on the right course in life. To give this student the opportunity to attend a Christian university, associate with quality people, and develop his potential had immense appeal. On the other hand, there were risks in taking on a convicted murderer as a special project. What if his "rehabilitation" was incomplete and he turned out to be a dangerous presence on campus? If his past became known, would the parents of other students object?

After conferring with other administrators, including the president of the college, he was left feeling that it would be his office that would make the final decision, and he would be supported either way. So he gleaned as much background information as he could on the youth; he spoke with people at Springer and Raton who had developed a relationship with Crawford; and when he heard nothing to discourage him from pursuing the matter further, he arranged to interview the kid himself.

And took an immediate, personal liking to him. The boy was polite and neat. He did not try to gloss over his past. He admitted that what he had done was wrong, he was remorseful, and he said he would never do it again. He seemed genuinely eager to get on with his life, and prove himself worthy of the trust his new friends placed in him.

"Sometimes you play your gut feeling," Laird would say later, explaining his decision. "Everything checked out, and it felt right."

Toward the end of his second year at Springer, Cody Vernon Crawford was released. He spent several months at the home of the Skows in Raton, helping "Doc" in the clinic and the missus around the yard and garden; and in time for the beginning of the next semester, he moved to Texas to begin classes at Lubbock Christian College.

For that first year he was not set up with a roommate; he lived by himself in a dormitory room. Nor was anybody, faculty or student, apprised of his past. In order to give him a fresh start, it was felt that no one should know that he was an "administrative experiment."

And from the reports of those who came into contact with him during his first year, he proved more than worthy of the chances that were taken on his behalf. Reserved and controlled at first—which was understandable, considering he had spent two years in a capsule—as he relaxed and began to feel more at ease around people he became more outgoing. Dean Laird had arranged for his part-time employment on the campus security force, patrolling the parking lots outside the college-owned dormitories, which helped him to build confidence. His circle of personal friendships widened as he took on volunteer work for a variety of compassionate causes. He signed up for the Big Brother program—to help some other kid who had a less than happy home life, he said. He worked as an aide in physical therapy for a local hospital—for the satisfaction of seeing people come back from being down, he explained. He responded to a challenge issued to new college students by a progressive preacher from a church fifteen miles on the other side of Lubbock to be a part of a ministry that reached out to minorities and the underprivileged: Rising early each Sunday, he would drive a bus around the ghettos of East Lubbock, picking up black and Hispanic church members who had no transportation of their own. Indeed, he was so active, so energetically filled with a "servant spirit," that it struck some who were close to him that maybe he was overcompensating for something.

Amy McCulloch, a schoolmate he dated several times who was one of the few students he confided in, felt, "Many of his decisions, it was like he was trying to pay recompense. I would think to myself, Why do you think you have to keep paying for what you did? He pushed himself so hard, to where, between his volunteer work and his schoolwork, he almost had no time for himself. . . . I felt like he knew in his intellect God had forgiven him, but emotionally accepting that grace was very difficult, and volunteering for this and that was his way of repaying the debt he felt he owed society."

This issue, in the general case, was not an uncommon one students at Lubbock Christian College faced: just how forgivable are we for our past mistakes. On the one hand they heard all the time they were forgiven the minute they asked to be forgiven, but there were other messages coming at them from the church that said God does not forget and true forgiveness was not that easy to obtain. It was something that a number of students were struggling with at the time, though few had as hard a time of it as Cody Crawford. The need to break free of the demoralizing circumstances of his past, to be liked and accepted as an equal, apparently became an obsession with him. And although he talked in the argot of the forgiven and saved, it seems, from the accounts of his companions at that time, that he was having trouble believing it himself.

Nor was this the only thing that Cody Crawford was struggling with. While in a short period of time he had achieved a substantial respectability, impressing a number of people that he was a youth leading a productive and exemplary life, the guys who lived in the same dorm with him, and the student who shared a room with him his sophomore year, Mike Begnalio, saw a very different side of him that subverted entirely the image of Cody Crawford as a paragon of Christian faith.

I met Cody in Tucson, Arizona, I think it was on spring break his freshman year, when I came there with a friend who went to the same church I did. When I told him I was going to attend LCC next year, he asked if I had a roommate. I said no, and he said how about if you and I room together. I said that would be fine with me, so that's how we became roommates.

I guess it was about the third night I was there, he thought out of fairness I should hear the entire story, in detail, as to his life. I had no idea what his background was. As he told it, it was, well, pretty bizarre.

He said he'd been a radical kid. He did not go real far back in his childhood, other than to say he smoked his first cigarette and had his first drink when he was a tiny kid. Mostly he talked about the preceding three or four years, beginning when he went up to the Denver area, where he wasn't doing anything in particular, just hanging out with friends and shooting heroin. From what he told me he was into heavy drugs for about six months. And that was where he stabbed his first man, was in Denver.

It was over drugs. The guy had drugs and Cody had no money. But he had to have the drugs, so he stabbed the guy. And he told me what it was like to stab somebody, and twist the knife, in extreme detail. He said it felt really good. The sound it makes as you turn the knife, he said it was like sticking it in a watermelon. A gush sound. He said you don't hear anything else when you do it. He said when you do it you hear that slurping sound as the knife turns and nothing else. And when you pull it out you can actually hear it close up.

He told me about the Indian incident too. On that particular night what he told me was, they had been doing acid. He said he didn't remember too much past the general picking up and beating up. According to him, he was in the backseat getting high and the other two guys were in front, when they came upon these Indians and did their thing. Afterwards, he said they dropped him back off at his house. He said he woke up the next morning with blood on his hands so he knew something had happened, but he was real fuzzy as to what had exactly transpired. He said he had just washed up and went to get breakfast when the cops called out over the bullhorn they had the house surrounded. He said he didn't have any idea how they figured it out. The only thing he could assume was the other two guys who had been with him that night had been busted somehow. As for the actual wrapping of them in burning rags and throwing them over the cliff, all that stuff he came to find out afterwards.

This was a part of my life it will be tough to forget. I was a young kid, never been away from home before, led a fairly sheltered life. I'd never been around a drug addict before, much less a murderer. I mean, I'm feeling real good about this guy, right? I'll tell you this, it was really bizarre for me at the time. I slept with one eye open for several nights afterwards.

And this was before he admitted he had homosexual tendencies. Oh, he liked women. He really wanted to be normal. It was just, the way he put it, there were no girls around when he was at the Boys School, he was at the age when that was the time to learn about that stuff, and that was what he did. He said they had pretty regular sex in there. With regularity, I mean. According to him, when he became one of the oldest, and because he was one of the biggest, he got the pick of the litter. He said he had his favorites.

He only approached me once, and he was nice about it, gave me lots of outs. Since I'm not at all, never have been, it really wasn't a problem with me. I explained, Look, this is not going to happen. And if it's going to be a problem, because I'm going to have to be in my underwear around here, I'll move out. He said, No, don't do that, I'm sorry, I didn't mean anything by it, I just can't seem to get out of the habit, I don't want to do that anymore anyway. I said, Fine. But I don't want to be feeling things in the middle of the night. Okay?

That was the last of it—except for the time I walked into our *room and caught him in bed with another student. "Don't get up," I said. "I'll come back after the date."*

Don't get me wrong. Cody was a mellow guy. He never gritted his teeth and talked like Dirty Harry. He was very calm when he spoke. If you met the guy on the street and talked to him for ten minutes, you would never believe he was the same guy who did the things he said he did. And I believe in his heart he felt he was forgiven. But just because you're a Christian doesn't mean you change your life-style. He still had some strange ways.

Like the things he thought were funny. He had an extremely twisted sense of humor. We would be watching TV and a horror movie would come on and blood would go squirting out and he would think that was hilarious. That isn't how it happens, he would say. Nothing bleeds that much.

And his fascination with nooses. To pass the time, he'd sit there with little lengths of string and make baby nooses. He was impressed with himself that he could make a noose so fast. And he could. He could make nooses faster than anybody. He taught me and we hung a few things, like a bag of flour, to see how well it worked. It worked pretty well. He thought it was neat that people saw him making a noose. He'd make one in class and hang his pinky and get a weird look on his face that would get a rise out of people. He had a key chain that was a noose, and a noose he'd made out of rope hung from the ceiling in our room.

And knives—he was really big on knives. He said he loved them, everything about them. He had three knives. One was a fourteen-inch machete that he kept hanging on the wall except when they came to inspect our rooms, and because we weren't supposed to have any knives, he'd hide it in his top drawer under his underwear. Another came from the Philippines and had a whale-bone handle. Once a week he would sharpen his knives—he kept them razor-sharp—and he was sharpening his knives the night he cut me.

As I recall it, either I wanted to go someplace and he didn't, or he wanted to go and I didn't, and anyway we were just fooling around and I grabbed my gym shorts and tossed them at him. He was on the bed sharpening a knife at the time and he lashed out and slashed my knee. I'll never forget his reaction. The first thing he said was, Oh, it's not so bad. I've done worse. But then, after I went and got stitches I went over to a friend's apartment and he showed up literally crying and beg-

ging forgiveness and pleading for another chance. Well, I believed it. My father was an elder, I was raised in the church, I was raised to forgive, and that's what I did. Supposedly I was a good friend when he cut me. After that I became his best friend because I forgave him and stayed his roommate.

Deep down, I'd say there was a lot of turmoil in Cody. He had a temper. Man, he had a temper. And he was a moody, moody guy. When he was down he'd be way down, and when he was up he was really up. There was no in-between with this guy.

As for his attitude towards what he'd done, I never got the sense he felt guilt or remorse. Never. In fact he bragged about being in Time magazine. He kept the copy that had an article in it about the Indian killings on his desk. He said the American Indian Movement had a price on his head. Six hundred dollars or some kind of small thing like that. But he thought it was kind of neat that they had a contract out on him. That was why he had to keep his knives sharp, he said. They were part of his self-defense in case the Indians came after him. I tried to tell him, that was a long time ago, they probably don't even remember your name. But he was very cautious, almost paranoid. He even said he'd heard they had put a curse on him, though he talked about that like it was a superstition. As far as I know he didn't do anything to counter it, or look into it further.

It's true, Cody would talk like his past was behind him, this was the present, and he wasn't that way anymore. And he was convincing that he was a changed person. But you could tell his history also made him feel important. It was part of being somebody. Like he got his identity from having a price on his head. From being in Time. From killing somebody and getting away with it, basically. When he first told me the story I think he really enjoyed my reaction. It was his way of telling me you're dealing with a celebrity here.

The way I ended up looking at it, his past trashed his life, but it also gave him his fifteen minutes.

Although he would continue to have his defenders impressed by his altruism who believed it grew out of a sincere desire to help others, who to this day see Cody Crawford as someone on whom Christian faith worked its wonderful magic, it was hard to ignore the stark, vivid, dismaying juxtapositions, in word and deed, that contradicted the appearance that his was a wholesome conversion. No question, religion gave his life a dimension it would otherwise have lacked. Gave him purpose and hope. But there were too many dark hints that he still suffered from a kind of malady over which his faith exercised a tenuous and uneasy control at best: The lightning changes of mood, the morbid sense of humor. The propensity for physical violence, the craving for kinky sex. The noose and knives, rather than crosses and pictures of Jesus, that adorned the walls of his room like the relics discovered by police in a flophouse after a cult killer has been apprehended. And not to forget the obligation to confess that at times came across like an exercise in self-dramatization, as when he blustered about his alleged drug addiction and nasty knife work, while at other times he operated on the edge of fantasy, as when he reduced a brutal and bloody series of murders to a drunken brawl and tried to blame it on booze and drugs. Never once did he acknowledge the horror of human suffering that he had caused.

All along there had been skeptics who felt that the change conformed too neatly to a predictable pattern: that of a disturbed kid who embarks on a life of drugs and crime, makes the transition to religion during his incarceration and becomes a "Jesus freak." They had greeted his remarkable progress with dubious regard because the change was not based on insight and understanding, an examination of personal motivation, or a development of internal resources. Rather, it had been accomplished by embracing an organizing philosophy, a belief system that provided a credo for living, a set of rules to follow. The appeal was obvious. It was a simple way of disencumbering him from guilt, of moving beyond the past. But because it never forced him to deal with the underlying reasons for his problems, in their minds it merely provided temporary relief, not an effective cure.

Possibly this is why, during this period, he took a sudden interest in writing his autobiography. It became an obsession with him. He would write daily in a diary, take notes on his thoughts. It was going to be the true tale of a reformed drug addict and repentant murderer whose life was changed thanks to Christ. A personal apocalypse expanded into a Christian parable. Possibly, still feeling he had yet to make full amends or reparation for his sins, he was trying to make them redeemable through literature. He would learn to bear his past by baring it.

Possibly. But we'll never know because events put an ending to his story before it was written.

For someone used to coming and going as he pleased and answering to nobody, the disciplined structure of life in an institution was a nightmare of confinement for Peter Burke. He saw the extent of his freedom as the right to choose what and how much food he wanted dished onto his plate at mealtime in the cafeteria. The only thing that separated the Boys School from the penitentiary, in his mind, was here he could wear his own clothes instead of a uniform. If he'd had someplace to go he would have slipped the collar: hotwired a car and hit the highway. As it was, he decided the way to prevail over the circumstances was to mind his own business, do his time, and get out.

And that's pretty much the way it went for Peter Burke during his two years in Springer: He did his time. He did not socialize with the other "students" and developed no friendships. This might have had something to do with dynamics in the lodge. (Because he was large for his age he was placed with an older group of boys, seventeen and eighteen years of age, who showed an intense curiosity about him and his crime. He didn't want to discuss either, so they harassed him. As a result he sought a lot of staff attention, for which his lodgemates resented him even more.) But there were also those who believed him incapable of genuine human contact.

To the counselors at Springer he was a fascinating conundrum. He remained true to the principle Never explain, never apologize, and in psychological sessions expressed little remorse for his deadly acts, or compassion for his victims. If he felt bad about anything it was getting caught and put in jail. So indifferent was he to life in general that he became the focus of staff debates on the beginning of evil, which in turn raised the nature vs. nurture theory of criminal behavior. Did it start with a bad seed? One too many X chromosomes? Or was he a victim of a dysfunctional upbringing? A casualty of neglect and abuse? Whatever was wrong, he didn't seem to feel what everyone thought you were supposed to feel if you had done what he did.

Only once did he give an inkling as to what had triggered his aggression in a savage direction. It began with a report of a nocturnal visitation. He guessed it was a dream, but as he recounted it, something woke him out of a restless sleep and when he opened his eyes he saw one of his Indian victims standing at the foot of his bed, come for revenge. Peter Burke was agitated for days, and for the first time opened up to a staff psychologist. "I know I shouldn't have done it," he admitted, "but I don't really feel bad." Then, as though he felt that needed clarification, he added, "But if they're just going to come to town and get drunk. . . ." His voice trailed off. When it returned, it sounded as though it came from a great distance. "My mom was an alcoholic. I hate anybody who drinks like that."

Burke had been at Springer for almost a year before he had his first visitors: his older brother Rollie and his sister-in-law Mitzi. After spending an afternoon with him, Rollie came away thinking his kid brother seemed reasonably content and had adjusted well to his conditions. Mitzi's impression differed vastly. "What I don't think Rollie saw was the controlled environment Pete was in. He didn't have many options to doing well. When I saw him I saw a con artist. Look at me. I can be good. If that's what it takes to beat the system. I didn't believe him for a minute. I saw his act as the best way to get out of the situation he was in. The more he appeared to be okay, the more points he got, and the sooner he'd get out."

Nor did Peter Burke fool the staff at Springer. Though he did not present a disciplinary problem, the evaluations on his report card indicate no one thought his prognosis was good, and indeed one went so far as to call him "a hopeless case."

Near the end of two years, when all three Farmington youths came up for review, Peter Burke was still at Step 3. No one thought he was ready to become a productive member of society, but neither did anyone feel major rehabilitation was likely no matter how long he was kept. And because there were no grounds to continue to incarcerate him, a search for placement in an outside community was initiated.

It was deemed best by everyone concerned that none of the youths should be allowed to go back to Farmington when they were released. It was bad policy to allow a youth to return to the same environment that had led to his offense. In this case a big consideration was also the risk of reprisals from the Indian community.

Pete's older sister Glenda was living in Dallas at the time, and when the issue of parole came up she expressed not only a willingness but a desire to take her errant brother in upon his release. She said she had not been around when Pete had gotten into trouble, nor had she given support to him earlier in life. Now she felt it was her time.

When he first moved into his sister's Dallas apartment she was all-accepting. She never told him to do anything, never disciplined him, never asked him about his murderous behavior, did not insist he continue with psychological counseling. She seemed to think that he had learned his lesson and, given a chance at a fresh start, would lose his bad habits. The only time she drew the line was when she discovered that after she went to bed he would sneak out, take her car without permission, and drive around to all hours of the night, returning just before daybreak. Do something smart like that again, she warned him, and he was on his own.

During this time he was enrolled in Richland College, but it was not how it looked. The only reason was money. Because his father had been a veteran he was entitled to benefits until he was age eighteen unless he was continuing his education, and as long as he was going to school he was eligible for payments until he was twenty-one. But even though he was classified a student he rarely attended classes; he was far more interested in partying and drinking. He may have detested alcoholics, but he also drank like one.

His destiny, as well as his rogue behavior, caught up with him one night at a party when he had tapped the beer keg at least a dozen times, was feeling mouthy, and smart-alecked the wrong guy. A surly biker whipped off the motorcycle chain he wore for a belt and the first lash caught Burke on the side of the head, spinning him around. The second dropped him to his knees. The third crumpled him onto his back. The fourth, fifth, and sixth blows to the head were distant thunder—just as it must have sounded to his Indian victims, who also continued to be pummeled once they were down.

It was morning when he came to and his head felt like a stake had been driven through the center. He figured he must have suffered a concussion and did not consider the injuries to be serious—not even when he woke up in the middle of the night on the floor, as though he'd been thrown out of bed during his sleep. Not even when, later in the week, he would be standing someplace and would start to tense up, his hearing would change, he would begin hyperventilating, and he would wake up lying on the floor. Not until he had a seizure in his sister's presence and she called an ambulance.

As it was explained to him, the trauma to his brain had

caused scarring which, in turn, was causing the epilepsy: massive firing of nerves in the brain in a disorganized way. It was not something that would get better, nor would it go away in time. It could only be controlled by medication.

After the beating the quality of his life, never good, only worsened. It took a period of experimentation to get the medication level right, during which he continued to suffer seizures that were accompanied by disorientation, mood swings, and memory loss. By the time the seizures were under control the damage to his brain was indelible. He had never been a quick mind, but neither had he been as slow-witted as he was now. When he tried to remember things his sequential recall was scrambled. He had always had a deadpan personality, but now his bearing and demeanor were so flat at times he seemed like a patient only partially come out of a coma.

Since he could no longer keep up the pretense he was a student, for money he took a job as a convenience store clerk, and he had worked there no longer than a month when he got into big trouble. A customer left her purse on the counter, and when she had not come back for it by the time his shift was over, he took it with him. In a way it was a reversion to behavior begun years before, when he had stolen money from his mother's purse. Then he had rationalized that if he didn't take it she would spend it all on beer anyway (the only time he'd been caught was when he took it before she'd had a chance to go to the liquor store); now he gave it no more thought than once again here was stuff he could put in his pocket and go out and buy what he wanted.

For a week he lived the high life on stolen credit cards. He thought about getting caught and told himself he should probably throw the cards away after the next purchase, but it was always going to be after he bought one more thing. The law rang down when he went into a store that checked his card, and rather than walking out with a TV he left in the custody of the Dallas police.

Because this was his first offense (he made no mention of the trouble he'd gotten into as a juvenile, and it wasn't on the computer records) he was put on probation for ten years. Less than three months later he was arrested again, this time for forgery. He had stopped by a buddy's house, stolen one of his father's checkbooks, and was writing blank checks for cash.

You might think that sitting in a jail cell, awaiting your turn in court, was a good time to wonder where your life was going, and the last thing you would consider would be something that would compound your problems. But Peter Burke's odd mix of defiance of authority and susceptibility to energetically decisive persons won out. While waiting for a court hearing he became pals with a cocky prisoner who was planning a jailbreak, and he decided to go with him. The day before his court date Burke asked for his street clothes, which were brought to him. An hour after lights out, he and his partner tied a sheet between two bars (it was an old jail, built in the 1900s, with the bars bolted to the outside of the windows) and twisted until they had created an opening wide enough for them to slip out of their second-floor cell. At a nearby used-car lot they found where the keys were kept, and they were pulling out of the lot when a police cruiser happened by. A long middle-of-the-night siren-screaming car chase was stopped by a roadblock. Escape attempt, burglary, and grand theft auto were added to the forgery charge, and Peter Burke was sentenced to five years in a Texas penitentiary.

As with everyone who enters the prison system in Texas, his first stop was Huntsville, a Confederate prison during the Civil War that had held Union soldiers, kept in service as the orientation unit for the Texas Department of Corrections. After he was given a physical exam, psychological tests, vaccine shots, and a haircut, he was shuttled by bus to Clemens, one of the work farms where inmates raised and harvested cotton and vegetables.

The routines at Clemens were rigorous. Reveille sounded at 5:30 in the morning, when the lights came on and inmate trustees walked up and down the cell block banging on the bars. Then they ran you down to the cafeteria to breakfast, ran you back to your cell, ran you out to the fields where they worked you like a slave under a broiling sun and an armed boss on horseback, ran you back for lunch, ran you back to the fields for another shift, then ran you back in at the end of the day. And when they said "Run" and you didn't gallop you were spurred up to speed by the sharp end of a three-foot nightstick.

A week of hoeing vegetables and Peter Burke had had enough. He "laid it down." When the work squads were called out, he stayed in his cell. Discovered there by a guard, he was asked if he had a medical pass to stay in. He shook his head.

"Then get your ass out of there," the trustee snapped.

"Fuck you," Burke shot back. "I ain't gonna work 'less I get paid for it."

In prison, no distinction is made between dangerous behavior and obnoxious behavior. Neither is tolerated. And refusing to work is a major infraction. After a thrashing that left him punched and kicked senseless, he was dragged along the hallway and bounced down three flights of stairs to solitary confinement.

Being thrown in solitary didn't mean a lot to Peter Burke. It wasn't any more uncomfortable than his regular cell. Smaller, maybe, but basically furnished the same: a bunk, a crapper, and a sink. The silence and boredom got tiresome, but he soon figured a way to beat that: He went into a kind of hibernation. Passed the time by sleeping, and even came to think of sleep as a way of shortening his sentence.

Food presented a problem at first but he even managed to work that out to his advantage. To keep you weak and lower your will to resist, when you were in solitary they fed you a full meal every third day and kept you on short rations the other two. It wasn't bread and water but it wasn't much better. But in his case, because he was taking in so little food he was metabolizing his medication faster, which brought on seizures, the doctor ordered him to be fed full meals three times a day.

The one thing about solitary he found he was not able to master was his thinking. In the hole you lived in your mind. That might not be much of a problem if you were cerebrally oriented, but he was more adept at blocking thoughts out than entertaining them, and after a month in solitary he was bored enough to go back to work.

Once he returned to the fields he found himself lacking the stamina to keep up with the rest of the squad. A hacking cough he had blamed on a cold would not go away and left him so drained he did not feel strong enough to work. So once again he laid it down.

The trustee sent him down to the security station where he was told to "stand on the wall." He obeyed instructions, stood with his toes and nose touching the wall, and waited for a superior to hear his complaint. Some inmates stood on the wall all day before they were heard; he only had to wait three hours.

"What's your excuse this time?" a voice behind him barked.

"I can't breathe. I'm tired. I can't work," he replied.

The response was a kidney punch that slammed him into the wall.

They thought he was out to test his will against their rules and tried to set him right. "You're going to go out and work if I have to drag you out myself."

There was a scuffle. One man had him in a headlock, another was lifting his feet. But he put up such a fight they ended up dumping him in solitary once again.

And he stayed down there for another month before he was able to convince his overseers he was seriously ill and they sent him to the infirmary. Even the doctor thought he was faking it, but to silence his complaining agreed to give him a chest X-ray.

The ambulance arrived in twenty minutes. He was not even allowed to go back for his gear. Tuberculosis was highly contagious and they did not want to take the chance he would infect other inmates.

He spent the next six months quarantined on a TB ward receiving therapy, and then he was shipped back to Clemens. Shortly after that he came up for parole and the board recommended his release. Having been turned down before for his rebellious behavior, he suspected the approval this time had something to do with their concern about liability.

Although on a five-year sentence he could have walked after ten months if he had behaved himself, Peter Burke had been in prison for almost two years. The first thing he did when he was released from prison was buy a new set of clothes with the $200 parting allowance he was given. He'd been issued a civilian outfit but no one had asked him for his size, or paid any attention to what matched, so he walked out wearing green checked pants, an orange shirt, and cheap plastic shoes. He felt like a clown until he slipped into a pair of Levi's, cowboy boots, and yoked shirt.

As it had been arranged, he was paroled out to a halfway house for drug addicts in San Antonio. There he met a fellow who had done drugs as a teenager until he was busted for heroin possession. He was clean now and they moved into an apartment together, but once on his own his roommate started shooting up again. Drugs didn't interest Pete. He'd even sworn off smoking pot when he found it induced seizures. And heroin didn't look like much fun: You shot up and nodded off. What was the kick there?

When drug dealers started dropping by, along with shady characters toting hot appliances, Burke knew his days were numbered if he stayed around, and stuffing his worldly belongings into a duffel bag, he hiked to the bus station and bought a ticket to Farmington.

He couldn't say why he went back, other than that was home, where he'd lived most of his life. He did not call ahead because he was afraid if somehow word got to the Indians they would be laying for him. When he arrived in town he walked back to the old neighborhood to look up guys he'd gone to school with. Some were gone—to college and the army—while others tensed up when they saw him standing in the doorway. Like he was a psycho killer in high school chum's clothing, someone who could suddenly flip out and attack them in a screaming frenzy.

When he phoned his older brother, Rollie didn't even invite him to the house. Instead they met at a coffee shop, where he was made to feel unwelcome. "There's nothing here for you anymore," Rollie told him. "People around here are never going to forget what you did. If you came for a visit, it's time to move on."

Peter Burke was not good when it came to reckoning with the consequences of his actions, and in particular he did not know how to deal with this rejection. If he'd read in the paper about someone who had killed a bunch of people he'd probably be wary too, but that wasn't how he thought of himself. When he looked in the mirror he didn't see a killer. He was no Charlie Manson. And yet that was how people saw him—as if they thought, Well, if he killed once he'll do it again. He didn't think it was fair for people to hold against him what he'd done as a fifteen-year-old. But neither did he have a clue as to how to go about changing their minds or escaping their judgment.

A next-door neighbor who had been friends with his mother, feeling pity on him, contacted a preacher who set Pete up until he could figure out what to do next. The clergyman got him a small apartment, a beat-up car, a job with a gas company in Aztec, and continued to look after him until he happened to mention his philanthropy to the chief of police in Farmington, who ran a check and found that Peter Burke was a fugitive. There was an outstanding warrant for his arrest in Texas because he had neglected to notify his parole officer when he left town.

So Burke returned to Dallas, but he didn't turn himself in. His sister no longer trusted him, making familial estrangement complete, so he stole a car and lived in it and opened a checking account for twenty dollars and wrote bad checks until it all caught up with him and he made the round-trip back to prison.

It was during his second term in the state pen that the proverbial beacon in the darkness shined its light on his bleak existence. There was a Bible-toter on his cell block, a black man who had found God and wanted everyone else to, too, and for some reason he took a liking to the troubled youth. When he couldn't talk him into attending worship services, he pleaded with him to enroll in a Bible correspondence course. Thinking it couldn't hurt, and knowing it would look good on his record when he came up for parole, Burke said okay.

To his mild surprise the things he found himself reading made a kind of sense. According to the Bible everyone was a sinner but if you asked the Lord for forgiveness you could be saved. He liked the sound of that. And according to the Bible if you prayed and believed you could change the shape and direction of your life. That too had an appeal.

And so he continued to read. And then he began to pray. And through the jailhouse preacher he was introduced to a network of Christian advocates of prison reform, which led to a correspondence with a kindhearted Christian lady from Seattle. And the next thing he knew she was offering to take him into her home upon his release, and because Texas was big on born-again inmates, he found himself up for early parole.

He didn't know whether it was a coincidence or an answer, all he knew was the breaks were going his way for a change and it looked as if his luck had turned around the time he began to read the Bible. So he took a private vow to behave in a Christian manner as long as it seemed to work in his behalf.

The conditions of his parole allowed him to locate in Seattle where his benefactors provided him with free housing, found him a job as a clerk in a convenience store, and allowed him free use of her car. Indeed, Peter Burke had everything he needed for a running start on a new life.

But even though he attended church regularly and tried to do what was right, his luck didn't hold. He managed to stay straight for just about two years, and then he began to revert to his former ways. He would go out and get drunk and someone would say something or something would happen, often he couldn't remember which it was, and he would do something stupid that got him into trouble. It was shortly after a late-night, back-street car race ended in a smashup that he was once again unable to resist the temptation of a forgotten purse, once again arrested for using stolen credit cards, once again had his parole revoked, and once again returned to a Texas penitentiary.

He put in his time, and when he was released he went back to Washington, but without the optimism he'd once had that good things lay ahead for him. He felt lonely, alienated, adrift, and for the first time uncomfortable with who he was and what he had become. He was weary of jail, but it seemed like he couldn't stop acting in ways that were damaging to himself.

Within six months he was facing more legal difficulties, this time a sex-abuse charge. And it was while sitting in a county jail awaiting a psychological evaluation that he became suicidally depressed. It seemed to him a black cloud plagued his existence, and whether he was in prison or out all he was doing was time. He decided if it was going to go on like this then life just wasn't worth the effort.

A bad trip. That was how Oren Thacker would describe his life after that Friday afternoon in April when Lieutenant Miller first pulled him in for questioning. He told them exactly what the deal was, figuring it couldn't go too badly for him because he didn't do that much, just rolled an Indian, and the next thing he knew they were asking him if he was a member of a Satanic cult. I don't know what you're talking about, he said, and didn't put it together until they brought up the stripping and the fire. Nah, it wasn't a cult thing, he told them, it was Crawford's idea. He said, Let's take the Indian's clothes off and burn them so he has to walk back to town naked, and it sounded like a funny thing to do at the time. Funny to kill a man? they had asked, and he swore that all he did was rough the guy up. Okay, maybe he'd have something more than a hangover in the morning, but no way did he kill anybody.

Then it kept snowballing and mushrooming and before he knew it they were locking him up and it was lawyers coming in and out of rooms and a psychologist asking him to put washers on pegs, and it turned into a real zoo. When it's going like that you don't know what to think, you just want to get off.

They said he was lucky he wasn't going to be tried as an adult, but he didn't feel so lucky when he was told he was going to spend the next year, maybe two, maybe more, in reform school. It was incomprehensible. Never would he have thought that someday he would do something that would land him in prison.

It was a pretty stressful adjustment at first. It was like everyone knew his name and what he'd done before he got there, and had their minds made up about who he was: some spoiled white boy who thought he could kill an Indian and get away with it. It was a crazy scene because the people thinking this way were lowlifes, thoroughly bad apples, shit-sticks from the word go. Some had robbed 7-Elevens, some were back for the third and fourth time. And here he was stuck with this barrel of monkeys and they thought he thought he was some kind of bad dude.

It was hard, because he tried to tell them he really wasn't into beating up on people, but they just looked back at him, Yeah, sure (this was before he came to realize that in the joint everyone pleads innocent). And they gave him a hard time, especially this one Hispanic kid who was about half-nuts from sniffing glue and had it in for him for some reason. Kept calling him "Indian killer." He could have taken the kid in a fair fight, but that wasn't the kid's style, he was a slasher. So this one day Oren was sitting in a chair in the dayroom, dozing, and he felt this itching sensation. When he opened his eyes and looked down there was all this blood streaming off his arm. He raised his hand for a better look and the wound opened up and he almost fainted, he could see all the way to the bone. The kid had walked up while he was sleeping and slit his arm with a razor blade!

After about three or four months they quit with the hazing, things settled down, and he was able to find the time and clarity to sort out his thoughts. Although he had never had a particularly strong consciousness of wrongdoing and guilt, he felt bad. Maybe he wasn't guilty of murder, but he knew he had screwed up royally and gotten caught. And it rocked his conscience back and forth because he didn't mean for it to turn out this way, but with knowing hindsight he could see he was partly to blame. No one had twisted his arm and forced him to go along that night.

As ashamed as he felt about what he was accused of, he felt the worst about what he'd put his folks through. His dad was devastated—wondered where he went wrong that his son had done this to another human being. His mom was scandalized—people looked at her and wondered what kind of lousy mother would produce a child who would do something so gross. And he worried that maybe the Indians would try to get to him by hurting them.

But there wasn't much he felt he could do about all that. What he could do, and decided to do, was make the best of a bad situation. Play it smart, play it right. The day was going to come when he walked out of this place, and as long as he was here there were things he could do so when that time came he wasn't completely disadvantaged. It would be a singular victory: He would prevent this misfortune from ruining his life.

So he committed himself to finishing his education. He was aware that he'd played the dunce in high school, and resolved now to pursue a General Equivalency Diploma. In addition to getting good grades in a variety of academic classes, he made the honor role in auto mechanics and graphic arts, and contributed to the school newspaper. He did everything from write stories to shoot pictures to run the printing press.

From time to time he saw Vernon Crawford, but they didn't have much to say to each other and he tried to have as little to do with him as possible. His ideas about Crawford went in a different direction now: He no longer saw the humor in his weirdness, but rather felt it was something dangerous—to himself and those around him. He also felt resentful when he measured his involvement against Crawford's: They were vastly different and yet they got the same sentence.

Helping to lessen his likeness to Crawford and Burke was the support of his buddies back in Farmington, some of whom he stayed in touch with. It cost money to call and took too much time to write so they would exchange tapes. They would send songs and messages, and he would tell them about what he was doing and what it was like where he was. Though they never brought up the incident, it was clear they believed that while he might have been an accessory, he wasn't in the same category as Crawford and Burke.

As dedicated as he was to doing right and well, still it wasn't easy. Even though he never came to see himself as a juvenile delinquent—he was a kid from a good family who tripped up, while they were mostly lost causes—he found that after eight or nine months he was starting to think and talk like one. He was even learning some of the tricks of the criminal trade. One kid taught him how to pick a padlock, and it was a snap. Another passed along his secret to breaking and entering: Go in before closing, hide out, then when everyone's gone collect your loot and bust out.

Not that he intended to use this knowledge. Any thoughts along those lines evaporated during a field trip to the state penitentiary in Santa Fe. They were given a tour of the facilities—walked along a row of cell blocks, up to death row, down to the gas chamber that had a door like on a submarine—

and it was obvious they meant business there. He guessed they were being shown this as a way of scaring everybody—saying, Look, if you don't straighten out, this is your next stop. But even though it left a strong impression, the lesson was unnecessary because he already knew that once he got out the correction system had seen the last of him.

It was because he knew this so certainly that as time went by his stay at Springer became increasingly tough to endure. Based on his record, he was counting on an early release; when it didn't come through he was crushed.

The prospect of spending an indefinite period of time at Springer put him in the doldrums. He was burnt out on the routines. There were days when he almost wanted to give up, to say, Do with me what you want because I don't give a shit anymore. His moodiness sharpened after he had been there for a year and a half and they still wouldn't tell him how much longer he had to wait.

That was the most difficult part: not having a specific date to look forward to. Having to go on day after day and not know where the top of the mountain was. Sometimes he felt like walking into the supervisor's office and saying, Look man, what're we gonna do here? Either give me twenty years or tell me twenty days, but I can't go on with this not knowing anymore.

And he existed in this fretful limbo, nerves stretched thin, for another six months before a release date was set, and an aunt and uncle from Minnesota promised the court they would take him home and put him on the right track.

By the time he left, his seniority and conduct had earned him a maximum number of privileges. He was leaving with a G.E.D. His counselors were optimistic: Having analyzed his "mistake" as stemming from immaturity and a weak sense of self, they had written in a final report, "He has developed more self-assurance . . . [and] can focus on the more positive aspects of his existence." He had even shaken the hand of Bruce King, the governor of the state of New Mexico, and snapped his picture.

But he put that all behind him when he dove into the back of his uncle's car. "Drive!" he said, pointing toward the Interstate, and he didn't look back.

For months, when he dreamed about what it was going to be like when he got out, all he thought about was the luxury of freedom: to be able to get up when he wanted, go out when he wanted, and not to have to stand in line. For close to two years he'd had to line up for everything. Line up for chow. Line up for inspection. Line up for class. If he thought he had to stand in line to get in, he'd pass up a movie.

But now that he'd been given his liberty he found there was a flip side that was unsettling. Without realizing it he had become used to schedules: The routines that he had once despised had given a purpose to each day, and without them he wasn't quite sure what to do with himself. Added to that, he found he missed having someone around in constant attendance. Having counselors to talk to, to give him advice and the reassurances he needed, had created a psychological dependency. He wasn't used to having to make his own decisions.

Perhaps the biggest problem facing him was now that he was on his own he was going to have to figure out how to make a living, which wasn't an easy task for any nineteen-year-old, much less one without a trade, without any job references, and who stuttered and faltered when asked where he'd been the past two years.

He was living in a suburb of Minneapolis with his aunt and uncle, who were regular churchgoers, and his horizon opened at their place of worship. It was a large Lutheran church with a congregation numbering almost 3,000, and when the need for a new janitor came up, he was hired. Maybe it wasn't something he was going to make a career of, but at least he could get started on something instead of just taking life a day at a time.

Although he had never been big on aspirations, now, as he swept the hallways and did the odd jobs that were part of maintenance, he found himself thinking about the photography he'd done at Springer and how much he had enjoyed it. This led to a long-distance phone call to his graphic-arts teacher, Damon Wicker, at whose encouragement and with whose help he purchased a camera and all the darkroom equipment necessary to start a business as a free-lance photographer.

He went so far as to have a box of business cards printed up, and he did make some money photographing weddings at the church, but it never really caught on and soon he was questioning whether Minnesota was the place for him. He felt he'd given it a chance and didn't see himself going anywhere. At this rate he was afraid he'd end up bagging groceries in a supermarket.

When he thought about where, of all places, he'd like to live he found himself thinking of Sterling, Colorado. It was a laid-back agricultural community stretched out along the South Platte River in northeastern Colorado. The range first of bison and Pawnee, and then of vast herds of cattle and ranchers, it was a place where pioneers had come for a fresh start, and where he wanted to go for his. It also helped that his grandmother lived there. She'd been the town's telephone operator for twenty-five years, knew everybody, and through her connections maybe he could find work.

So he left Minnesota and moved in with his grandmother in Sterling, helping her around the yard and eventually hiring on at a local hay mill. It was his first real job; the pay was good and so were the benefits.

Not long after that one of his co-workers set him up with his sister, who worked at a nursing home. She had a girl-next-door wholesomeness, she was a caring person, and she had a compatible sense of humor. He thought it was hilarious when she told him about a lady who had walked out of the nursing home, entered a stranger's house, fixed herself a tuna-fish sandwich, and was watching TV when the occupants came home. The first blind date led to another date and that to marriage.

All in all, Oren Thacker couldn't complain. Most of the time he felt like he had managed to close the book on his past and begin a new one. And from where he sat, in a trailer on the outskirts of Sterling, the view of pastures as well as his future should have put him at ease. But the fact of the matter was something dark nagged at his spirits. There were moments when he felt shadowed, and he was continually looking over his shoulder in fear that something he could run from but not hide from was about to catch up with him.

Since he had been sketchy with his wife on the details about the trouble he'd gotten into as a sixteen-year-old, and kept his in-laws completely in the dark, he was concerned that one day the truth would come tapping and betray him.

Then there was the matter of how to handle conversations that referred to his high school years. Whenever he listened to other people reminisce about their high school sweethearts and graduation ceremonies he remembered how he had been jerked out of class his junior year and that was it. No goodbyes, he was gone. It left him with an acute sense of loss at having missed out on an important part of growing up, and made him wistful and sad to think he had been cheated out of this heritage.

On occasion he'd been asked about his prom. The theme was "Southern Comfort" and the boys all went as Rhett Butler, the girls as Scarlett O'Hara, he recalled. Who did you go with? was usually the next question. He would have to reply, I didn't go. Why not? Well, it's a long story. Some let it drop, but others pressed. Tell me. To which he would grimace, appearing to search his memory, when in reality he was making up a story or trying to figure out how he could change the subject without answering.

But more frightening than exposure and more disturbing than the gap in his life was a vibration that continued to emanate from Indian country. He too had heard that AIM had a contract out on them, and he had also been told by his Farmington friends that the word around town was a Navajo shaman had put a hex on all of them. It made him uneasy to think that someone or something might be stalking him, but he didn't know how to begin to deal with it and tried not to pay it much mind. He thought about it only at those times when something happened to him that so defied the odds of probability he had no choice but to wonder if maybe he *was* jinxed and the forces acting on his fate were *not* unconscious. Which was what he thought when he notched another unintentional death.

11

THE
NAVAJO WAY

Almost a year passed before the report prepared by the New Mexico Advisory Committee to the U.S. Commission on Civil Rights was released. It took the form of a 171-page document titled *The Farmington Report: A Conflict of Cultures*, and there was no mistaking its conclusions: A guilty verdict had been reached. The authors did their best to adopt a reflective tone, putting the events that initiated their inquiry into a historical and sociological context—"It was perhaps inevitable that someday the presence of conflicting races, cultures, and value systems would lead to confrontation and violence"—but in their judgment the facts supported the charge that murder and related violence the previous year had taken place in an atmosphere heated up by racial discrimination and economic deprivation of Navajo Indians. Long-standing conflicts in culture and conflicts in community interest had been ignored for years, they wrote, and when Farmington was finally forced to face its moment of reality, its white citizens and their elected officials were ill-prepared to deal with the ensuing crisis and handled it poorly.

The news coverage was extensive, appearing in major papers across the country; not surprisingly the report caused an uproar in Farmington, where it was praised by a few as the gospel truth, but damned by most as a pack of lies.

Those who agreed with its findings took the position that it had had to come to something terrible before Farmington would acknowledge there was anything wrong at all; then, once it had blood on its hands all the town wanted to do was wash it off; and now maybe the community would engage in the kind of self-scrutiny that would transform the entire episode into a coming-of-age story that brought Navajo and Anglo together on a higher level of human and cultural sensitivity and understanding.

A seething Marlo Webb, stung by the suspicion that critical comments in the report contained concealed accusations that *he* was somehow more responsible than others, spoke for the rest of the community, expressing indignation at the suggestion that they should be held accountable for the depth of anguish that existed among Indians in northern New Mexico. He countered quickly with a rebuttal, branding the report a "collection of half-truths, innuendos, statements out of context, falsehoods, and unrealistic and illogical conclusions. . . . There is just enough thread of truth in the report to lead an uninformed reader to wrong conclusions that the West is still being won over dead bodies and at the expense of the Native Americans."

He proceeded to attack the credibility of the Committee: "What more could you expect from such a beautiful job of staging and coaching handpicked witnesses. It was evident from the start that [they] came on the scene determined to justify [their] prejudgment of the situation and would take any steps to see that a predetermined outcome was reached." And in a final attempt to slander his accusers, he characterized *their* bias: "This is a typical example of how the ever-growing cancer of bureaucracy is dominating and directing our country and the lives of its citizens. . . . This commission would appear to want to drag each of us down to the level of the lowest common denominator and obviously is advancing the cause of socialism in this country. They advocate that government fill all of the needs of the individual rather than achievement through individual effort. This would be impossible to finance and completely contrary to the American way of life, and the greatness achieved through the free enterprise system and self-achievement of the individual."

In the end he assured the Committee members that Farmington had no intention of following its recommendations, and would ignore the report.

Hear-hears from the city council and the chamber of commerce were followed closely by an editorial in the *Farmington Daily Times* labeling the report "a disservice to the people of this state in general, and Farmington in particular," and calling upon New Mexico's congressional delegations to launch a full-scale investigation "into the operations of the U.S. Civil Rights Commission, into the New Mexico Advisory Committee, and the manner in which the report on the Farmington area was prepared.''

Public quarreling assured the issue sustained high visibility, and shortly after the mayor reacted, John Foster Dulles II registered his profound disappointment. "Very frankly, we are quite depressed at the mayor's reaction," he stated to the press. "We saw this report as a very small stepping point. A starting place, if you will.''

In most of its comments the Committee took the moral high ground. This is a tool with which people can begin to right wrongs, the members said, a way of engaging the people of Farmington and Navajo Indians in a meaningful dialogue on civil-rights issues. But even though they liked to say their report was written in hopes it would pave the way for improvement in racial relations, privately they knew it was unlikely.

At a press conference, asked for his assessment of the situation given Farmington's response, Sterling F. Black, the chairperson of the Advisory Committee, shook his head sadly. "There appears to be little awareness on the part of the general population or elected public officials of the complex social and economic problems," he said. And he warned that this could lead to further violent confrontations between young Navajos, "who are aware of the indignities and injustices, and want something done to better the situation," and establishment leaders, "who say, There are no problems existing, people in this town get along very well with each other, there are no indignities, there are no injustices, and there is nothing to be done to remedy these complaints.''

Black ended by saying that he and the other Committee members "feel this is a mistake. We feel that we are going to have a clash if the two forces continue to move in opposite directions along the same line.''

Committee member Gerald Wilkinson, who had expected no different from the mayor, was less circumspect. "The mayor is upset because this is the truth," he declared. Then he acknowledged the contributions of members of the Coalition for Navajo Liberation, casting their struggle as a skirmish in the war of change from which they had emerged victors: "This report confirms that everything you said about discrimination is true. You were right and the mayor and the city officials were wrong.''

Wilkinson had prepared for this moment. Once he had everyone's attention, he read from a statement in which he attempted to place Farmington, its behavior in the past and its choices in the future, in perspective.

For many years Indian people have been going to Washington with complaints to government officials. Many of the old photographs show Indian chiefs posing with government officials in the Capitol. The old chiefs believed that if they just told the government about their problems the nation's leaders, being good men, would do something about them. . . . History shows, however, that the public, when confronted with these problems in the old days, did very little. Today they are doing very little.

It is very strange how the government spends millions to educate us and once we are convinced of certain principles, like "liberty and justice for all," the government deliberately destroys them for us.

Now another opportunity presents itself. The U.S. Civil Rights Commission, an agency of the federal government, funded by the taxpayers, has informed the public that all the charges of racism, discrimination, and brutality made by the Navajo people of Farmington, and more, are true. If the government does not respond, then the American education system that teaches us that this country wants justice and will act on situations of injustice, once it is informed, is a lie. . . .

The Civil Rights Commission has shown in its report beyond question that Farmington is a racist and sick community which treats its Navajo citizens in many respects like animals. . . .

Farmington has been shown to be a blight on the state of New Mexico and a parasite on the Navajo Reservation. Insecticides sooner or later are usually found to control blights and parasites. Whether what cures Farmington will be more violence or reasonable programs and a sharing of power with Indian people is up to the city fathers.

At the end of the report the Committee had listed recommendations it felt should be adopted to relieve and rectify the existing situation. But with little optimism that this would happen without federal enforcement, it forwarded the report to the full Commission in Washington, D.C., which in turn passed it on to those governmental agencies whose job it was to make sure federal laws against discrimination were complied with for action. Within the year a number of lawsuits were filed by the Justice Department accusing the county and city of pursuing policies and practices which discriminated against Indians, and ordering them to discontinue these practices and take immediate steps to correct the present effects of past discriminatory policies.

Were red powers of darkness truly involved in this story? Was a curse put on the three youths by shamanic means? Had each finally come to a grievous end because of the spiritual biddings of a Navajo medicine man?

Over the course of my research these questions came to obsess me. The idea and aura of a supernatural court of appeals carried sinister but fascinating implications, and unless I came up with an answer that was personally satisfying, I knew the tale would be incomplete.

Once again I found myself looking for someone who could provide me with crucial insights, an interpreter well-versed in the mythic lore of the Navajo tribe who would give me a better understanding of the forces at work here from the Indian perspective—a cultural defender, if you will, who could make the case for witchcraft.

If indeed relatives of the victims had sought ceremonial redress, I did not expect to be lucky enough to locate the individual in charge. Whether or not the reporter's information was reliable, I doubted anyone in the know would identify him for me. For that matter, based on what I could surmise, the ratio of people who understood Navajo metaphysics in depth was small; those who knew about the ways in which medicine men were able to master malevolent spirits, smaller; and those willing to discuss these matters even less if they existed at all. There is no record of any white observer witnessing the Navajo practice of witchcraft, and even though I wouldn't go so far as to call this phase of my investigation a witch hunt, I cannot deny that what I really wanted was someone to say to me, "Talk to him. He can tell you about the secret ways."

Without a guide or clearly marked trails, confronting cultural territory posted with No Trespassing signs, I turned to academic sources of help: libraries and museums; cultural anthropologists and Navajo scholars. I even read the novels of Tony Hillerman. What I learned was that for the *Dineh*, everything in the universe is alive, every created object, whether animate or inanimate, is credited with possession of spiritual powers. This faith goes back to their understanding that the universe was created and shaped by dynamic and purposeful deities who continue to be present and active, and who can influence the course of events in the everyday world. Medicine men and shamans are held to be the "magical mediators" between man and these supernaturals, and through ritualistically prescribed ceremonies they are believed to be able to activate Holy Powers.

Most Navajo ceremonies line up under two headings: Those that are precautionary and protective, such as the Blessing Way, which is designed to ensure health, prosperity, and well-being; and those that cure a patient of an evil or illness, such as the Enemy Way. In these rites a medicine man recites songs and chants which put a "patient" in tune with the Navajo deities, restoring him to harmony with all creation, and once again he may "walk in beauty." This is known as the Navajo Way.

All these ceremonies are designed to impact health in a positive way; they are conducted to attract good or deter evil. But there are also supernatural techniques for practicing bad medicine rather than good, and those people who are able to manipulate spirits for evil purposes are known as witches. It is said they are active mainly at night and they often wear the skin of a wolf or coyote, actually turning into those animals, which is why they are also called "skinwalkers" or "Navajo wolves." It is said their most effective technique for killing is to rob a grave of corpse flesh, which they grind up into a poisonous concoction that they blow in powder form on their victims, killing them.

While many of these tales seem improbable, their ability to inspire fear among Navajos remains strong. Even acculturated Navajos who have lost faith in the traditional approach to medicine are reluctant to discuss witchcraft in other than generalities. Indeed, the individual who would eventually give my archival understanding updated energy made me feel that seeking an initiation into the mysteries of Indian magic and power could be dangerous business.

Early one spring morning I paid a visit to the old San Juan Mission cemetery. There are those who have gazed across all those wooden crosses staked in the sand among rocks and cactus and seen a bleak and haunting symbol of the Navajo tribal past. As whites have their Boot Hill memorializing the desperadoes of yesteryear, this, they have said, ought to be called Moccasin Hill, because it conveys some of the same grim dimensions of history and myth: Many of those interred here also were victims of the Wild West. But the truth of the matter is there are no famous Indian renegades buried here, and the only grave with any notoriety that I am aware of belongs to Herman Dodge Benally.

I have stood at the foot of his grave many times, pulled by the ambience, hoping, I suppose, for some kind of spiritual contact. At no time have I seen phantoms, nor have I heard incorporeal voices, but nevertheless I always sensed that this was a place where unusual things *could* happen. This time I found myself remembering a story told to me by the wife of a Baptist missionary who had attended the funeral for Benally's father.

From what she heard, he had been drinking and passed out in the road and was run over by a truck. He had not been much of a churchgoer, but he had been baptized so he was buried at the mission cemetery. The actual interment had been a crude affair, she said, recalling a hole in the ground beside a pile of dirt that barely accepted a plain pine box lowered with ropes that landed at the bottom with a sickening thud. The service had been delayed because Benji, his oldest son, had not shown up and no one knew where he was. But now it proceeded rapidly, as if everyone was anxious for it to be over and done with. She remembered how unpleasant it was to have to stand there paying her last respects and watch two Navajo men fill the hole with dirt a shovelful at a time. The clods drummed on the casket, sounding like someone beating his fists on the inside of the lid and wanting out.

A cry from a distance brought everyone's head up, and all turned to watch Benji running out from the mission down the path to the cemetery. He kept stumbling and falling and picking himself up and running again. He was drunk. He was feverish and wild-eyed. And when he arrived at graveside he wanted to see his father one last time.

The request horrified Christian and Navajo mourners alike, and for a terrible moment no one knew what to do. Then, on his own, one of the gravediggers jumped into the hole, scraped the dirt off the top of the casket, and wrenched the lid open.

As appalling as the circumstances were, everyone, including the missionary's wife, edged forward to gape into the hole. Her recollection of the sight would remain with her forever. "The Navajo will live in poverty, then turn around and spend a fortune on a funeral. The father was dressed better than I'd ever seen him dressed when he was alive. He had on new jeans and a new shirt. There was a Pendleton blanket draped over his shoulders and a fancy belt buckle and a silver bolo tie. And he was wearing an expensive piece of jewelry on his wrist: a beautiful turquoise bracelet that had been broken into pieces with a pair of pliers before he was buried so skinwalkers wouldn't come and steal it. Benji stood there with tears running down his face, his lips moving, but no one could hear what he was saying, and then . . . and then it was as if he had just caught a glimpse of what was to come for him, that he too would die violently, because he turned and ran away, stumbling and falling, the same way he came. It was just a dreadful experience.''

When I had finished paying *my* respects I wandered among the nearby graves looking for the father's. Some were mounded, some settled into a depression, all ringed with river rocks and marked by a white cross on which a name was spelled in metal letters. I read as I walked slowly among them: Shorty Clah, Key Silversmith, Mary Blueeyes, Navajo Jim, Hosteen San Juan. I didn't see a single epitaph, but some didn't need one: Baby John Pete, Stillborn Willie, Yellowman's Wife. Just think about those names.

It's left to the relatives of the deceased to keep up the graves, and I found myself drawn to those festively garnished with silk flowers and pinwheels. The only graves with marble headstones belong to those who served in the military.

There is no official line separating the old area from the new, but you can tell them apart by the broken stone outlines, the lean to the crosses in the old section, as if it is more of a struggle for them to stand upright, and the letters on many of the names are falling off. The oldest section is across a small arroyo and could almost be mistaken for the newest. A few years ago a group of college youths from back east came west to do missionary work for the summer, and they took it upon themselves to dig up the old slab boards that truly did give the cemetery a Boot Hill look, and replace them with matching white crosses that were staked out in orderly rows without regard for the bones they belonged to.

At some point in my meanderings I stopped and looked around: at a line of dogs loping along a ridge, tracking the scent of the city dump a mile away; at distant flat-topped mesas that looked as if their peaks had been leveled by the grinding weight of the turquoise sky. . . . Footsteps snapped me out of my reverie. A man was walking up the path that led out from the mission, carrying a shovel and a posthole digger. Although we had never met I recognized him as the mission's caretaker. It was his job to keep an eye on the place, and although I had never actually caught him watching, I was sure that included keeping an eye on me.

At the edge of the cemetery he dropped one tool and started using the other. I walked over and got my first good look at the man. The poor fit of his clothes gave him the appearance of a peasant, but beneath them his stout build and vigorous movement attested to a hidden strength. He could have been forty and he could have been sixty, the ambiguity due as much to the southwestern sun as to the wrecked features of his face—his nose looked shaped by hands other than his creator's and faster than his own. But he had quick eyes that flashed intelligence when he looked up at me.

"Ya-tah-hey," I said.

"Hi," he replied.

I introduced myself and so did he. His name was Pinto Begay. I asked him what he was doing and he said he was going to put up a fence around the cemetery. As I soon learned, when they first began to bury people here the land belonged to a man who gave verbal permission to the mission to use this part for its burial grounds, but there was no agreement in writing. He had long since passed away, and his heirs had recently sold the land to a company interested in it for the mineral rights. When they informed the mission of their intention to mine the underground gravel, the members protested, the tribe got involved, and the upshot was the company was told if it wanted to excavate gravel here it had to pay for the relocation of the graves. A compromise was then worked out: The owners agreed to let the cemetery stay as long as it was not expanded by additional burials and the outer perimeter was fenced.

I looked toward a huge open gravel pit in the near distance where heavy equipment was taking bites out of the foothills and spitting them into dump trucks, and wondered how much of the activism in 1974 could be credited for providing the experiential base from which Navajos handled subsequent conflicts with Anglos.

"So now everyone will be happy," Pinto Begay said in a soft-spoken voice. And then, for no particular reason I could tell, he added, "Even the Navajo wolves."

My glance revealed my surprise at his blithe reference to a forbidden subject.

"Oh? And why will they be happy?"

He emitted a quick little laugh before showing me a droll and enigmatic sense of humor that was out of the ordinary. "This is their happy hunting ground. They come here at night and sit at the edge of the graves and sing up bodies."

I stared at him. "Do you believe that?"

He grinned, showing me great gaps where front teeth were supposed to be, before he went back to his work. "That's what I hear."

I was aware that while Navajo will sometimes treat the topic of witchcraft with offhand jocularity in casual situations with whites, they tended to deflect discussions, so I had no great hopes when I asked him if he would mind elaborating.

He looked at me with a curiosity I imagined was intensified by the suspicion I did not know how big an answer that request entailed.

"White people always want to know what they can't understand," he chuckled.

It was a line that had the ring of a refrain. I was certain it had been used before to put off inquisitive ethnographers and anthropologists.

"It's because I want to understand that I'm asking," I said in earnest.

After a pause he asked, "What is it you want to know?"

Figuring I had nothing to lose, I told him exactly what I wanted to know: "If the kids who killed the Navajos in Farmington back in 1974 were witched?"

The question did not appear to surprise him, leading me to believe that he knew a lot more about me and why I was there than I was aware of.

"That's a little like asking a priest or clergyman to tell what was confided to him by a confessor," he replied.

I felt light-headed with anticipation, wondering if maybe this man was an apparition and I wasn't really having this conversation.

"I realize that," I said. "But you asked."

He seemed to weigh his answer before he spoke. "I'll go this far. When it came on the news that the first one died, there was confusion in the Christian community, but Navajo traditionalists were walking around with smiles."

Over the course of the fall semester of his sophomore year Cody Crawford's mental state seemed to deteriorate, in large part due to an obsession with the notion Indians were out to get him. He told fellow students he was afraid to travel alone, and whenever he drove anywhere he carried a club under the front seat of his Volkswagen. "If they try to take me," he promised Amy McCulloch, "I'm gonna take a bunch of them with me."

Most thought his fears were of his own making, but they were also beginning to see Cody as self-involved, creepy, and prime for therapy. Adding a religious dimension to his life had not cured him of his nasty ways. While he was capable of quoting Scripture in class from memory, on more than one occasion he had repulsed classmates by telling dead-baby jokes at parties.

And it wasn't fun to be around someone whose morbidity included frequent references to his own death. He would say things to the effect that he knew it was coming. Things like, "What's it matter? I don't have a lot of time left anyway." He even sent his parents an anniversary card that read more like a farewell note, thanking them for all they'd done, asking them not to worry because better things were in store for him.

The timing of the letter was as cruel as it was prescient. By the time his parents received it he was lying comatose in a hospital.

A classmate by the name of Robert Isbell was along when it happened.

Cody was one of those guys that, well, kind of like an alcoholic: He doesn't want to help himself, you can't help him. I'd try—I could tell you stories you wouldn't believe, how many times I said, Come on, let's do this, or let's do that. And everybody around him would be positive and lively and wanting to do things, because there's not a lot of negative people at LCC. It's a fun place to be. There were more girls than boys there, a lot of them overprotected girls from West Texas Church of Christ homes, very, very pretty, friendly, and innocent. To tell you the truth it was like Heaven. If you didn't feel like doing anything else you could just sit around and talk to girls. . . .

But Cody got depressed real easy and I don't know why. He had a lot of people going out of their way to be friends with him, take him under their wing, especially when he'd go into a slump. He was kind of a yo-yo type guy. Like if he was a salesman you'd have to pump him up every day just to get him through his shift, you understand what I'm saying?

Maybe it was because he didn't have a girlfriend, or his

*grades were bad, or he thought he was no good, I don't know
what was on his mind. I wouldn't see him for a coupla days and
then I'd go down to his room. What're you doin'? Ah, I'm just
layin' here, I ain't doin' nothin'. It wasn't like he was a zombie
or something. I mean, he was communicating with society as
far as the dorm went. But he just wouldn't have enough energy
to put his clothes on or go to class. He'd lounge around in a
T-shirt and his gym trunks.*

*And when he was depressed all he talked about was dying.
You or me, we might say, Ah, I'm bummed out. But he'd say,
Maybe I'd be better off dead. Or he'd make comments like,
Maybe I won't be around next year. Things that were blatant
enough and out-of-left field enough that you'd think, What are
you talkin' about, you're gonna die? When you're twenty years
of age you don't think about dying. Most kids that age think
they're bullet-proof. Nothin's ever gonna kill me.*

*The night it happened he hadn't been out of the dorm in five
days. Hadn't been to class in five days. He'd just been sitting
in his room. He'd buy food from the vending machine and he'd
sleep a whole lot, and he'd watch TV. He'd just been sitting
around lethargically, in a depressed state. So I said to him,
Come on, let's go jogging, get you out of this. We had jogged
together before earlier in the year, when I got him to running
to lose some weight, but he had quit.*

Okay, he finally said.

*I was wearing a white fishnet shirt, red trunks, white shoes
and socks, and Cody had on blue—blue shirt, blue shorts, blue
socks, blue sneakers. As we left the dorm we started to jog
through a parking lot, and here's an example of the kind of
things he'd say. A car was coming toward us, it was dark and
its headlights were on, and there was no reason at all to say
something like this, I mean I would never have thought of it,
but he said, If you hit me there's going to be a big bloody spot
on you. Like he was talking to the car. That's just not something that would come out of a normal person's mouth. What
in thunder? I thought. Where are you coming from?*

*We were going to jog around the campus, and we were
jogging down the shoulder of a residential street that ran along
the eastern side of LCC, where there was nothing but a cot-
tonfield on one side and houses on the other, and whenever we
heard a car come up behind us we would move over to the
gutter or up onto the sidewalk. But in this one particular area
there wasn't a sidewalk, and there were no streetlights, so*

*when I heard a car coming I moved over into the gutter. And
I'm running along and all of a sudden I hear this PONK, a big
thud. I can see the picture of him right now. I can see Cody lit
by the headlights as he flies through the air. It's in my head and
I can't get it out. There he goes.*

*When he hit the ground it wasn't like he just sprawled. I
mean, he didn't nosedive and grind himself into the pavement.
He rolled perfect, like when somebody jumps off a trampoline
and lands on their hands and rolls a couple of times. That's
why I expected him to get up. That's why, when I ran up to him
I said, Man, he hit you hard, or something like that.*

*It didn't register nothing. I could see blood coming out of
his nose and mouth, so I said, Man, are you okay? Still nothing. Holy cow, I thought. And then I started thinking, Don't
move him, don't do anything, just wait till the ambulance
comes.*

For three days Cody Crawford lay in a coma, kept alive by a
respirator. His parents, called the night of the accident, arrived
the next day and maintained a bedside vigil at the hospital. All
day long fellow students came and went, talking to him in
normal tones. Hey Cody, you're looking good, they would say
when they walked into his room. Told that a person in a coma,
though he may appear unconscious, can sometimes understand
what is said, they acted as if the patient were sitting up in bed.

The doctors knew better. Crawford had been hit on the back
of the head by an oversized mirror bolted to the passenger door
of a motorhome, and X-rays showed that upon impact the brain
stem had been severed from the spinal cord. He would never
regain consciousness. But as long as the life-support systems
kept him breathing visitors continued to act as though recovery
were possible.

On the third night his heart quit and the decision was made
not to keep him alive by artificial means.

A funeral service was held in Lubbock, after which the
casket was driven back to Farmington for a second service. Six
LCC classmates served as pallbearers, and shortly before the
funeral they were given a briefing by a plainclothed policeman.
Although the mortuary had received no threatening phone calls,
the thought of angry Indians avenging themselves on Crawford's embalmed corpse was enough to prompt precautions.
The students were told there might be trouble and if a group
of Indians showed up they should simply put the casket

down and walk away, leaving everything to those in charge of security.

Nothing out of the ordinary happened, at least from the uninvited. But the preacher delivering the eulogy, Reverend Gene Reneau, startled everyone when he departed from the traditional words of consolation to lecture the Crawford family. In attempting to account for how such a brief life could include such violence, he seemed to be saying that Vernon Crawford was a product of his upbringing, and those whose influence shaped him should accept a certain amount of responsibility for his fate.

The matter of Vernon Crawford's fate would continue to be discussed in the months after he was buried in Greenlawn Cemetery in Farmington. Although the police had investigated the accident as if the circumstances were suspicious when they learned Crawford believed he had reason to fear for his life and kept weapons stashed in his dorm room, in the end they concluded it had been a freak accident. The driver had been a local elderly man who said he never saw the jogger until after he hit him.

Others, however, were unable to accept that the accident was an entirely random event. Searching for an alternative interpretation, they said the Almighty has limits: If we sin and repent but are not going to follow through, or if we are going to revert back to our old ways, God would rather take us out of this world and on to Heaven. They were mostly Church of Christ friends who felt that Cody Crawford's fate had the ring of Divine Judgment, but there were Navajos who believed the same.

Late one February afternoon, I stopped by the San Juan Mission in hopes of catching Pinto Begay in a conversational mood. It so happened he had just finished his chores for the day, and the month was being treated to unseasonably warm temperatures, so we went for a walk.

Following a dirt road that tapered to a path that led, eventually, to an arroyo winding among low rolling hills, we headed for the sandstone bluffs that floated like islands in pale blue fathoms of western sky. At times I felt like a beachcomber, noting the way the wind-ruffled sand appeared to hold the goodbye wave lines of a receding tide and the tiny seashells and nautilus fossils scattered among the jackrabbit bones. But my questing curiosity was unwavering and went directly for an elucidation of his tantalizing admission that when Vernon Crawford had been killed it was seen by Navajos in the area as a validation of traditional powers.

Before answering, he seemed to want to put the emotion driving the Navajo response in a larger context, for he went to great lengths to remind me that the desire of a crime victim to find and punish the responsible party was a natural human reaction.

"Christians may talk about how forgiveness is a virtue, Vengeance is mine, said the Lord, and all that; but when you see them interviewed on the TV, standing on the steps outside the courthouse, they all want revenge. They want the guy electrocuted, or sent to prison—punished to the maximum. That's human. Anyone who is a victim will feel better after some form of retribution."

Navajo were no different in this regard, he went on to say, except for the way these emotions fit into their religious worldview. "For the Navajo, the ideal is to live in cosmic harmony. As long as you stay in harmony with your creator, your family, yourself, you're doing all right. But if somebody interrupts that harmony, there is no forgiveness. The way a Navajo thinks, if he's had evil done to him he has to get rid of the evil in order to get back in harmony with the universe."

As if he thought maybe I was having trouble following the concept, Pinto Begay put it another way. "If someone does you wrong, and I'm thinking the Navajo Way now, if someone comes along and knocks your life-cycle out of whack, you never just let it go. He has to answer for what he did. You get back at him. You even the score. Then, after you have balanced out what he messed up for you, you can get back in harmony with the rest of your life. You can put your world back in order."

I didn't say anything for I was thinking about the Navajo concept of justice and how it compared to the eye-for-an-eye doctrine of law and order.

"Does that mean whatever is done to you, you do to him?"

"Yes, but that doesn't mean you have to necessarily be the one to do it. If the law-enforcement authorities do their job that can be good enough."

"And if they don't?"

There it was, the heart of the mystery. The scenario as I put it together now went this way. The slayings had produced disharmony. They disrupted order, creating chaos in human relationships. To the Navajo way of thinking there had been no justice. The evildoers had not been made to pay for their evil acts. Some kind of action needed to be taken to rectify the situation. What was it?

"Traditional remedies," he answered. "They resorted to ritual means to equalize this matter."

"You know this for a fact?"

"I know it."

At this point Pinto Begay made an important distinction. He said that in the traditional Navajo culture wrongs were settled by payment rather than revenge. An injured party and his next of kin were compensated in goods or services in an amount sufficient to cover the economic loss created by an offense. Harmony and balance could thus be maintained because people felt equal. But this principle didn't work in settling wrongs committed by foreigners who raided the Navajo, or in wars with tribal enemies. There, rituals were involved, appeals to the supernatural deities for help. They were called "war ceremonials," and because they were used against outsiders, this was not knowledge freely passed on to non-Navajos. In fact, the use of religious power in warfare was perhaps the most secret and dangerous of Navajo ceremonials.

I pondered this new information, wondering if I should let it go at that or push for ceremonial details. I decided to let my source set the limits.

"So when there are no physical means of getting hold of an outsider and making him pay for his crimes, and it has to be done through ritual, how do you exact punishment? How do you actually get to the criminal?"

"Here you're dealing with the dark side of Navajo religion," he said. "You're not dealing with the same forces you deal with in the Blessing Way, where you ask a Holy Person to put everything in harmony and give you life. What you're asking for is harm, and this is an evil act. This involves witchcraft."

Peter Burke planned to kill himself by drug overdose. The young nurse who brought him his medication in jail was supposed to make sure each patient took his ration of medicine, but she was new on the job and instead of checking she would sit and visit with him. It seemed never to occur to her that someone would pretend to swallow his pills, palm them secretly, and pocket them for a time when they could be taken all at once.

Ironically, it was her naïveté and like for him, the very qualities that enabled him to collect a lethal dose, that made it impossible for him to go through with his plot. He knew that after his body was found there would be an inquiry and she would be found negligent. A suicide on her first watch: It was something she would carry with her forever, personally as well as professionally; and uncharacteristically, knowing that if he did commit suicide he would leave her with that legacy made his death uncomfortable enough for him to postpone.

He hadn't thought about what she would do with the information, but it surprised him when he told her what he had been planning and gave her back the pills and she went straight to her supervisor and turned him in. Perceived as a danger to himself now as well as society, they marched him to solitary. So instead of getting her into trouble, I get myself in trouble, he thought as he once again found himself buried alive. Don't trust nobody, was the moral he drew. You get fucked over every time.

In his mind the sex-abuse charge was bogus, with the emphasis on "in his mind." He remembered the incident differently than the victims. About the circumstances, everyone was in agreement. He and a friend got drunk and went to an ice-skating rink. At one point he fell down and two little girls, age eleven and twelve, laughed at him as they skated by. He got up and chased them, and what happened when he caught up with them was where his version differed. He said he shoved them from behind. They went home and told their mothers this vile man had grabbed their breasts.

During his police interrogation he denied the charge, saying, "If I did that, wouldn't I remember?"—this, after he had already informed them he was an epileptic on medication who had memory problems. His court-appointed attorney requested a psychological evaluation, and a profile was compiled by two psychologists whose specialty was sex offenders. His attorney gave him a copy, which he read with curiosity:

Peter Burke has a history of a sad, lonely boy whose father died when he was five years old, and his mother died from illness associated with alcoholism when he was fifteen years old. Left pretty much to his own devices, even as a small child, Peter developed into a loner who is often the victim of circum-

stances in which he finds himself. An unassertive, inadequate person, Peter has pretty much accepted what has been thrust upon him by other more dominant, purposeful individuals. Noting an early tendency to "stay by myself, I don't have associates," Peter has been in trouble with the law since age fifteen. He has been incarcerated either in county jails or penal institutions for seven out of the past ten years. Perhaps because of his own "victim" stance in the world, he has found that "I'm always mad. I keep it inside. I don't show it. I try not to show anything. I just get madder and don't say anything." When he is not in custody Peter lets his angry feelings build to a point where "I just go out and get drunk after it builds up."

As regards to the instant offense, he observes he was feeling pretty mad at the world that day, "I didn't have a job, I had a bunch of bills, and the night before I went to a party and got drunk."

By way of a sexual history, Peter reported that he has never had sexual contact with a female. His first sexual experience occurred when he was twelve years old. An older boy induced Peter to perform oral sex upon him. At age fifteen Peter began seeking out sexual contact from other males and engaged in various masturbation activities with them. Other than that, this man states that the majority of his sexual contacts have taken place while he is in custody—the usual pattern being that Peter is the passive recipient of sexual advances from other dominant males. A professed homosexual, Peter stated he masturbates to fantasies of males and added that when not in custody he rarely approaches other males for sexual contact.

In short, Peter has consistently portrayed an antisocial attitude and response pattern for much of his young life. A loner and a drifter, Peter has wandered rather aimlessly through life with few, if any attachments, and deriving structure and support solely from his periods of incarceration. He shares our concern that because of this latter peculiarity he may indeed have become "institutionalized." That is, Peter Burke may not be able to function in a self-directed manner when outside the confines of an institutional setting. He has little or no energy with which to handle the stresses and strains of everyday life, he has a poorly developed self-concept, and suffers from vast and unmet dependency needs. Again, unfortunately these latter needs are met, albeit indirectly and incompletely, when Peter is incarcerated.

In summary, Peter Burke is a seriously disturbed young man

*who is in need of immediate psychological assistance. While
the alleged sexual abuse might be best characterized as an
obnoxious, offensive response as opposed to an act motivated
by sexual needs, it was nonetheless an assault upon another
person that is consistent with this man's antisocial personality
functioning. While little can be done in the short run to adequately address the chronic style of functioning of this alienated, lonely man, it is strongly recommended that immediate
steps be taken to address the severely depressed state of this
individual. Looking down the road a bit further, as a prospec-
tive out-patient . . . this young man will need strong, support
ive supervision while on probation, and even then his prognosis
for successful adjustment would be extremely guarded.*

When he read their report he shrugged. It could have been
worse. If they had known what he'd done as a juvenile, he
thought they probably would have recommended the chair.

Even though he maintained innocence, on the advice of his
attorney, he copped a plea. His idea of a defense had been
common sense: "I wouldn't have done it in broad daylight,
would I? That would be dumb." His attorney sighed as though
his patience were being tested. "Look. Who's a jury going to
believe? Two—got that?—TWO teenage girls? Or an ex-con
who can't remember what he had for breakfast? You go to trial
and you're found guilty, you'll get five years minimum. Plead
and you'll do one."

So he pled and was sentenced to a year in the county jail. A
year that was spent for the most part in solitary confinement for
his own safety. Somehow word got around he was in for sex
abuse, other inmates took that to mean he was a baby-raper,
and he was threatened with castration so they moved him out
of the cell-block dormitory into a single cell.

It was 1985 when he walked out of jail straight into the
catch-22 that had kept him in a financial hole his entire adult
life. When he sought legitimate employment, if he was honest
and told them he was an ex-con with epilepsy, no one was
going to hire him. But if he didn't tell them and they found out,
it would prove he wasn't trustworthy and they would fire him.

So he found a room in a crummy downtown hotel, compli-
ments of a low-income assistance program, or else he would
have been on the street; and he'd been there for three or four
months when he got a call from the employment division about
a job caretaking a terminally ill man. The dynamics of the

situation made it sound like a sentence. The old man had emphysema, he did not have long to live, he was severely depressed, and he just wanted everybody to leave him alone so he could kill himself. A nurse came in three times a week, but no one within the family was willing to take on the role of keeping him company for the time he had left, so they were looking for someone to be the old man's live-in companion.

At the interview Peter Burke was quiet and withdrawn so their take on him was limited, but they were desperate enough not only to offer him the position, they didn't even ask for references.

Once he got used to the idea of living in someone else's house, it wasn't so bad. One of his responsibilities was to feed the old man, but he was bent on starving himself to death and refused his meals. Some might have found him depressing to be around, but Peter didn't. Having recently contemplated suicide himself, he thought he understood how a dying man probably felt—he just wanted to forget everything—which made him more tolerant than he would have been otherwise.

The best part of the job, however, was getting to know the rest of the family: the old guy's son Dave and his wife Deb, and their daughter, Penny, who was his age. In contrast to his own family experience, these people were open, expressive, and affectionate toward each other; and more than that, they encouraged him to be the same. He had never been an outgoing person, so it wasn't easy. But the more time he spent around them the more he loosened up and felt comfortable with this new way of relating.

In time he felt he had to be honest with them and tell them about his past, and he was painfully frank and unsparing in his revelations. He told them the story of his life, including his years in prison. And he confessed to crimes he'd never been caught for. The only thing he left out was the trouble he'd gotten into in Farmington. And to his amazement and relief, his past transgressions didn't even faze them. All that mattered to them was who he was now.

Their acceptance ingratiated them to him and to show his appreciation he put himself at their beck and call. If they needed something done, anything, he was available. If they wanted an errand run, he volunteered. An odd job or favor? All they had to do was ask.

By the time the old man died there was a seat at the dinner table for him as if he were one of the family. Certainly some of what they were expressing was gratitude for the thankless job he had done, but they also made him feel like he belonged. That feeling was actualized when they invited him to move in with them. Dave and Deb were property managers of a 150-unit apartment complex and they needed a maintenance man to mow the lawns and do various repairs. If he was interested in the job, they would offer him the apartment adjacent to theirs and free meals in trade.

Still unaccustomed to showing emotion, all he said was Okay.

As comfortable as Dave and Deb were with the hired hand, the daughter Penny was ambivalent. She worked as a corrections counselor in a maximum-security institution, and she recognized Peter Burke as a type. She'd seen a lot of men like him at work. Suffering from psychological damage that usually came out of a history of abuse or neglect, they had difficulty forming relationships, difficulty maintaining employment and motivation, and lived day to day, rarely thinking ahead, rarely making plans.

But there was also something about Peter Burke that endeared him to her. She saw how hard he was trying to fit in, and felt if she asked him to do something for her he would just about go to the end of the world to do it. Obviously marked by profound losses, probably someone who had never known the sustaining pleasures of work and friendship or the love of a woman, she was touched by his vulnerability and her heart went out to him.

Although she could tell he had serious problems that interfered with his ability to function normally in life, she had been raised in a family where helping other people was number one. And so, when an intimate relationship developed between them, she didn't question whether or not it was a healthy one for her, she was too focused on him. Indeed, as well as his lover, she became his mentor.

She pointed out his lack of social graces. "You're rude, you don't pay attention when people talk to you, you walk around with a scowl on your face. No wonder you don't have any friends. And you never say you're sorry, about anything!"

It was true, he never apologized to nobody for nothing. Someone didn't like what he did, fuck 'em. It never occurred to him to say I'm sorry. But it had never occurred to him that he was different from other people either. It was the way he'd always been.

Not anymore, she told him. If he was insulting or inconsiderate, he was going to hear about it. And hear about it he did. She didn't let him get away with any nonsense. And she was ruthless in her refusal to let him play on her sympathies. She said she heard that shit at work all the time.

Sometimes she confused him, like when she tried to psychoanalyze him and attributed a lot of the way he was to his dysfunctional upbringing; but then, when he did something she disapproved of and he tried to use his childhood as an excuse, she'd say, "Oh no, you're a big boy now. You know better than that." Other times she pierced him to the core, like when she complained that she never knew what he was thinking because he never said anything, and he explained he never said anything because he never thought anybody cared what he thought. She just stared at him, tears welling. But he knew that running beneath all her comments and criticisms was a genuine caring and interest in his welfare and improvement, and that was a first for him.

Their relationship lasted two years. It took her that long to realize she was playing the role of a caretaker, she was going to fix things, make him better, and in the process she had neglected herself. Trying to heal other people and make their lives well and happy fed only part of her. And she also had come to the conclusion the relationship wasn't meant for the long run. Although Peter had made progress, she doubted he would ever be able to hold a job that gave him stability, and she was afraid he would become completely dependent on her.

It was a painful decision for her. She knew she was his best hope and felt she was abandoning him. But for her own sake she put an end to it.

He took her decision stoically, blocking out the hurt the way he had his entire life, by just forgetting about it. That was something that had not changed. Besides, even though he knew he would miss his relationship with Penny, as a matter of survival what was most important to him was that he continue to be accepted by her family. By now he thought of her parents as *his* mom and dad, her grandparents as his too. His connection to the family was like a lifeline: Without it he might as well be dead.

My first impression of Peter Burke was that he looked like someone in need of a blood transfusion. He was tall, gaunt, and thin-lipped. His eyebrows came together in a V that made him look perpetually cross. Dark-brown eyes stared insolently from under the brim of a ball cap that hid a receding hairline, and a stringy ponytail hung limply to the middle of his back. But it was the low energy level that hit me strongest. He had no vitality. Everything about him seemed slow: the way he moved, thought, spoke. It was as if it was almost too much of an effort to keep up with—what, life?

This must be what it's like after a lobotomy, I thought, as we talked about his life: whole sections of memory blank, thought-lines snarled. But he also impressed me as making a genuine effort to be honest. At one point he said he didn't lie anymore because he didn't care about anything enough to lie. I believed him, for that and another reason: Lying also took energy.

Picking up on this point during a conversation, I reminded him that missing in all his attempts to be honest was the admission of his crimes against Indians. Had he successfully blocked that out too?

The scowl that was his most natural expression intensified. "That's not something you forget," he admitted. "I mean, I don't sit around thinking about it, but I can't leave it behind either."

"Guilty conscience?" I wondered.

He thought about that. "No. The reason I don't forget is I always have to remember not to mention it."

I looked at him. "Did you ever give any thought to the men you killed—who they were, for instance?"

It was as if I had introduced an idea he had never had before. He shook his head.

"Did it ever occur to you they might be family men?"

To this he nodded, but seemed to have to wait for the corroborating information to make its way into consciousness. It was hard watching the effort to remember: It was as if his mind were fumbling in the dark for a light switch, bumping into things. Finally he found what he was looking for and said while sitting in solitary in Texas he had come across a passage in the Bible that said something to the effect if you kill someone you have to take care of his family, and that *had* started him to thinking, Did those Indians have families?

"And?"

At first he thought if they had a wife and kids they shouldn't be in town getting drunk, they should be home. But then he remembered his own mother would get drunk in town sometimes and not make it home. And since there was nothing he could do about any of it anyway, he went to sleep and forgot about it.

I continued to question Peter Burke, shifting to an examination of his attitudes toward Indians, whom he denied hating as a race. "The fact that they were drunk is what pissed me off." No, he said, he had not gone out with the intention of killing them, but he did want "to beat them up real bad."

The emotionally distant way he spoke about the murders caused me to think that what very well may have taken place was a complete dehumanization, and in Peter Burke's mind what he had committed was an act of vandalism. Those were not human beings he killed. All he'd done was commit a crime against property.

The only thing he seemed to care about, and that made him the least anxious, was what his "adopted family" would think if they found out he had not been totally forthcoming with them. It went back to that dreadful conundrum about truthfulness. He didn't tell them because he was afraid they would not be able to get past it. *He* had been able to put it in the category of another lifetime, just as the law treated it, as if it didn't exist because he'd been a juvenile; but he wasn't willing to take the chance that the most important people in his life would see it differently.

Other than a fear of losing the support of his family, not much else seemed to matter to Peter Burke. Penny was right, there had been some progress. He had stopped drinking, for instance. And whereas before he did things without thinking them through to their consequences, now he not only thought about getting caught, he expected it would happen if he broke the law again. It had taken him a long time to learn that, but he knew even if he got away with some stuff it would be only for a while. "You don't ever make a clean escape," he explained. "Even if you don't get caught, you carry it around with you. One way or another, you're going to pay for it."

I thought that represented a major growth in his thinking, and followed up by connecting it to an earlier subject: Did he look at how he had ended up and see any connection to the Indian murders he had committed?

He took a long drag on a Pall Mall cigarette and seemed to be trying his hardest to untie a knot in his thinking. But he never succeeded. He exhaled in a long sigh. "I don't know. Maybe. I ran out of excuses a long time ago. That was Penny's doing. After her I can no longer blame anything that happens on anyone but myself.''

For a long time I studied Peter Burke, watching him smoke, knowing he was unaware of what might have pursued him, just as he was unconscious of the human drama he had provoked when he was fifteen. It never occurred to him to wonder why his life seemed to hold more threats than possibilities. And it struck me as I gazed upon this lonely, alienated, reclusive, grown-up Peter Burke that the death penalty is not necessarily the ultimate punishment. That in certain cases the extension of life can be a more severe sentence, especially when accompanied by the diminishment of personal power, intrusions that make one ill, disorder in one's thoughts, and turbulence to one's emotions. Peter Burke had long ago ceased to be a fully functioning person. He exists marginally in this world, someone who has lost his soul.

The final thing I asked him the last time I saw him was how he wanted his epitaph to read. His reply was fitting: "Life sucks, but it's better than jail."

Witchcraft. The prospect awakens classic horror scenarios involving devil worship, black magic, incantations, and secret rituals performed under a full moon. *Voodoo*.

As it turned out, the prevalence of these popular notions explained Pinto Begay's forthcoming candor: Once he learned of my interest in the witchcraft angle, he was afraid it would lead me to incorrect impressions about Navajo witchcraft. He said he recognized it was a significant part of the broader story that ought to be understood because it was an expression of the Navajo people's deepest feelings, and he did not want to see it sensationalized.

"How is Navajo witchcraft different?" I asked.

In response to this he made several important distinctions that he said needed to be kept in mind at the outset. First of all, although each medicine man had his own specialty, the same way white doctors specialized in diseases of the heart and brain, all were familiar with some aspects of witchcraft but not all would use them. He cited his grandfather as an example. "He would have nothing to do with this witchy stuff. The way he explained it to me, he said his gift wasn't given to him for that purpose. It was given to him to put people back in the right order, it wasn't meant to be used against somebody.''

Not that the ones who were willing to deal with the "dark

side," as he put it, should be branded as witch doctors, however, for in certain cases witchcraft could be a force for good. The context in which a shaman used his ability to contact and manipulate evil spirits needed to be taken into consideration. Here, for example, a non-Navajo had done something evil to a Navajo that was tantamount to an attack from an outsider. Navajos, in turn, took the action they did only after they felt Anglo methods had failed to right the wrong in Navajo terms. They did not see what they did as an invocation of the powers of evil to help kill someone so much as an appeal to their gods to give them a victory over their enemies. In a sense, this was war.

Finally, he wanted to make sure I knew that the categories of good and evil, as personified by God and Satan, were not viewed the same way by the Navajo. Evil was not negative in a moral or ethical sense. Rather, there was harmony and order on one side and chaos and confusion, which produced premature death, illness and misfortune, on the other, and almost all the Navajo deities had both inclinations. They could punish as well as reward, be helpful as well as hurtful. No god was wholly good or wholly bad, but a mix. Just like human beings.

Once that was understood, he allowed me, through a series of questions, to unravel in terms comprehensible to me the intricately nuanced process of "witching" someone.

"Is there a particular name for the ceremony we're talking about?"

"No," he replied, reminding me that the sing used in this case was a blend of a war ceremony *and* witchcraft. "Depending on the medicine man and how he figures it out, he will use different parts of different ceremonies. It's 'a ceremony.' They don't name it more than that."

"Only one?"

"In the ritual that involves witchcraft, where you're dealing with evil spirits, there is always going to be bad stuff left over. So the first ceremony is usually followed by a Blackening Ceremony to get rid of the evil hanging around."

"I've read that the witching part can take various forms—focusing evil thoughts, sprinkling corpse powder on a victim. Is that what happened?"

"Everything goes into it. Thoughts count a lot. The medicine man will tell the victim's family to start concentrating on what they want to happen to that person, and he does his thing."

"Does that involve corpse powder?"

"It's said that's the quickest way to get to someone. But there are other ways. If you can get hold of some of the victim's hair or clothing, that works too."

"But that requires a personal encounter. What if you can't get any of that? What if the individuals you want to target are impossible to contact physically?"

"That doesn't matter. A spell can be cast."

At this point he told me about the sorcery side of witchcraft, by which a medicine man could target victims at a distance by chanting sorcery formulas over special charms. He said in these cases, when nothing materially associated with the victim was available, his name would suffice. "A person's name is more than a means of identification. It carries that person's power." That was why, in traditional Navajo society, no one was ever called by his given name. He was addressed by his kin term or a nickname.

In addition, he said ritualistic items that symbolized the intended victim were used.

"You mean effigies?" I asked, picturing doll-like images that were tortured.

"Sort of," he said, and described how a fist-sized stone was selected. On one side the likeness of the victim to be witched was scratched, while on the other side a death symbol was etched: a graphic that represented a powerful and dangerous force. A line was then drawn connecting the two. To the heart if the person was to die. Another line over the top connecting the death symbol to the head assured that the victim would realize, before he died, where the direction of his death was coming from.

In the working of these spells, he said each sorcerer had particular powers that assisted him. It could be the sun, the dark of night, lightning. Some had animal allies, like the snake, bear, coyote. The final step in the ceremony, he said, involved the burial of the effigy in a grave. An Anglo grave if the intended victim was white. And sometimes with an object that represented the way he was to die, such as a car part if he was to die in an auto accident.

I studied Pinto Begay's face for a glance or a tic that underscored a coded meaning to this last bit of information. Did he know that Vernon Crawford had been killed in an auto-pedestrian accident? Had a piece of car been buried with his effigy? He gave me nothing to add.

"And death is the outcome?"

He shrugged and smiled slightly. "So it's said. But death isn't the only way it has to work. It can also cause injury and illness, misfortune and hardship. In some cases it steals your shadow. Takes away the living part of where your strength lives and makes you foolish and weak. The idea is to bring you down."

I nodded slowly, thinking about Peter Burke, before asking about the sorcery formulas. Could he describe them more precisely for me?

Here the ceremony rounded back again into its favored element, mystery. Pinto Begay would not go into specifics, implying either some things are better left undescribed, or he was not familiar with those particular chantways. I still don't know which it was.

The way it happened to Oren Thacker this time, he was driving his pickup home from work one day, his brother and brother-in-law were sitting in front with him, and they were about six miles outside of town cruising down a four-lane highway when they came up fast on a little boy riding his bicycle on the shoulder of the road. Maybe it was the sun blazing on the horizon that blinded the kid, but you'd think he would have heard the swish of an oncoming car; at any rate, just as he was being passed he turned his bike and pedaled onto the highway. Oren swerved so sharply the door on the passenger side flew open and his brother-in-law almost fell out, but he was saved when Oren's brother grabbed him by the shirt. As soon as the truck spun to a stop on the grass median, Oren jumped out and ran back. The little boy lay in a heap beside his mangled bike, and one look told him neither would ride again.

Oren was devastated. He couldn't believe he had contributed to another death. Even though it wasn't his fault and he wasn't even cited for reckless driving, he felt sick with responsibility.

It was a sickness made worse by the press coverage of the accident. Apparently when the door to his truck opened his one-year-old daughter's stuffed doll had fallen out, and when the photographer from the local paper arrived at the scene, assuming it belonged to the child victim, he used it as a prop for a heart-wrenching picture that was printed on the front page the next day. In it, the doll lay on the road beside the broken-up bike, and the accompanying article identified Oren Thacker as the killer.

That wasn't the main reason he left Sterling and moved to Tulsa, Oklahoma. The main reason was the price of cattle dropped coincident with a rise in the cost of feed, and the mill fell on hard economic times. He also wanted to live closer to his family, and his parents had recently departed Farmington for Oklahoma City, following the money the way wildcatters always did. But just as they were glad to leave a town where they had been tainted by dishonor and shame, so was he.

In Tulsa he built a new life from the ground up. After a stint in industrial maintenance he went into painting, interior and exterior. Soon he landed a contract with a property management group, representing over 200 apartments, to repaint each unit whenever there was a turnover. It was steady work—most construction jobs were here today, gone tomorrow—and the conditions were comfortable: He worked inside where it was cool in the summer and warm in the winter. It also proved to be a lucrative business, and in short order he was able to put a down payment on a three-bedroom house and buy his wife a Volvo and himself a Supercab Ford.

The Tulsa years had their downs as well as ups. On one job he was fixing a tire on a jacked-up forklift when it collapsed and smashed his elbow. Then, later on, he was driving to one of his painting jobs and there was a piece of sheetrock lying in the road that must have fallen off someone's truck, and when he slid on it he put on his brakes, skidded, and slammed into another car. (The first thing that ran through his mind was this might be yet another fatality, so he hurried over to make sure the driver was okay. To his relief he was, but in his concern he neglected to collect any witnesses to support his version of what happened, and by the time the cops showed up the other guy had three witnesses backing his story that Oren had run a red light.) But whenever he stopped to think about his situation he would feel good about it. He'd been happily married for over a decade, his pride-and-joy was healthy, both cars were paid for, and the appraisal on his house had doubled.

As for the trouble he'd gotten into as a sixteen-year-old, he felt he had more or less succeeded in making good on the vow he made at Springer not to let this misfortune ruin his life. That determination, the styptic effect of time, and his dedication to following a straight path, treating people with fairness and decency, had stopped the bleeding of his conscience. This was not to say that it was the same as putting it all behind him, however, for the truth of the matter was his heart continued to beat with secret rhythms of guilt and worry.

Although he no longer felt like someone living in exile, barred by law from returning to his hometown, ostracized for bringing disgrace to the community, he did still carry the burden of a criminal past around with him at a personal cost. At times when he was quiet he was engaged with an elsewhere that those around him had no knowledge of. Although he passed himself off as an ordinary citizen, he lived with an offstage presence, a shadow wearing black-and-white stripes. It was always in the back of his mind that someone could run a check and it would show up on his record that he had a murder conviction in his past, leading to an embarrassing exposé.

It had also aged him. Where once people thought him immature for his age, now they were surprised when they learned he was the younger brother. He seemed so much older and more serious than his brother, they told him; and he knew what they meant. Some of the things that come with age came to him while he was doing time, number one being he no longer took his life or the future for granted.

He was not superstitious by nature or inclination ("I think we make it on our goods and bads; I try to look ahead, not back"), but even if he did not conceive of his individual fate as the handiwork of anyone's doing but his own, he did admit to sometimes feeling like a marked man. Marked in the sense that the world was a dangerous place for him. His experiences had left him with an edgy alertness for potential reversals of fortune. "I don't take chances anymore," he says. "I avoid any situation that could lead to trouble."

Any temptation that comes up that holds risks, he steers the other way. Once an enthusiastic drinker, now, if a friend said let's stop for a drink at a bar and it's late at night, he passes. You never know what might come up, but the odds are it won't be good. As he approaches an intersection his foot automatically lifts from the accelerator and hovers over the brake in anticipation of the unexpected. He knows only too well that a lapse in attention can at any given moment produce unintended and disastrous consequences. It's happened before.

Maybe that was to be *his* punishment, I thought during our last conversation. Fear of the unguarded moment, and constant vigilance.

But when I asked him about his penance he said something

else. While continuing to distinguish between the nature of his involvement and Crawford's wacky dementia and Burke's inhumane indifference, he acknowledged that he had yet to pay his dues for his part in the crime. He went on to talk about two possible forms of vindication, each of which used his experiences to say something larger. One was to get involved in some kind of social work that would allow him to advise troubled adolescents, as someone whose words carried the weight of lived experience. "What I'd say is, when you're brought up to know right from wrong and get old enough to go out on your own, then you gotta stand behind what you know is right. Don't let anybody talk you out of it. Be your own person. Don't let nobody think for you. Don't go along with somebody just because you don't want to think on it yourself. Because shit happens fast, and before you know it, it can explode in your face and your life will never be the same again."

The other, he said, was to give something back to Indian people, that they might better understand what was going on with him, and that it could turn other people away from participating in more of the random atrocities that stain their history. He closed by saying, "I guess that's why I'm talking to you."

The opportunity to interview a Navajo informant who was knowledgeable about native theories and philosophies, who was willing and able to articulate and translate them into terms that were meaningful to me, and who appeared to be intimately familiar with the events of immediate interest provided the basis for further conversations with Pinto Begay. He never claimed he was actually present at the ceremony that was performed, and in fact he denied it, insisting, "I didn't attend because it was none of my business." He did admit to showing up at the celebratory feast held at the home of a relative of one of the victims after Vernon Crawford's funeral, however, and described how a sheep was slaughtered and mutton stew was served with fry bread; people came from near and far to partake in the festivities; and at one point an elder spoke, saying, "What we set out to do has been accomplished. Everything that happened is in our favor." He likened the occasion to a Thanksgiving dinner.

I had no way of knowing if his denial was the better part of discretion, and he had been in attendance at the ceremony; but I do know at key points he spoke with such authority and particularity that it *seemed* he was providing me with an eye-witness report. It also occurred to me that even if he had been there, I doubted he would have said so. If I were in his place I'm not sure I would have.

But I had no reason to doubt that Pinto Begay was being truthful with me, and nothing he said in answer to my questions or in explanation of events contradicted anything I had read or heard about Navajo beliefs. Among any population if you talk to more than one individual you are apt to get some difference of opinion or interpretation, but so far I had detected no significant departure in his accounts of what had happened from what could have happened according to the studies and literature on the *Dineh*.

As long as he was willing to fill in the blanks for me, I wanted to continue our dialectic. Specifically, I wanted to hear more about the nature and operation of a so-called curse. Was he really claiming that the supernatural functioned like a court system, and medicine men carried invisible ceremonial arrows in medicine-quivers? If so, I wanted to know precisely how it was supposed to work. There was something spookily splendid about the idea of native peoples recruiting help through song and prayer from their mythological gods, but I could not accept every claim to sorcery uncritically, and needed to be shown some form of meaningful manifestation before I was a believer.

"This evil power—does it take a tangible form? Or does its force rely on the power of suggestion?"

"Fear is a big part of it. Word gets back to the victim that a ceremony was done to get him. He starts thinking about it: What are they going to do to me? When are they going to come after me? Pretty soon he's a man possessed. Then they've got him."

I wondered if belief was a necessary component of the power he was describing. Did the target need to believe in the power, or at least be aware of a curse before he could be hurt?

"There is power in any type of faith," he replied. "If you believe something, it creates power."

"But if you do not believe something is going to happen, would these ceremonies have any power on their own?"

"You have to remember, there is power on the other side too. There are people there who believe something bad is going to happen."

"Is it all a matter of belief, then? Is it all in their heads? All of their own making?"

Pinto Begay grimaced, as if the answer was both yes and no: Yes, it was a matter of belief, but no, it was not confined the way my jargon suggested. And he proceeded to advance the proposition that there were occasions when information could be transmitted from the consciousness of one person to the physical body of another.

As I listened to him attempt to explain the metaphysical assumptions with which Navajos thought and according to which they viewed events that occurred, I was struck by the fundamental difference between the nature of their world and the principles it operated by and that of my own. According to him, the Navajo believed that thought alone could have an impact on the structure of reality and the causation of events because an energy connected the mind to matter in a way that allowed the one to control the other.

I had to think about that for a few minutes, and then I responded in an obvious way: I wanted proof, evidence of a direct line of provocation from the ceremonies performed to the fates of the slayers.

"How is someone supposed to know this is what happened?"

"By looking at what happened."

"I mean, does the supernatural leave its signature?"

Pinto Begay laughed. He knew what I had in mind: if not scientific accountability in the form of laboratory verification and reproducible results, at least plausibly objective support. And he shook his head and said he was sorry, I wasn't going to catch sight of the spirits, they did not announce themselves, did not leave a calling card; but there was no doubt in the minds of those with the right kind of vision when the hand of fate belonged to the Holy People.

With nowhere else to turn, I turned to the three boys' fortunes.

"But it wasn't three for three. Three Navajos died, but only one of the killers is dead."

He gave me a so-what shrug. "Maybe it wasn't necessary for all three to meet a violent end for balance to be restored. Maybe a different ceremony was done for each. There's no telling what the medicine man did, or what he wanted to have happen."

I remembered the meeting with the medicine man who had

seen a bear when he looked at the picture of Vernon Crawford, a deer when he saw Oren Thacker's photo. Could the *hataali* who did the witching ceremony have peered into a glass of water or crystal, seen the heart and soul of each, and administered punishment according to what he saw?

"A medicine man might do that," Pinto Begay replied.

"So justice may not have demanded three lives for three lives. It might have been meted out according to the character of each one's crime."

Pinto Begay nodded. "That could be."

At this point, for the first time, I told him what I knew of what had happened to the three boys. I said that Crawford, whom I perceived to be the instigator, was dead. Burke, who had been able to inflict human suffering without flinching, was more than halfway there and diminished by spiritual annihilation. And Thacker, who admitted complicity but denied guilt, seemed at times to be caught in misfortune's web, and privately contemplated ways of atoning for his past.

Pinto Begay squinted pensively. I think this was the first time he had heard about all three fates, but he did not appear surprised. "It's possible the medicine man saw there were degrees of evil here, so he went for the leader first to make sure he would never cause it again; he crippled the second; and as for the third, he didn't get off free, maybe the spirits are taking care of him their way."

"If that were the case," I asked, "in your opinion would justice have been served?"

He took his time answering. "That would be justice the Navajo Way. Then the universe could be put back in place, and those who suffered restored in beauty."

AFTERWORD:

The Broken
Circle

Paleontologists assure us that much of the Navajo Reservation is a prehistoric lake bed, and in times past plant-eating dinosaurs chomped on ferns growing on the sandy shores, while winged reptiles roosted in the surrounding forests. The climate changed, they say, and over hundreds of millions of years the scene went from wet to dry and most of the animals died off.

Perhaps. But gaze across the vast barren stretches of the reservation today and it is easier to imagine the creation of the desert landscape as the result of a single cataclysmic night: a fiery lightning storm that smoked the sea into a column of steam ascending from the earth; a planet-splitting quake that drained an entire ocean into a subterranean abyss . . . and dawn broke on a world where mammals and people would emerge.

It is not just the bewitching expanses that a fanciful imagination will fill with an abundance of observation and invention—out here life itself sometimes seems to be imbued with an otherworldliness. Spend enough time among people who believe in and fear the presence of a spirit world, and it's not always easy to be sure about what's real and what's not.

On the surface level if you consider the price each of the youths had to pay, it proves nothing. Crawford and Burke, by virtue of their histories and personalities, were going to continue to live at risk in society, and what happened to Thacker is consistent with his character. But it *is* uncanny how actions appear to bear out theory when you realize that *if* there were such powers, and if they *could* determine the course of events, the outcome might not look any different.

To the Navajo people there is nothing to argue about. What is important is what is achieved, and to the degree they regard the ritual as successful, the truth of Navajo religion was revealed in a way that not only provided retribution, it renewed cultural traditions.

The process by which a dramatic event is incorporated into the collective memory is different for every culture. For the Navajo it usually follows the time-honored pathway of storytelling. Personal testimonies are passed along the extensive kin network and down through generations, growing into family myths that eventually become part of tribal folklore. The way the Chokecherry Massacre is recalled among the Navajo has transformed a story of white crimes into a tale of red justice that reclaims the wonder and magic of the old beliefs in supernatural power, while providing an authentic spiritual strengthening to the tribe.

For us Anglos, the power lies in the pen. The meaning and promise of an event remain elusive until committed to paper. What we want from a story like this is not only a record of the efforts of those who believed the future could be different by means of struggle, but a reckoning of the achievements, put in a context that illuminates their significance and gives them contemporary relevance.

In that regard, Farmington did not emerge as a model community, but neither did it stay the same. Social injustice was not eradicated, and what progress in racial relations was forthcoming would be less the result of moral conscience and the good will of the city than of continuous pressure by various citizens' groups, civil rights organizations, and concerned individuals. But perhaps it is a mistake to expect a dramatic change in perspective and behavior. For towns and individuals alike, maturation comes gradually, over years and with experience. More often it is the case that events like those described in these pages compose a point on a line moving people in a direction that brings them closer to, if not racial harmony, then greater racial tolerance, and deeper human connections. This is my reading of the legacy for white Farmington.

There is a final yield, more personal. Along the way of assembling this account, I too came to think of this story in Navajo terms, with reference to the concept of a circle. Circles occupy an important place in Navajo symbolism, and a closed circle is carefully avoided. The guardian spirit in a sandpainting loops around but always leaves an opening. The pathline that frames the designs on Navajo pottery is always interrupted by a "ceremonial break." I've even heard of a Navajo alcoholic who said he never screwed the lid back on a bottle of liquor once it was open in order to avoid closing the only passageway.

The idea behind the custom is that when a circle is closed there is no way for evil spirits to get out, they are trapped within; and the break in a circle serves as an escape route, a spirit path for bad to depart and good to enter.

In a fashion parallel to a closed circle, for seventeen years rumor and gossip, grudges and emotions, family secrets and tribal taboos have surrounded and contained this story; and as I put these words down, I see them as the final strokes that leave an airing break in the encircling line.

ACKNOWLEDGMENTS

To those Navajo people whose contributions gave me "eyes of adequate understanding" into the Navajo world and Navajo feelings, ,ahéhee,. I especially want to express my appreciation to Rena Benally, Wilbert Tsosie, John Redhouse, and Pinto Begay.

I also want to thank the many people in Farmington who were generous with their time in sharing information and insights—those who are identified in the pages that follow, as well as those who requested anonymity or were not specifically mentioned by name. In particular I want to acknowledge my indebtedness to Bob Miller, a lawman whose cooperation broke the case for me, narratively speaking.

A nod to "Pete" Myers, the western artist who ended up giving me a lot more than an ominous postscript to my Farmington Story; and a special note of gratitude to Shirleen Deal, who performed exceptionally as an unofficial research assistant. Three other individuals who figure prominently in the story and who provided me with an insider's point of view also deserve to be singled out: Judge Frank Zinn, Dr. Walter Winslow, and Marlo Webb.

I am additionally beholden to the following people who served as expert consultants: Dave Brugge, an acknowledged authority in Navajo history and thought and an invaluable source of information and interpretation; Ned Siegel, a Santa Fe psychologist who was a repository of insight into his profession; and Don Barliant and Janet Bailey, literate and literary friends on 24-hour call for reactions and advice. Last but hardly least, Rita Feinberg, my Washington, D.C., associate, who handled several FOIA requests for me, and acted as a point person in my dealings with federal agencies, deserves recognition.

A short list of others who should not be overlooked: Carolyn Brewer, Frank Demolli, Norm Marin, Forrest Fenn, the National Indian Youth Council.

Finally, when an editor influences the development of a book in the way a writer hopes for, and in the way Michael Korda did for this book, he too deserves honorable mention.

There is another way to think of acknowledgments, and that involves a statement regarding methodology. Although this book is a factual account of a true story about real people, at certain places in the text my reconstruction of a scene or situation is not based on direct personal observation, but on the best recollections of the participants a number of years after the fact, backed up wherever possible by secondary sources, written material and records, all arranged by me in a plausible and revealing order.

Finally, the only characters in the book whose names have been changed are: Pinto Begay, Barbara Alvis, Dave, Deb, and Penny, the three teenagers who committed the crimes, and the members of their families.

INDEX